D0492258

The Tides of Reform

Making Government Work, 1945–1995

Paul C. Light

Yale University Press

New Haven and London

Set in New Caledonia type by Northeastern Graphic Services, Inc.

Printed in the United States of America by Vail-Ballou Press, Binghamton, New York.

Library of Congress Cataloging-in-Publication Data

Light, Paul Charles.
    The tides of reform : making government work, 1945–1995 / Paul C. Light.
        p.   cm.
    Includes bibliographical references and index.
    ISBN 0-300-06987-1 (cloth: alk. paper)
            0-300-07657-6 (pbk.: alk. paper)
    1. Administrative agencies—United States—Reorganization.
    2. Administrative agencies—United States—Management.   3. Civil service reform—United States.   4. United States—Politics and government—1945–1989.   5. United States—Politics and government—1989–   I. Title.
JK411.L54   1997
353.09—dc20   96–38557

A catalogue record for this book is available from the British Library.

10 9 8 7 6 5 4 3 2

To Robert Katzmann

Contents

Tables

Acknowledgments

Writing the acknowledgments is always the most enjoyable part of a book project. Because I write mine only at the end, it is a time to remember all the people and institutions who made the endeavor possible.

This project began at the University of Minnesota's Humphrey Institute, where a small team of graduate students gave their talents and energy to collecting the primary materials needed to code the 141 statutes on which this book is based. Lisa Zellmer led the team, with help from Elizabeth Hubbard and Russell Langsam. The project could not have been better assisted.

In addition, my colleagues at the Institute provided a welcoming environment in which to work through the basic questions embedded in the project. Sharon Anderson, John Brandl, James Jernberg, Judy Leahy, and Sam Myers all deserve my heartfelt appreciation.

The project was finished at The Pew Charitable Trusts, where a host of colleagues eased the final analysis and writing. Rebecca Rimel and Nadya Shmavonian, president and executive vice president, respectively, protected me as I carved time from my schedule to write the book, never wavering in their enthusiasm, while my director colleagues and so many others in the Trusts provided warm support as I struggled to do two jobs at the same time. My staff in the Public Policy program was particularly supportive, never questioning my lack of focus, always generous with their own energy in keeping the unit alive. Elizabeth Hubbard, who journeyed to Philadelphia with me from Minnesota, Stephen Del Rosso, Caitlyn Frost, and Jennifer Bolton all have my gratitude.

The book has benefited from various reviews along the way, including two anonymous reviews for Yale University Press, as well as readings by Patricia Ingraham, Robert Katzmann, and Laurence Lynn. I also benefited from assorted presentations of the work, especially a lecture given at Kathleen Hall Jamieson's kind invitation at the University of Pennsylvania's Annenberg School of Communications. I also appreciate the support of John Covell, who embraced this book as a senior editor at Yale University Press, and Dan Heaton, who added to its readability and clarity as manuscript editor.

My family suffered this project gladly, as always. Sharon, Kate, Max, and Wheeler were always there for me and created a safe harbor as I struggled with the tides.

The book is dedicated to Robert Katzmann, who encouraged me to undertake the original book in the trilogy and has been ever encouraging of my work. He, more than anyone, is responsible for my body of work on government management reform.

Would that I could hold these individuals responsible for the content of the book. Alas, I can only thank them for their support, and must acknowledge the words and analysis that follow solely as my own.

The Tides of Reform

Introduction

This book is based on the notion that there is not too little management reform in government, but too much. Contrary to conventional wisdom, Congress and the presidency have had little trouble passing reform measures over the years, moving almost effortlessly from one reform philosophy to another and back again, rarely questioning the contradictions and consequences of each separate act. If government is not getting better, it is most certainly not for a lack of legislation.

The large centralized bureaucracies against which Congress and presidents now inveigh were not built in a day.[1] They were built statute by statute, rule by rule, as four separate tides, or philosophies, of reform worked their will on the coastline of administration: (1) scientific management, with its focus on tight hierarchy, specialization, and clear chains of command, (2) war on waste, with its emphasis on inspectors, auditors, cross-checkers, and reviewers, (3) watchful eye, with its embrace of sunshine and openness, and (4) liberation management, with its cry to let the managers manage, albeit with a bit of market pressure. Even the effort to liberate government from rules and hierarchy has been known to generate rules and hierarchy.

These four tides are not mere variations of a single reform philosophy. Each has a different goal—scientific management puts efficiency above all else, war on waste celebrates economy, watchful eye seeks fairness, and liberation management puts a premium on performance. Each has its own institutional champions—the presidency has been a comfortable home for both scientific and liberation management, the Senate for watchful eye, and the House for war on waste. Each even has its own patron saints—Herbert Hoover for scientific management, Jack Anderson for war on waste, Ralph Nader for watchful eye, and Richard Nixon and Al Gore for liberation management.

Apart from their current relevance, all four tides have been present in one form or another since the first days of the Republic. The war on waste began in the Continental Congress, which appointed the nation's first inspector general in the wake of a procurement scandal involving George Washington's Continental Army; the first expression of what would later be labeled scientific management came at the Constitutional Convention, in debates about the president's authority to appoint and control officers of the executive branch; the notion that these officers should be free to manage their departments as they deemed fit was a centerpiece of administrative philosophy from Washington through John Quincy Adams; and the first effort to open government to the sunshine came when Andrew Jackson introduced rotation in office, replacing the semipermanent senior leadership corps with party faithful in what quickly became labeled the spoils system.[2]

Much as reformers and blue-ribbon commissions might claim otherwise, there is truly nothing new under the sun when it comes to making government work. Human beings have been reforming government ever since they invented government.

Administrative historians should not be the only ones concerned with the tides of reform, however. In an era of scarce resources, decisions about *how* government works have become just as important as decisions about *what* government does. With little room to create new programs and little appetite to cut old, administrative arrangements become a new battleground for conflicts that once would have occurred in the budget and appropriations process.

Opponents of activist government can always find good press coverage in the war on waste and the seemingly inexhaustible supply of fraud, waste, and abuse uncovered by today's inspectors general. Advocates of activist government can have their administrative cake and eat it too by campaigning against machine bureaucracy through liberation management, even as they attempt to rescue government through employee empowerment and customer service standards. Opponents can offer privatization as a way to inject market pressure into moribund monopolies; advocates can offer some new administrative office as a guarantor of coordination and careful spending. These debates are not just semantic. To the extent that government can improve its performance, the public will allow greater activism, perhaps even national health insurance; to the extent government is seen as creating more problems than it solves, the public will likely remain unyieldingly hostile to expansion.

These debates continue to ebb and flow in large part because Congress, the presidency, and administrative scholars have never quite resolved when and where government can be trusted to perform well. In the absence of much evidence one way or the other, the four tides continue to wash ashore in contradiction, with scientific management and liberation management trusting government and its employees to mostly do well, war on waste and watchful eye assuming just the opposite.

WHY THE TIDES MATTER

Watching the tides of reform can be just as fascinating as watching the tides of the ocean. Both have a rhythm that is simultaneously soothing and powerful, and both have impacts both small and large, depending upon the climate and gravitational pulls.

Watching the tides of reform also helps make historical sense of the onslaught of reform over the past fifty years, putting great statutes like the Administrative Procedure Act of 1946, the Freedom of Information Act of 1966, the Ethics in Government Act of 1978, and a host of other statutes into some semblance of order.

Watching the tides is about more than aesthetics, however. It is also about asking how the tides vary over time, and whether the assorted pieces of reform actually add up to a more effective government. The answer rests in large part on four basic findings that flow from this book.

First, unlike the tides of the ocean, which simultaneously erode and reshape the shore, the tides of reform mostly add administrative sediment, whether in the form of new statutes, rules, paperwork, or administrative hierarchy. Over the years, the reforms have piled up rather like driftwood at the seashore, as have the administrative agents of reform, from the newly created undersecretaries and administrative assistant secretaries in the 1950s to evaluators and policy analysts in the 1960s, inspectors general in the 1970s and 1980s, and chief financial officers and chief operating officers in the 1990s.

Because their effects are cumulative, the four tides can produce the very things they hope to eliminate. Scientific management can produce a thickening of administrative hierarchy as the quest for narrow spans of control between supervisors and subordinates generates layer upon layer of needless management, thereby confusing rather than tightening accountability to the president; war on waste can engender so much fear inside government that employees do every last thing by the book, even to the point of needless waste and inefficiency; watchful eye can produce a rain forest of rules regarding public access to information, thereby reducing sunshine in government; liberation management can create a paralysis of teamwork in which agencies spend so much time and energy empowering their employees that process, not performance, becomes the cherished outcome.

Second, the tides of reform tend to come in comprehensive statutes. Rare is the Congress or president who can resist a governmentwide reform when a single agency experiment might do. Even when government undertakes a pilot project to test reform—the 1993 Government Performance and Results Act, for example, which mandated ten experiments in its effort to design a measurement and planning system for federal agencies—the temptation is to go governmentwide. Not only did Congress require full governmentwide implementation in 1997 regardless of the results of the pilots, but the Office of Management and Budget ended up authorizing seventy-one pilots in twenty-seven departments and agencies, virtually assuring that any lessons learned from the pilots would *follow,* not precede, full implementation.

Third, the tides are often at cross purposes. Congress and the presidency are perfectly capable of building a new administrative structure one year and cutting it down the next, opening government to the sunshine one year and closing the curtains the next, loosing the inspectors general to be junkyard dogs one year and leashing them back the next. Those who do not like a given reform rarely have to wait long for Congress and the president to change their minds. Indeed, there are often contradictions in omnibus reform statutes, like the 1978 Civil Service Reform Act, which contain contributions and contradictions from all four tides.

The result is that each reform statute creates intended and unintended consequences in making government work. It may be that the latest installment in the war on waste (for example, an increase in inspector general staffing) undermines the most recent contribution from liberation management (say, a campaign to get federal employees to take more risks); it may be that the latest effort to strengthen coordination (like creating chief operating officer posts in every department and agency) merely adds another layer of management in the way of the greater sunshine in government (for example, expanded freedom of information access to records).

Finally, there is at least some evidence that the tides of reform are accelerating—that is, that the interval between the last reform statute and the next is shrinking. Congress and the president appear to be less patient, reforming past reforms more frequently and shifting direction more quickly. The more government is reformed, the more Congress and the president think it needs further reforming.

These four patterns in the tides of reform lead to one simple prediction about the future: as surely as high tide follows low, today's effort to build a new administrative hierarchy will be followed by tomorrow's campaign to thin the bureaucracy and liberate managers to manage, and vice versa. Because Congress and the presidency simply do not know what does and what does not actually make government work, and because they have no overarching theory of when government and its employees can or cannot be trusted to perform well, they will move back and forth between the four reform philosophies almost at random. Reformers who command the tides to stop become little more than modern versions of the great Danish king Canute, who ordered the tides to stop and was washed out to sea.

Thus, even at the height of scientific management in the 1940s and 1950s, when Herbert Hoover reigned nearly supreme as the architect of a tightly rationalized administrative state, Congress and the president produced two of the nation's most significant watchful eye reforms: the Administrative Procedure Act, which subjects agency rules to intense public scrutiny, and the Federal Tort Claims Act, which makes federal employees liable for their actions and, in turn, laid the groundwork for future legislation on bribery, graft, and corruption, as well as freedom of information in the early 1960s. Even as one tide comes in, it is already destined to move out in due course.[3]

So, too, for liberation management, which crested in 1993 with the appointment of the National Performance Review (NPR), headed by Vice President Al Gore. Even in its call for an end to scientific management, the NPR made its own compromise with machine bureaucracy. There on page 91 of *Creating a Government That Works Better and Costs Less* is a call to create "a coherent financial management system, clarify responsibilities, and raise the standards for financial officers," a call that Herbert Hoover would not only applaud, but could have written. There on page 89 is a requirement that every federal department and agency "designate a chief operating officer" as a "senior official with agencywide management authority," a recommendation with clear echoes to the Hoover Commission's 1949 call for the creation of administrative assistant secretaries for management in every department.

Ultimately, the ebb and flow of reform is a natural by-product of the competition of ideas. What goes around comes around. Much as today's liberation management sees its antagonist in the machine bureaucracies created in the

1930s, those bureaucracies were in part a reaction to the watchful eye reforms of the Progressive Era in the early 1900s, which were in part a reaction to the state building of the 1860s and 1870s, which was in part a reaction to Jackson's spoils, or rotation, system of the 1830s, which was in part a reaction to the scientific management of George Washington, John Adams, and Thomas Jefferson. And so it goes on down through history.

Yet just because the ebb and flow is natural does not mean it is regular. Just as the tides of the ocean are affected by climate and position of the sun and the moon, so, too, are the tides of reform affected by the political and budgetary climate and the position of the Congress and the presidency. As trust in government plummeted in the 1970s and 1980s, for example, war on waste and watchful eye rose to high tide, crashing ashore in several hurricanes of reform under Ronald Reagan.

During the same period, Congress and the presidency appeared to reverse position in the gravitational pull of reform. Congress, not the presidency, became the most active originator of reform ideas, with the Senate and House exerting very different gravities on the legislative debate. Understanding these meteorological and gravitational pulls on reform is essential, therefore, for offering possible remedies to the effects of the tides described above.

MEASURING THE TIDES

This book is written to help tide watchers better understand the ebb and flow of reform, and to help Congress and the president better protect government against the effects of accretion, comprehensiveness, contradiction, and acceleration outlined above.

It is based on an analysis of 141 federal management statutes signed into law from 1945 to 1994. The initiatives were collected using a method modeled on work by Yale political scientist David Mayhew in studying policy reform in general. His book *Divided We Govern: Party Control, Lawmaking, and Investigations, 1946–1990,* shows that Congress and the president are perfectly able to produce reform under both divided and unified party control.[4]

Mayhew built his list of 267 reform statutes using two "sweeps" of history. First, Mayhew looked at what the *New York Times* and *Washington Post* thought was a major reform at the moment of actual passage, soaking into three decades of microfiche to isolate the then-contemporary judgments of significance. Second, he examined judgments made by scholars in their histories of reform, poring through dozens of books about the most important statutes of a given period, such as Lyndon Johnson's Great Society. Laws discovered in either sweep made Mayhew's list of 267; laws encountered in both were deemed to be particularly significant and were singled out for additional emphasis.

An Inventory of Reform

The core of this book is an inventory of federal reform statutes passed between 1945 and 1994. Like Mayhew's list, *The Tides of Reform* is based only on public laws, not executive orders or other less permanent vehicles of reform. Generating a list of 141 reform statutes is challenge enough without developing a scheme for sorting through executive orders, OMB circulars, and departmental initiatives. Readers will search in vain for a detailed discussion of Harry S. Truman's desegregation orders, Reagan's regulatory reform initiatives, or the host of lesser orders that have clearly reshaped federal administration. As with Mayhew's work, this is a book about statutes.

Unlike Mayhew's, however, this book uses rather different strategies for making the two needed sweeps through history. There is no effort here, for example, to generate a list of major statutes by perusing the *New York Times* or *Washington Post,* if only because federal management reform is rarely the stuff of which contemporary *Times* and *Post* coverage is made. Although both papers do pick up major statutes, like the Civil Service Reform Act or the Social Security Independence and Improvement Act of 1994, they are virtually useless as sources on less visible reforms, such as the 1987 Computer Security Act or the 1990 Negotiated Rulemaking Act. These statutes, while significant for management reform, hardly merit back-page coverage for major newspapers, let alone the front-page celebration that eased Mayhew's task. This unevenness becomes more acute the further one goes in history—for example, when neither paper had a federal management page (the *Post* now does) nor a government management beat (the *Post* now does).

Thus, the first sweep of history must involve some alternative source of then-contemporary judgments of significance. That source here is the *Congressional Quarterly Almanac.* First published in 1945 as nothing more than a loose-leaf collection of already published quarterly reports, the *Almanac* was not technically an almanac until 1947, when *Congressional Quarterly* began compiling a distinctly separate summary of the year's legislative action. By the 1960s, the *Almanac* had become the preeminent source of legislative history on government reform, in part because there are so few alternatives, but also in part because *Congressional Quarterly* became more adept at separating the major management initiatives from the minor.

Making a second sweep of the history of federal management reform is infinitely easier, largely because there is ample public administration scholarship on federal management reform, much of it collected into edited volumes over the years.[5] Alas, unlike other areas of public policy scholarship, public administration has not developed the kind of legislative case studies that might deepen a history of major reform statutes. Notwithstanding such seminal contributions as John Rohr's analysis of the 1946 Administrative Procedure Act, Chester Newland's detailed assessment of administrative reform in the early Reagan years, or Marver Bernstein's classic review of administrative reform in 1970, public administration and management scholars have generally focused more on the *functional impacts* of reform than on the *history*.[6]

Although one can find clues to the major reforms in impact-oriented research, any list of reforms emerging from traditional public administration scholarship must be supplemented by other sources. One such source is the now-defunct Administrative Conference of the United States, which published its 1,029-page second edition of its *Federal Administrative Procedure Sourcebook* in 1992.[7] (Created as a mixture of scientific management and watchful eye, the Administrative Conference was a victim of the war on waste led by the new Republican Congress in 1995.) A second source is the General Accounting Office, which occasionally takes stock of the major and minor reforms, including a particularly valuable look back at the 1970s taken early in the Reagan administration.[8] A third source is the congressional record itself, particularly hearings and debates that involve broad summaries of past legislative intervention.[9]

This second sweep can be further supplemented here by my own interviews with key legislative and executive staff, as well as past research on the war on waste and scientific management movement, personal experience on Capitol Hill, which included a two-year stint with the Senate Governmental Affairs Committee as a lead staffer on executive organization and management, and, finally, work as a senior adviser to the National Commission on the Public Service (Volcker Commission) and National Commission on the State and Local Public Service (Winter Commission).[10]

Together, these two sweeps of history produce a list of 141 initiatives, including both statutes and reorganization plans, for further analysis. These initiatives are summarized in Appendix A.

Readers are forewarned that the author's personal experience working for Congress and commissions yields an obvious potential for bias. Building this list involves judgments about what gets in and what does not. Because such judgments are ultimately influenced by my own views of the world, views clearly linked to my own work on Capitol Hill, the final list of 141 major initiatives is best viewed as one scholar's snapshot of history.

As a result, the final list in Appendix A no doubt misses statutes that other scholars might add and most certainly adds some statutes that others might ignore. Having worked on the 1988 Presidential Transitions Effectiveness and Department of Veterans Affairs Acts, for example, I may have had a self-interest in adding both to the list. Other scholars might debate whether both statutes belong.

The question, of course, is whether the list can sustain the analysis that follows. I am confident that readers will discover that the differences between the four tides of reform are often so dramatic that the addition or subtraction of one or two statutes along the way would have little impact on the overall results. Moreover, Mayhew's list confirms twenty-six of the 141 initiatives in Appendix A. The overlap would certainly have been even greater had Mayhew allowed reorganization plans into his tally—he would likely have counted establishment of the Department of Heath, Education, and Welfare (1953), the Office of Management and Budget (1970), and the Environmental Protection Agency (1970) as major initiatives. Though not formal statutes in a technical sense, reorganization plans are a form of legislation and were included in the sweeps conducted for this book.

Interestingly, all but two of the reforms on both lists involved scientific management initiatives of one kind or another. Fourteen of the twenty-six created entirely new agencies or departments, seven reorganized existing agencies into something new, two changed the budget process, and one reformed the federal personnel system. Although the Department of Education Act was an exception, using a scientific management rationale to reward a powerful lobbying group, twenty-three of the twenty-six involved an effort to bring greater sense to the structure and operation of government. Of the other two statutes on the overlapping lists, one can be defined as a watchful eye reform (the 1974 Freedom of Information Act), and one can be labeled part of the war on waste (the 1981 Omnibus Budget Reconciliation Act). So much for what kinds of management reform reaches the *Times* and *Post* and retrospective studies.

A statute's failure to make Mayhew's list does not make it anonymous, however. The 141 initiatives in Appendix A include such stalwarts as the Administrative Procedure Act of 1946 and the Federal Tort Claims Act of 1946, both of which were ineligible for Mayhew's list because they fell in a Congress not covered by his research. Appendix A also includes the original Freedom of Information Act of 1966, which was a one-sentence statute that laid the basis for future expansion, as well as the Federal Pay Comparability Act of 1970, the Government in the Sunshine Act of 1976, the Inspector General and Ethics in Government Acts of 1978, the Paperwork Reduction Act of 1980, and the three bills that are collectively labeled the Reinventing Government Package of 1994.

So defended, the list also includes such virtual unknowns as the Presidential Transitions Act of 1964, the Office of Federal Procurement Policy Act of 1974, the Competition in Contracting Act of 1984 (a blend of war on waste and liberation management), and the Federal Employees Liability Reform and Tort Compensation Act of 1988 (which liberated federal employees from some of the provisions under the Tort Claims Act). If not equal in notoriety, all the statutes share a rough commitment to making government work. Although perhaps not always as significant as the items on Mayhew's list, the 141 initiatives listed in Appendix A stand as a fair inventory of the top federal management reforms covering the second half of the twentieth century.

Two further caveats are in order before turning to a brief overview of the measures used in this book. First, Appendix A includes seven cases in which multiple reorganization plans were combined into single entries. Twenty reorganization plans were combined into just such an entry in 1950. Although none of the plans can stand on its own as a single entry, the sum is clearly greater than the parts. All of the plans were issued under the aegis of the first Hoover Commission and reflected a high point in scientific management history.

In a similar vein, the three bills that made up Gore's National Performance Review package are summed into one entry in 1994. All three were introduced as part of an omnibus package on the same day, and though eventually broken into three separate bills to accommodate the legislative process, all three passed as consecutively numbered bills on the same day, and were signed into law as consecutively numbered Public Laws, also on the same day and in the same signing ceremony. (The two 1984 bills that expanded competition in contracting are also combined.)

Second, assorted federal pay increases and repeated reauthorizations of the 1939 Reorganization Act (a now-expired statute that once gave presidents authority to recommend structural changes in executive organization under various legislative approval schemes) are included on the list of 141 reforms only if they were particularly visible or part of some broader legislative controversy. Thus, the 1949 reauthorization of the Reorganization Act was included because it was a linchpin of Truman's promised implementation of the Hoover recommendations.

Plotting the Tides

The challenge for a book on the tides of reform is not to create a persuasive list of initiatives, for the universe of possible statutes is only so large. Even with occasional disagreements about the specific entries in Appendix A, most scholars would likely come to a similar list, be it somewhat larger or smaller. Rather, the challenge lies in using the list to both plot the tides of reform and understand their underlying dynamics.

One way to do so is to compare each of the 141 initiatives cast ashore in this book, so to speak, against a common set of measures. When did each pass? Was there any legislative controversy? How was each one implemented? What were the actual impacts? By coding the answers to a standard set of questions, the 141 initiatives can help draw a clearer map of the past and perhaps even predict a bit of the future. Although sorting such a diverse list of reforms often involves difficult judgments, the effort is well worth the risk as a first step toward understanding the ebb and flow of the tides of reform.

Toward this end, the 141 initiatives were coded into 37 variables broadly measuring (1) time of passage, (2) legislative history, (3) reform philosophy, (4) change strategy, (5) size and scale of the initiative, (6) implementation approach, and (7) impacts. The variables run the gamut from the year in which a statute passed and the margin of legislative support to its subject matter (procurement, ethics, budget, etc.) and impact in shifting power toward Congress or the president. A simple percentage listing of how the 141 initiatives fall into the different variables can be found in Appendix B.

Time is the easiest category to collect. One needs only to look up the date of passage and code it by decade, era (pre- versus post-Watergate), or president (Truman on through Clinton). Legislative history is also relatively simple to chart, although identifying the origin of a particular idea (presidency, Senate, or House), interest group involvement, and the degree to which the legislative debate was routine or controversial requires deeper analysis of the *Almanacs* and whatever other histories might exist.

Identifying the underlying reform philosophy is much more difficult. Pinpointing the tide of reform that carries a given statute often requires a close inspection of committee reports, hearings, and the statute itself. So, too, does identifying the accountability mechanism (compliance, capacity, or performance) and the general view of government represented in the legislative record. Answering these questions becomes even more daunting when one discovers that almost a third of the 141 statutes represent more than one tide of reform. Major reform statutes such as Civil Service Reform are often viewed as freight trains (or should we, to accommodate our dominant metaphor, say cargo ships?) for smaller measures that may directly contradict the primary thrust.

Identifying a statute's underlying change strategy is a refreshingly simple task by comparison. Does the statute focus on the structure of government, its procedures, or both, or does it merely create a blue-ribbon commission? If the answer is structure, does it create a new agency, merge two or more old agencies, create a government corporation, or some variant of elevation, demotion, or abolishment? If the answer is procedure, does it create a new system, broaden an existing system, simply reauthorize, or enact some variant of deregulation? And regardless of its structural or procedural focus, what specific area of public administration and management—procurement, budget, ethics, pay, rulemaking, debt collection, tort claims—does the statute address?

The scale and implementation of reform are also easy categories to measure. Is the reform big or small? Is it a totally new idea or an adjustment of an established or old initiative? Does it have a sunset or is it permanent? Does it cover a single agency, as do most of the overlaps with Mayhew's list, or several agencies, or is it to be implemented governmentwide? Is the administrative approach centralized or decentralized, and is there any evidence whatsoever that Congress and the president meant to use the given reform as an experiment in making government work?

It is the final set of measures, those dealing with the impacts of a given statute, that is simultaneously the most important and most frustrating for this analysis. After all, a critical question in a book subtitled *Making Government Work* is just how well the 141 statutes did in achieving just that. The general consensus among politicians and scholars alike is "not very well." No one has yet topped Marver Bernstein's statement of the case, and no one likely ever will: "The history of management improvement in the federal government is a story of inflated rhetoric, shifting emphasis from one fashionable managerial skill to another, and a relatively low level of professional achievement."[11] The statement is as relevant today as it was when it was written in 1970.

The challenge is to find ways to measure the impacts of reform. At one level, all of the statutes examined in this book were a success. All were passed, all were implemented, and all had at least some impact. Contractors to the federal government got their money faster under the Prompt Payment Act of 1982, small businesses got more opportunities to bid for business under the Small Business and Federal Procurement Competition Enhancement Act of 1984, veterans got better letterhead and a seat at the cabinet table under the Department of Veterans Affairs Act of 1988, and a significant number of near-retirement federal employees got buyouts of up to $25,000 under the Federal Workplace Restructuring Act of 1994.

Woe be to the scholar who would dare put a "success" or "failure" stamp on any of these bills. Even the Energy Security Act of 1980, which created the Synthetic Fuels Corporation, cannot be labeled a failure, even though the corporation was abolished in 1986. After all, the corporation was created, produced a few drops of fuel, and arguably did its share in creating a deeper national commitment to alternative energy sources.

Yet being implemented is hardly a robust measure of impact. The fact that contractors got their money faster or that small businesses got a chance to bid is hardly a robust measure of how well these reforms made government work. This book uses a series of alternative questions that might yield some broader sense of impact. Did the given statute shift the balance of power to the presidency or Congress? Increase or decrease the cost of government? Expand or contract the role of government? Thicken or thin the federal hierarchy? Accelerate or slow the administrative process? Enhance or reduce interest group and public access to government? Improve or reduce government morale? Strengthen the line (delivery) or staff (advisory) units of government?

Not every question can be answered for every statute. Some impacts simply could not be discerned or were so small as to be negligible. Consider the 1974 Congressional Budget and Impoundment Act. Although the new budget process and creation of the Congressional Budget Office clearly shifted power toward the Congress, it had no discernible impact on the cost and role of government, interest group and public access, or general government morale.

As Appendix B suggests, the Congressional Budget Act was hardly the only one of the 141 initiatives that was difficult to measure. More than half show up as "no impact/not discernible" for those three factors. That so many initiatives simply do not show up on these simple measures of impact may suggest a broader problem for the study of making government work. As advocates of the Government Performance and Results Act of 1993 argued, the absence of clear performance measures makes it nearly impossible to know whether anything that government does has the hoped for result.

Lacking a bottom line against which to measure results, whether in the form of the kind of ersatz profit-and-loss statements required under the Chief Financial Officers Act of 1990 or in blunt statistics on customer satisfaction, fraud, waste, and abuse reduced, or public trust restored, the search for clear consequences of reform will always be difficult. And because the field of public administration has never developed a deep commitment to experimental design, advocates will likely continue to claim great impacts that are virtually impossible to refute through careful analysis. Indeed, even when an idea clearly fails, advocates are well within their rights to argue that it was never given a fair chance.

1

The Tides of Reform

Making government work has been a rallying cry of reform from the very beginning of the Republic. Although good government was Alexander Hamilton's great passion in *The Federalist Papers 69–75*, it was actually Thomas Jefferson who called for the nation's first reinvention, a fitting role given his penchant for creating gadgets of one kind or another. What Hamilton was to building the administrative state, Jefferson hoped to be to reforming it.[1]

Inaugurated as president after one of the most hotly contested elections in history, Jefferson articulated a vision of a smaller, less centralized government. With all the blessings that Americans share in this "chosen country, with room enough for our descendants to the thousandth and thousandth generation," Jefferson asked in his first inaugural address, what else could the nation want? "Still one more thing, fellow citizens," he answered: "a wise and frugal government, which shall restrain men from injuring one another, shall leave them otherwise free to regulate their own pursuits of industry and improvement, and shall not take from the mouth of labor what it has earned."

In the modern vernacular, Jefferson wanted a government that worked better and cost less, one that taxed lightly, paid its debts on time and in full, and sought "economy in the public expense." The effort to make government work has not stopped since. Nor, for that matter, has the campaign for economy and efficiency.

Ultimately, Jefferson's rhetoric far outweighed his success. He did cut taxes and downsize the military, but his Louisiana Purchase doubled the size of the nation, requiring a rapid expansion of the General Land Office, which would later become part of the Interior Department. It was this expansion that spawned the corruption that would sweep Andrew Jackson into office and entrench the two-party system in 1828. Remembered mostly for introducing the spoils system, Jackson was actually a champion of making government work and would have been equally comfortable with the administrative orthodoxy of Herbert Hoover and the watchful eye of Ralph Nader.

Jackson saw reorganization as the cure to a host of administrative evils. As Matthew Crenson writes, almost every department was reorganized at least once during his administration, the War Department twice, and the State Department thrice. "The reorganization plans themselves are of little lasting importance," writes Crenson of the effort. "Their significance lies instead in what they suggest about the state of administration. The capacity to reorganize implies an ability to deal with administrative operations in formal and abstract terms. Existing administrative arrangements have to be made explicit before they can be deliberately changed." Jackson's reorganizations "clearly disclosed his fondness for unity of command and a certain devotion to administrative autocracy."[2]

Watchful eye also influenced Jackson's reform agenda. Jackson clearly saw rotation in office—spoils—as a way of both rewarding the party faithful and restoring a watchful accountability to government. By disrupting the continuity of service established under Washington, Adams, and Jefferson, the Jacksonians hoped to restore a simpler time. "They regarded their administrative handiwork, not as an attempt at modernization, but as the restoration of something old and respectable," Crenson writes. "They aimed to purify the federal establishment of all its new-fangled complexity," or as Jackson himself put it, "to restore 'the government to its original simplicity in the exercise of all its functions.'"[3]

It was toward this aim of moral purity that Jackson and his lieutenants also created codes of conduct and accounting systems in the departments. Consider the following examples drawn from the Post Office code of conduct:

1. Every clerk will be in his room, ready to communicate business, at nine o'-clock A.M., and will apply himself with diligence to the public service until three o'clock P.M. . . .

3. Newspapers or books must not be read in the office unless connected directly with the business at hand, nor must conversation be held with visitors or loungers except upon business which they may have with the office. . . .
5. The acceptance of any present or gratuity by any clerk from any person who has business with the office, or suffering any such acceptance by any member of his family, will subject any clerk to instant removal. . . .
8. Strict economy will be required in the use of the public stationery or other property. No clerk will take paper, quills, or anything else belonging to the government for the use of himself, family, or friends.[4]

Codes of conduct and accounting systems required monitors, of course, leading to the rise of the first counterbureaucracies in American history, mostly in the form of an increased number of special assistants to department secretaries.[5] Although the Continental Congress invented the first statutory inspector general, it would be nearly two hundred years before a federal legislature would create the second.[6] In the interim, it would be up to the secretary's staff to prevent fraud, waste, and abuse and to assure ethical conduct.

Ultimately, Jackson rejected two of Jefferson's cherished administrative ideals.[7] First, Jackson saw economy and efficiency not in tax cuts and downsizing but in the administrative rigor that would come from organizing government wisely. Second, he saw administrative accountability not in continuity of service and letting the managers manage but in the watchful eye that would come from rotation in office. In many ways, therefore, Jackson's reforms can be seen as a reaction to Jefferson's war on waste and liberation management, which were themselves reactions to the growth of government under Washington.

DEFINING THE TIDES

The United States emerged from the 1830s with the broad contours of four competing philosophies of government reform: scientific management, war on waste, watchful eye, and liberation management. The claims of presidents, Congresses, blue-ribbon commissions, and good-government advocates notwithstanding, making government work has long involved a rather broad mix of options.

This is not to argue that Jackson had a careful rationale behind every reform, or that his inventory of alternatives was either consistent or based on a clear body of theory. Quite the contrary. Jackson's agenda was a pastiche of untried ideas driven by his longing for times gone by. "With respect to the technology of management," concludes Crenson, "the Jacksonian period was prehistoric. It is doubtful whether Old Hickory's contemporaries recognized the existence of any 'technique of management' separate from the commands of the law, the rules of accountability, and ordinary common sense."[8]

It was left to the late 1800s and the Progressive Era to produce the deeper theories underpinning the four tides of reform discussed in this book. The theory emerged, in turn, as the federal government grew from barely 50,000 employees in 1870 to more than 250,000 by 1900. Having labored for a half century under Jackson's spoils system, which itself can be described as a primitive form of watchful eye, the United States joined the industrialized world in adopting merit as the underlying anchor of government employment in 1883.[9]

Historians celebrate passage of the Pendleton Civil Service Act as a signal moment in the march of scientific management, but it also involved a war on waste, a bit of watchful eye, and an ultimate hope for liberation management. For a period lasting into the 1930s, when scientific management finally emerged as the dominant philosophy of the next two decades, the tides were nearly inseparable. Consider, for one example, how Woodrow Wilson linked the four ideas in his 1887 call for "a science of administration which shall seek to straighten the paths of government, to makes its business less unbusinesslike, to strengthen and purify its organization, and to crown its dutifulness."

Through a blend of scientific management (straightening the paths of government), war on waste (making government business less unbusinesslike), and watchful eye (purifying government organization), government would be free to give its employees the "large powers and unhampered discretion" that Wilson saw as the "indispensable conditions of responsibility":

> Public attention must be easily directed, in each case of good or bad administration, to just the man deserving of praise or blame. There is no danger in power, if only it be not irresponsibility. If it be divided, dealt out in shares to many, it is obscured; and if it be obscured, it is made irresponsible. But if it be centered in the head of the service and in heads of the branches of the service, it is easily watched and brought to book. If to keep his office a man must achieve open and honest success, and if at the same time he feels himself intrusted with large freedom of discretion, the greater his power the less likely is he to abuse it, the more is he nerved and sobered and elevated by it. The less his power, the more safely obscure and unnoticed does he feel his position to be, and the more readily does he relapse into remissness.[10]

The vision of a permanent civil service unencumbered by politics, recruited through open competitions, and directed through formal job descriptions lasted for the better half of the twentieth century. As the legal scholar Robert Vaughn argues, the vision "established the premise that an employee was an agent for broadly defined public interests; it created special responsibilities; and it emphasized the importance of public employment, creating a moral calling for public service."[11]

Yet notwithstanding Wilson's rhetorical flourishes about honor and accountability, it was a vision that also included a strong element of war on waste. As Stephen Skowronek argues, war on waste, not scientific management, was the dominant philosophy of the period and was tied to virtually every administrative reform enacted: "Retrenchment, broadly construed, meant disposing of the excess baggage of wartime government, strengthening the government within a clearly delineated sphere of action, and imposing a strict regimen of economy and efficiency on the administrative apparatus."[12] Consider, for example, how Rhode Island's Thomas Jenckes, one of the earliest advocates of civil service reform, explained its goal: "Let us seek to obtain skill, ability, fidelity, zeal and integrity in the public service, and we shall not be called upon to increase salaries or the number of offices. It is safe to assert that the number of offices may be diminished by one-third, and the efficiency of the whole force of the civil service increased by one-half, with a corresponding reduction of salaries for discontinued offices, if a healthy system of appointment and discipline be established for its government."[13] (Ever was it thus that saving money is the underpinning of most reform.[14])

The Progressive Era also reflected a strong element of watchful eye reform, whether in the form of the direct election of U.S. senators, as ballot initiatives, or in a deepening of the codes of conduct pioneered by Jackson. Here it was Theodore Roosevelt who rose to the occasion, pushing simultaneously for fuller implementation of the merit system and stronger presidential control of administration.

Roosevelt also appointed the first of what would be a long list of twentieth-century blue-ribbon reform commissions, this one led by an assistant secretary of the Treasury Department named Charles Keep. The Keep Commission established the basic rationale for virtually every reform commission that followed, including the National Performance Review (NPR). Simply put, it was to be the president's duty, and the president's alone, to make government work. Ironically, Roosevelt's effort to gain control of the General Land Office became his downfall. After a two-year struggle to reorganize the Interior Department, Roosevelt's reform effort came apart as Congress rejected every last recommendation of the Keep Commission.

Most importantly perhaps, Roosevelt foreshadowed the future break in Wilson's public service vision by issuing a gag order against lobbying not *of* but *by* federal employees. The order, issued in 1902 and again in 1906, forbade federal employees "either directly or indirectly, individually or through associations, to solicit an increase of pay or to influence or attempt to influence in their own interest any legislation, either before Congress or its committees, or in any way save through the heads of the Departments or independent agencies under which they serve, on penalty of dismissal from government service."[15]

On the surface, the gag order appeared to reflect a rare alliance between the president and Congress against lobbying by public employee unions. But, as Skowronek argues, the alliance was on the surface only: "This politics was bounded by labor's efforts to manipulate Congress and the President to gain autonomy for itself, by the benefits championed by the President to build the merit service into a centrally controlled career service, by the inescapable question of whether Congress or the President was the proper locus of personnel development and administrative oversight, and by the constitutional limitations on the prerogatives of any one branch to gain control over the merit employees."[16] The tides of reform that had come together ever so briefly in Woodrow Wilson's vision were starting to move apart. The president was becoming the champion of scientific management, particularly as it related to centralized control and unified command, while Congress was moving steadily toward watchful eye, particularly as it related to opening government to the sunshine of public scrutiny.

By the 1950s, scientific management and watchful eye were completely separate as philosophies of reform. Scientific management was the guiding tide in shaping the rapidly expanding welfare state, while watchful eye emerged as the tide of choice for restraining government. The other tides grew more distinctive, too, as one reform commission after another sought to distinguish its recommendations from what had come before. As the commissions piled up—the Keep Commission on Department Methods was followed by the Taft Commission on Economy and Efficiency in 1910, the Joint Commission on the Reorganization of the Administrative Branch of the Government in 1920, the President's Committee on Administrative Management (Brownlow Committee) in 1937, the first Hoover Commission on Organization of the Executive Branch of Government in 1947, the second in 1953, and a host of study groups, task forces, and commissions named for Ash, Grace, Volcker, and Gore in the 1970s, 1980s, and 1990s—the four tides grew further apart.[17] Ash gave scientific management a last hurrah (so far) in 1970, Grace escalated the war on waste in 1983, and Gore defined liberation management in 1993.

By the end of the 1980s, the four tides had enough weight to be considered separate, often competing philosophies of reform, each with a different goal, inputs, institutional champions, defining moments and statutes, patron saints and advocacy organizations, even most recent contradictions. These separate histories help form a portrait of each tide that I shall consider in order.

Scientific Management

Scientific management is the easiest of the four tides to define, if only because it has been recommended by so many blue-ribbon commissions. Its advocates are heroes to the field of public administration, great scholars such as Luther Gulick and great practitioners such as Louis Brownlow; its legislative gains evident in even the most cursory inspection of the statute books (table 1.1).

To this day, scientific management continues to exert remarkable influence in Congress and the presidency. As table 1.1 suggests, its basic goal is "efficiency," a goal that appears at or near the top in virtually every reform report of the past one hundred years, including the NPR report. Like Andrew Jackson in the 1830s, today's reinventors long less for a new kind of government than for the agile agencies that existed in the days before watchful eye and war on waste thickened the controls on government.

Thus, even in its broad statement of liberation, the NPR report pays its respects to the old aims of scientific management. The second sentence of President Clinton's preface promises not just "a new customer service contract with the American people" but "a new guarantee of effective, efficient, and responsive government."[18] Efficiency is rarely far from the first droplet of reform.

Table 1.1 Key Characteristics of Scientific Management

Goal	Efficiency
Key Input	Principles of Administration
Key Products	Structure, Rules
Key Participants	Experts
Institutional Champion	The Presidency
Defining Moments	Brownlow Committee, First Hoover Commission
Defining Statute	1939 Reorganization Act
Most Recent Expression	1990 Financial Officers Act
Most Recent Contradictions	1988 Department of Veterans Affairs Act, 1994 Social Security Independence and Improvement Act, 1994 Reinventing Government Package
Patron Saint	Herbert Hoover
Patron Organization	National Academy of Public Administration (Standing Panel on Executive Organization)

All reformers worship efficiency as plain old good politics, but what separates scientific management from the other tides is its absolute commitment to a set of discernible management principles that can guide reform. Although the principles can be traced back to Frederick Taylor and his stopwatch, they received their greatest boost from *Papers on the Science of Administration,* edited by Luther Gulick and Lyndall Urwick.[19]

In describing the chief executive's job as POSDCORB (an abbreviation of Planning, Organizing, Staffing, Directing, Coordinating, Reporting, and Budgeting), Gulick and colleagues offered two basic principles as hard truths about government reform. The first was specialization. "Why divide work?" Gulick asked. "Because men differ in nature, capacity and skill, and gain greatly in dexterity by specialization; Because the same man cannot be at two places at the same time; Because the range of knowledge and skill is so great that a man cannot within his life-span know more than a small fraction of it. In other words, it is a question of human nature, time, and space."[20]

The second was coordination of work, which included recommendations for creating unity of command, narrow spans of control, and staff assistance for the executive. "From the earliest times," wrote Gulick, "it has been recognized that nothing but confusion arises under multiple command. 'A man cannot serve two masters.'" If obeying the one true master meant excluding Congress, so be it. And if the effort to keep the span of control to just six subordinates meant a vast thickening of the federal hierarchy, also so be it. "Just as the hand of man can span only a limited number of notes on the piano, so the mind and will of man can span but a limited number of immediate managerial contacts."[21]

The key products of such principles are inevitable. Coordination creates structure, specialization creates rules. Neither is imposed through a mean-spirited distrust of public employees but through a compassionate recognition of the limits of human nature. Narrow spans of control allow employees to keep in touch with their one master, while staff assistance allows that one master to stay on top of the job. Because of their natural limitations, frontline employees would be among the last people the master would wish to consult on how to do their jobs better. In this "president-comes-first" image of administration, it is experts who are the key participants on behalf of a unified command. They are the ones with the knowledge, the skills, and the organizational history to create the proper mechanics for utilizing human capital well. Congress is always welcome to pass statutes giving the president more authority, of course, but not to give itself a greater role in what is a single master's job.

There can be little question that scientific management had its glory days during the 1940s and 1950s. Its defining statute, the Reorganization Act of

1939, was designed to give the president much greater freedom to shape the executive branch to the principles of administration. Whatever the complaints of social scientists like Herbert Simon, who belittled the principles in a famous article titled "The Proverbs of Administration,"[22] scientific management was clearly an idea whose time had come.

And coming from the three-member Brownlow Committee, which numbered Luther Gulick as its chief theoretician, the Reorganization Act was a linchpin of implementation. The bill had five classic scientific objectives, with a bit of war of waste thrown in at the top as a selling point:

(1) To reduce expenditures to the fullest extent consistent with the efficient operation of the Government;
(2) To increase the efficiency of the operations of the Government to the fullest extent practicable within the revenues;
(3) To group, coordinate, and consolidate agencies of the Government, as nearly as may be, according to major purposes;
(4) To reduce the number of agencies by consolidating those having similar functions under a single head, and to abolish such agencies as may not be necessary for the efficient conduct of the Government; and
(5) To eliminate overlapping and duplication of effort.[23]

These objectives were deemed so important that the statute itself suggested that they could "be accomplished more speedily" by giving the president reorganization authority than "by the enactment of specific legislation." Such a broad grant was not without congressional critics, of course. "Advocates of this bill tell us that bureaucracy threatens to destroy this government," one House member argued. "Let me say to them that dictators are made by just such measures as this one. And let me add, a dictator would do a quicker and more complete job of destroying Our Government than any bureaucrat who ever lived."[24] Similar charges when the bill was first introduced actually led Roosevelt to issue the following statement:

A. I have no inclination to be a dictator.
B. I have none of the qualifications that would make me a successful dictator.
C. I have too much historical background . . . to make me desire any form of dictatorship . . . in the United States of America.[25]

The conflict was eventually resolved with a two-house legislative veto. The president would have authority to reorganize federal agencies *provided* that the House and Senate did not pass a concurrent resolution against a given plan within sixty days. The act changed over the years, mostly in an effort to limit the president's authority as Congress became more assertive, and it was allowed to lapse from time to time. Congress prohibited use of reorganization authority to establish new departments in 1964 and restricted the number of reorganization plans to one every thirty days in 1971.[26] In spite of the limits, the basic statute remained active until the mid-1980s. Unable to resolve the loss of the legislative veto following the Supreme Court's decision in *Immigration and Naturalization Service v. Chadha,* Congress finally let the reorganization authority lapse.

Although scientific management has mostly been at low tide since the 1940s and 1950s, it has hardly disappeared from the statutory ocean. Its most recent expression came in the Chief Financial Officers Act of 1990, which established a single "master" for financial reform in every department. By creating a new deputy director for management in the Office of Management and Budget, the act also sought to centralize presidential control over financial operations, thereby reinforcing the principle of unity of command.

The act was not a pure scientific management statute, however. Annual financial statements would give Congress and the public a better look at agency operations, and inspector general audits of those statements would, sponsors hoped, cut into fraud, waste, and abuse. As Senator John Glenn (D-Ohio) argued as the bill moved toward final passage, "This legislation is intended to create an organizational structure and provide an important oversight mechanism to insure [that] the executive branch adopts adequate financial controls. This bill is a clear expression that Congress wants better accounting and more clear accountability lines within the executive branch of Government."[27]

The bill itself led with the following two findings: "(1) General Management functions of the Office of Management and Budget have not received sufficient priority and need to be significantly enhanced to improve the efficiency and effectiveness of the Federal Government," and "(2) Billions of dollars are lost each year through fraud, waste, abuses, and mismanagement among the hundreds of programs in the Federal Government."[28] The mix of rationales was picked up in the press coverage of the bill. The *Congressional Quarterly Almanac* titled its story on the act "Financial Centralization," while the headline in *Government Executive* was "Chasing Wayward Billions."[29]

As with the three other tides discussed in this book, scientific management has never been so strong as to prevent contradictions and reversals of past statutory success. The Social Security Independence and Improvement Act of 1994 is the most recent example. What Congress joined together in 1953 by combining the Children's Bureau, Social Security Administration (SSA), and Education Administration into a single Department of Health, Education, and Welfare (HEW), the 1994 act continued to pull asunder by giving SSA its independence. (Congress had started the dismantling in 1979 in passing the Department of Education Act.) According to Senator Daniel Patrick Moynihan (D-N.Y.), SSA's independence was the only way to fix a "brain dead" agency "lost in the exurbs of the Department of Health and Human Services."[30]

Given their loyalties to the president as the "one true master" of the executive branch, scientific management advocates particularly opposed the creation of an independent board to oversee the new agency. Not only would the proposal insulate the agency from direct presidential control, but the Standing Panel on Executive Organization of the National Academy of Public Administration (NAPA), a patron saint of scientific management, also argued that an independent board would impede administrative efficiency by creating multiple power centers at the top of the agency.[31]

Although the NAPA panel won the battle against the board, it lost the war against independence. Starting in 1995, the Social Security Administration would operate as a cabinet-level agency under a single administrator. Moynihan succeeded in making the case that SSA needed to be protected from the rising politics surrounding the United States' largest entitlement program. As such, the Independence and Improvement Act is best viewed as an expression of watchful eye, not scientific management. By elevating SSA to cabinet status, Moynihan and other champions of the program would be able to hold the agency more accountable, if only by making decisions more visible to the public.

War on Waste

As noted earlier, war on waste may be the nation's oldest reform philosophy, for the first inspector general predates ratification of the U.S. Constitution itself. And, as we have also seen, rare indeed today is the management reform that does not pay lip service to the war against fraud, waste, and abuse. Cutting costs has become *the* essential selling point for passing almost any effort to make government work.

Consider the reinventing government campaign as an example. Although the vast majority of the first report of the Gore NPR deals with efforts to liberate "good people caught in bad systems," the title itself reveals the shotgun marriage needed to win public support. It was not just *Creating a Government That Works Better* but one that *Works Better and Costs Less*. According to the report's primary author, David Osborne of *Reinventing Government* fame, the demand for savings was unrelenting and self-driven: "The truth is, we wanted more 'war-on-waste, save-money' philosophy than we were able to get into the report. We needed it to make the report credible to the media, Congress, and the political community. The White House kept killing proposals to eliminate programs and functions so as not to offend particular congressmen. So our 'costs less' content kept taking big hits. That's why I and my writing team pleaded with Gore to put the 252,000 personnel reduction goal in the report. Had we not convinced him, I don't think the report would have been credible in Washington."[32]

War on waste is far more than an undertow in other tides, however. As table 1.2 illustrates, it is a robust reform tide in its own right, complete with its own defining moments, statutes, patron saints, and interest groups. The broad goal of war on waste is simple: economy in government. Whether defined as preventing fraud, waste, and abuse, or as plain old budget cuts, it is a goal that has walked hand in hand with efficiency ever since the Taft Commission on Economy and Efficiency in 1910.

One can argue that economy, not efficiency, has always been the root goal of federal management reform. It was certainly the cry of many proponents of civil service reform in the late 1800s, and it was front and center in the drive for budget reform in the 1920s. "To the politicians and the general public, the argument was single and simple—economy in government, to which efficiency and legality would contribute," writes Frederick Mosher about the 1921 Bud-

Table 1.2 Key Characteristics of War on Waste

Goal	Economy
Key Input	Generally Accepted Practices
Key Product	Findings (audits, investigations)
Key Participants	Inspectors General, the Media
Institutional Champion	Congress
Defining Moments	Welfare Fraud Hearings
Defining Statutes	1976 Shriners' Hospital for Crippled Children, Conveyance (Office of Inspector General at Health, Education, and Welfare), 1978 Inspector General Act
Most Recent Expressions	1989 Department of Housing and Urban Development Reform Act, 1992 Federal Housing Enterprises Financial Safety and Soundness Act
Most Recent Contradiction	1993 Hatch Act Reform Amendments
Patron Saints	W. R. Grace, Jack Anderson
Patron Organization	Citizens Against Government Waste

get and Accounting Act, a key scientific reform of the era. "It was proclaimed that a budget system would lower the costs of government or at least keep them from rising as quickly; it would thus keep taxes down, prevent deficits, and lower public debt."[33]

The war on waste takes as its inputs the rules governing generally accepted practices, most notably in the accounting "yellow book." It is mostly by measuring compliance with these rules that the government's auditors and investigators are able to uncover the fraud, waste, and abuse that produce yearly records in dollars saved or put to better use.[34]

War on waste also involves a rather different set of participants and champions from the other three tides. At the risk of metaphor overload, inspectors general (IGs) and the media are the foot soldiers in the war, and Congress, not the president, is the field general. It is a point well illustrated by the hearing activities of the IGs. The IGs or their staff testified before Congress 339 times between 1977 and 1988, of which 250 appearances (or 74 percent) occurred at the subcommittee level. Although the IGs divided their testimony almost evenly between the House and Senate, their prime "customers" were mostly the same: information-poor subcommittees for whom an IG would make a lead witness and an audit or investigation a possible headline.[35] However, as I will show in Chapter 5, it is the presidency that benefits most from war on waste. Congress may be the key designer, but most of the statutes used in the war tend to strengthen the presidency.

Ironically, the rise of the war on waste as a separate tide of reform was inspired by a key scientific management statute passed in the early 1950s. In enacting the Budget and Accounting Procedures Act of 1950, Congress effectively removed itself from auditing the day-to-day activities of the executive branch. The General Accounting Office previously had been responsible for auditing every agency transaction, a duty that required the services of nearly twelve thousand full-time employees. Not only did an increasingly liberal Congress want these staffers for other purposes, the division of responsibilities offended the Hoover Commission, which adopted "performance budgeting" as one of its top recommendations.

Distilling a complex statute into its simplest terms, performance budgeting meant that it was the president's duty to track expenditures from appropriation to final audit, a shift that might explain why President Truman was led to declare the 1950 act "the most important legislation enacted by Congress in the budget and accounting field since the Budget and Accounting Act, 1921, was passed almost thirty years ago."[36]

(It is important to note that performance budgeting in the 1950s bears little relationship to performance budgeting today. As the budget expert Allen

Schick notes, the Hoover ideal was about "(1) casting budget categories in functional terms, and (2) providing work-cost measurements to facilitate the efficient performance of prescribed activities. . . . Performance budgeting derived its ethos and much of its technique from cost accounting and scientific management."[37])

Whatever the impact of the 1950 Budget and Accounting Procedures Act on improved financial management, it blinded Congress to the kind of detailed information that it had once used to track agency activity. It is hardly surprising, therefore, that Congress soon created a new set of eyes for inspecting the books, a set that would reside not on Capitol Hill but in offices of inspector general within the agencies themselves. Nor is it surprising that Congress soon amended the Administrative Procedure Act of 1946 to assure public access to executive branch information. These statutes were the natural consequence of Congress's need to know.

The defining statute in the war on waste was an obscure 1976 measure whose primary purpose was to convey ownership of the land underneath a Shriner's hospital in Salt Lake City. Attached to that statute was creation of an IG at HEW, the first of dozens of statutory IGs across government. Although IG legislation shows up only three times in Appendix A, IGs have been embedded in at least thirteen other statutes since 1976, creating a total of sixty-one in agencies large and small by 1994, with at least one now overseeing the House of Representatives itself.

The IG mission is evident from the 1978 Inspector General Act, which established offices in twelve departments and agencies. It is to conduct and supervise audits and investigations of basic programs, promote the economy, efficiency, and effectiveness of those programs, and keep the department or agency head and Congress fully, currently, and mostly simultaneously informed about problems and deficiencies in those programs and operations. (Note that the public is not included in the list of clients.)

Beyond the obvious responsibilities under their individual statutes, all of which are modeled on the 1978 act, the IGs are responsible for a host of duties established elsewhere, some of which involve other tides of reform. They are responsible, for example, for auditing the financial statements required under the Chief Financial Officers Act (scientific management), assessing the internal control reports required under the Federal Managers' Financial Integrity Act (war on waste), overseeing the broad impacts of the Competition in Contracting Act of 1984 (which carries a bit of liberation management), investigating citizen claims under the False Claims Act of 1986 (war on waste), and assuring protection under the Whistleblower Protection Act of 1989 (watchful eye). Under legislation requiring energy conservation in the executive branch, an inspector general is even responsible for making sure the lights are turned off at night.

In spite of their broad statutory responsibilities, the IGs have but one basic tool at their disposal: monitoring. "They are to look, not act; recommend, not implement," as I have written elsewhere. "The IGs were neither created as line, or operating, officers of their departments and agencies nor given any powers to suspend, or otherwise interfere with, program activities."[38] All they could ever do is provide information.

As the war on waste heated up during the 1980s, however, many IGs became purveyors of the kind of information that creates front-page headlines and columns by war on waste patron saint Jack Anderson. Encouraged by a savings-hungry White House besieged by red ink, the IGs began to favor a body-count war on waste, piling up yearly records in their statistics on dollars saved, cases opened, and audits completed, but not quite knowing whether government was even remotely less vulnerable to the fraud, waste, and abuse they sought to deter.

That the IGs should become specialists in detection, not prevention, is hardly surprising given the nature of the times. Indeed, it was an investigation of welfare fraud in 1974 that led to enactment of the original HEW model. If HEW was not rife with fraud, as Representative L. H. Fountain (D-N.C.) later explained in his subcommittee's findings, it was most certainly rife with vulnerability to fraud. "We found that basic data needed by both Congress and HEW for effective action against fraud and abuse was simply not available. HEW officials could not provide information on which to base a meaningful estimate of losses from fraud, waste, and abuse. In fact, they could not even give us an accurate count of the number of programs the Department was administering."[39]

Lest the reader conclude that Fountain was expressing a variant of scientific management in his argument for the consolidation of the audit and investigatory function under one umbrella, it is important to note that the IG concept was neither designed to unify the president's control nor to narrow the span of control. Although Congress did combine audit and investigative functions into a single office, headed by a single presidential appointee, the new IGs were explicitly independent of the president's unified command.

To the contrary, the HEW IG was to report to the secretary and Congress nearly simultaneously, rendering the IG anything but part of a single chain of command. Little wonder, then, that every agency called to testify before the House on the 1978 expansion testified against it.[40]

The war on waste enjoyed its greatest popularity in the 1980s, stirred by the record-setting reports from the IGs and the efforts of J. Peter Grace, chairman of the Private Sector Survey on Cost Control in the Federal Government (the Grace Commission), who fittingly published his 1984 report under the title *War on Waste*.[41] New statutes creating IGs continue to be popular on Capitol Hill to this day, as do statutes designed to crack down on cheaters and defaulters, and the war on waste remains a highly attractive way for selling just about any management reform.

War on waste was thus a secondary theme in efforts to rescue the Department of Housing and Urban Development (HUD) from internal corruption in 1989. Crafted in large part by new HUD Secretary Jack Kemp, who described his department as a "swamp" of fraud, the reforms imposed a broad inventory of new fines, penalties, and rules on financial transactions, all of which would be subject to close inspection by Congress and the IG.[42] Of particular note is the severe narrowing of the secretary's authority to allocate monies from two special housing funds, authority that had reflected an early liberation of a kind. Although the rest of the statute concentrated more on reorganization and tighter chains of command as its reform strategy, thereby making it primarily a scientific management approach, war on waste clearly influenced substantial portions of the effort.

In spite of its popularity, the war on waste has not remained without contradictions. Consider the successful effort to liberate federal employees from the political restrictions of the 1939 Hatch Act. As noted earlier, the Hatch Act was not the first effort to limit the political activities of federal employees.[43] One year after issuing his second gag order against union lobbying in 1906, Roosevelt issued another order to provide that "no person in the Executive civil service shall use his official authority or influence for the purpose of interfering with an election or affecting the result thereof."

Driven by worries about the political consequences of a growing federal workforce, this effort to assure the neutrality of the civil service was eventually expanded into the 1939 Hatch Act. After the statute was upheld by the Supreme Court on two separate occasions, opponents returned to Capitol Hill for redress.[44] After two presidential vetoes, the first in 1976 by Gerald Ford and a second in 1990 by George Bush, Hatch Act reform finally passed and was signed by Clinton in October 1993.

Allowing federal employees to carry posters at political rallies, distribute campaign material or stuff envelopes, or participate in voter registration drives or phone banks may seem like small liberation. But the overall effect is away from the tight controls of war on waste and scientific management and toward greater freedom for the individual employee. Hence, liberation appears in clear conflict with war on waste.

Conflict may be inevitable given the competing views of employees embedded in each philosophy. Whereas war on waste operates largely from distrust, liberation is driven by trust. Even as Osborne and the NPR used war on waste to sell its recommendations, they made the case for reorienting the IGs. "The inspectors general have certainly uncovered important problems," the NPR report argued. "But as we learned in conversation after conversation, they have so intimidated federal employees that many are now afraid to deviate even slightly from standard operating procedure."[45] After a year of negotiation with the NPR staff, the IGs issued a "vision statement," in which they committed themselves to becoming "agents of positive change striving for continuous improvement in our agencies' management and program operations, and in our own offices."[46]

Congress was not part of the negotiations, however, and continues to press the IGs to be junkyard dogs. In the summer of 1995, for example, the new Republican chairman of the House Government Operations Subcommittee on Commerce, Consumer, and Monetary Affairs introduced H.R. 4679, The Inspector General Reform Act of 1994, to "expand the mission of the Inspectors General, to provide for greater independence for Inspectors General, and to make Inspectors General more effective and accountable."[47] Much as the vice president might want more cooperative, even visionary IGs, the reality is that the IGs owe substantial loyalty to a Congress that often wants war.

Watchful Eye

If watchful eye and war on waste share a broad distrust of government and its employees, and if both find strong support on Capitol Hill, they clearly diverge on just how to make government work. Where war on waste puts its faith in strong enforcement by counterbureaucracies, watchful eye puts its faith in simple sunshine (table 1.3).

By making the internal operations of government more visible through disclosure and open meetings, for example, and by providing remedies through the courts, watchful eye advocates have no more confidence that government will get better on its own than that the inspectors general can be trusted to protect whistleblowers. It is a lack of confidence clearly revealed, for example, in the 1989 Whistleblower Protection Act, which made it easier for federal employees who report fraud, waste, and abuse to prove that they were fired or demoted as a result.

As table 1.3 suggests, watchful eye claims fairness, often based on due process, as its overall goal. It is in the effort to prevent the arbitrary exercise of power that the tide has gained its greatest statutory momentum, particularly in statutes designed to provide freedom of information for ordinary citizens. And it is in a general rejection of government's ability to protect what it deems

Table 1.3 Key Characteristics of Watchful Eye

Goal	Fairness
Key Input	Rights
Key Product	Information
Key Participants	Whistleblowers, Interest Groups, the Media, and Public
Institutional Champions	Congress and the Courts
Defining Moments	Vietnam, Watergate
Defining Statute	1946 Administrative Procedure Act
Most Recent Expression	1989 Ethics Reform Act
Most Recent Contradictions	1990 Administrative Dispute Resolution Act, 1990 Negotiated Rulemaking Act
Patron Saints	John Gardner, Ralph Nader
Patron Organizations	Common Cause, Public Citizen

as the basic rights of access that watchful eye calls on whistleblowers, interest groups, the media, and the public to enforce its goal. With the courts as its key enforcer, watchful eye seeks to make government work almost entirely from the outside.

Although table 1.3 lists the Vietnam War and Watergate as defining moments in watchful eye history, the underlying pressures for open government have existed at least as far back as the muckraking traditions of the Progressive Era, if not beyond. And, as noted earlier, efforts to purge politics of internal corruption through codes of conduct go back at least to Andrew Jackson.

Moreover, as table 1.3 also indicates, the defining statute for freedom of information was passed in 1946 as the Administrative Procedure Act (APA). That act is signally important in the history of watchful eye, for it established four key purposes against which to measure future reform. According to *The Attorney General's Manual on the Administrative Procedure Act,* which was published in 1947 and remains an essential reference, the act was designed:

(1) To require agencies to keep the public currently informed of their organization, procedures, and rules.
(2) To provide for public participation in the rulemaking process.
(3) To prescribe uniform standards for the conduct of formal rulemaking and adjudicatory proceedings (i.e., proceedings required by statute to be made on the record after opportunity for an agency hearing).
(4) To restate the law of judicial review.[48]

Passage of the act reflected an enormous struggle between advocates of scientific management, represented by Franklin Roosevelt's Attorney General Francis Biddle, and watchful eye, represented by former dean of the Harvard Law School Roscoe Pound.[49] The struggle involved two very different portraits of the public service, one that saw government employees as self-aggrandizing power maximizers, the other that had a more trusting view.

At least with regard to administrative procedures, it was also a struggle that lasted for the better part of a decade, producing a half dozen major reports, a presidential veto in 1940, and a rough compromise in 1946. As the administrative law scholar Walter Gellhorn assesses the result, "What was forestalled was more significant than what was enacted. For the most part the new statute was declaratory of what had already become the general, though not yet universal, patterns of good behavior; nudging the laggards did no harm, though my own guess is that changes for the better were of small dimensions."[50]

What was forestalled was a code of administrative ethics designed to control what Pound saw as government's tendency to:

(1) "decide without a hearing, or without hearing one of the parties, or after conference with one of the parties in the absence of the other whose interests are adversely affected";

(2) "make determinations on the basis of consultations held in private, or of reports not divulged";

(3) "make determinations of fact seriously without a basis in substantial evidence of in any evidence of rational probative force, much less sustained by the reasonable weight of the evidence as a whole";

(4) "set up and give effect to policies beyond or even at variance with the statutes or the general law";

(5) "determine facts not on the basis of hearing and evidence but on the basis of preconceptions or assumptions of facts to fit the assumed exigencies of a policy";

(6) "make no separation of facts and law, or of facts, law, and policy to be applied to facts"; and

(7) "make the same mistakes in judicial settings about separation of facts and law, etc."[51]

Pound's rhetoric clearly raised the "decibel count" of the debate and led Congress to pass a tough first version of the act.[52]

It was not enough, however, to convince the president. Nor did Pound's indictment translate easily into an ethics code. According to a majority of Attorney General Biddle's Committee on Administrative Procedure, which was convened in part to prepare a case for the expected presidential veto in 1940, such codes tend to "become merely hortatory": "They appear to prescribe a uniform procedure and to erect standards; but, in fact, and in application, they dissolve and permit whatever in the opinion of the administrator is practicable and necessary. . . . Or the code commands the obvious, in situations where disobedience of the command will, without the code, vitiate administrative action. . . . The majority does not believe that legislation is useful which says either 'do as you please' or 'do nothing which is lawless.'"[53]

Defeating the code of ethics changed the course but did not weaken the intensity of watchful eye. Having lost on codes of ethics, advocates of watchful eye began to concentrate their energy on full disclosure and open government, using the APA as a platform for prohibiting the withholding of executive branch information in 1958 and assuring freedom of information in 1966, and consolidating existing bribery, graft, and conflict of interest laws into a single statutory base in 1962. These twin towers of future watchful eye reform encoded the central principles of disclosure and prohibited behavior. If not a formal code of conduct per se, these early legislative successes clearly established certain minimums for behavior.

In spite of these early precedents, there was something special about the Vietnam War and Watergate that accelerated the pressure for open government. Perhaps it was what the nation learned from the Pentagon Papers, which documented the deception regarding Vietnam, and the *Washington Post*'s Watergate investigation, which showed how far a president might go to deny the truth. Perhaps it was the success of John Gardner and Ralph Nader, both of whom became patron saints of watchful eye by questioning the truthfulness of government. And perhaps it was simply the repeated use of executive privilege by Presidents Lyndon Johnson and Richard Nixon to deny access to information about the war, particularly about the Gulf of Tonkin incident that had laid the basis for Johnson's escalation and Nixon's secret bombings five years later. In releasing a survey of 284 instances of executive branch refusals to provide information between 1964 through early 1974, Senate Judiciary Chairman Sam Ervin (D-S.C.) noted the "range of devices, subterfuges, preposterous extensions and assumptions of authority, and outright evasiveness used by the bureaucracy to thwart the Congress in its legitimate inquiries," an inventory that surely had some influence as Congress toughened the Freedom of Information Act in 1974.[54]

In all likelihood, of course, the rising tide of watchful eye reform reflected a blend of all three causes and more. Just as Congress had invented the IG concept to compensate in part for its loss of information in the wake of the 1951 Budget and Accounting Procedures Act, so, too, did Congress turn to sunshine in government in the 1970s to secure access. However, unlike the IG act, Congress did not turn to a counterbureaucracy to provide the focus. It chose an entirely decentralized catalyst in the form of whistleblowers, interest groups such as Gardner's Common Cause and Nader's Public Citizen, the media, and individual Americans.

Not all of the watchful eye reforms were mutually reinforcing, however. At almost the same moment Congress was strengthening the Freedom of Information Act, it acted to protect individuals against arbitrary invasion of privacy in the Privacy Act of 1974. Although theoretically compatible in their shared pursuit of protection, the Privacy Act had a very different goal from its legislative contemporary. Compare how the two Senate committees, Judiciary and Government Operations, explained the goals of their respective bills:

> [Freedom of Information Act] S. 2543 would amend the Freedom of Information Act (FOIA) to facilitate freer and more expeditious public access to government information, to encourage more faithful compliance with the terms and objectives of the FOIA, to strengthen the citizen's remedy against agencies and officials who violate the Act, and to provide for closer congressional oversight of agency performance under the Act.

> [Privacy Act] The purpose of S. 3418, as amended, is to promote governmental respect for the privacy of citizens by requiring all departments and agencies of the executive branch and their employees to observe certain constitutional rules in the computerization, collection, management, use, and disclosure of personal information about individuals.[55]

The resulting tension has not gone unnoticed by legal scholars and practitioners.[56] Some have even argued that the Privacy Act was a partial repeal of the Freedom of Information Act, which was strengthened at virtually the same moment in legislative time.[57] Far more compelling is the notion that even the purest tide of reform often carries conflicts, in part because no tide is ever fully separable from that which has come before or that which will come after, and in part because no tide is the pure property of any single committee, chamber, or branch. In this case, two competing committees endorsed slightly different visions of the same goal, resulting in a continuing conflict over just how much to protect the individual against the public's right to know.

Watchful eye is not just contradicted on occasion from within. As table 1.3 argues, it is clearly contradicted by recent efforts to spur negotiated rulemaking as an alternative to the adversarial process that eventually emerged under the APA. Advocates of "reg-neg," as it is sometimes labeled, do not see themselves as unalterably opposed to APA; rather they view reg-neg as a way to shorten the rulemaking process and reduce court appeals.

With alternative dispute resolution as their alternative, reform advocates finally persuaded the Senate to take the lead on two statutes passed in 1990. The first of the two, the Administrative Dispute Resolution Act, argued that "administrative proceedings have become increasingly formal, costly, and lengthy, resulting in unnecessary expenditures of time and in a decreased likelihood of achieving consensual resolution of disputes," and that "alternative means of dispute resolution have been used in the private sector for many years and, in appropriate circumstances, have yielded decisions that are faster, less expensive, and less contentious."[58] The second statute, the Negotiated Rulemaking Act, made its case in slightly different terms: "Adversarial rulemaking deprives the affected parties and the public of the benefits of face-to-face negotiations and cooperation in developing and reaching agreement on a rule. It also deprives them of the benefits of shared information, knowledge, expertise, and technical abilities possessed by the affected parties."[59] Although both statutes merely encouraged more dispute resolution, they did represent a clear break with the past. By their nature, for example, negotiated rulemaking processes are less "inspectable" from the outside. Although not quite a return to smoke-filled rooms, such negotiations do provide insulation from the adversarial pressures of the traditional notice-and-comment process under the APA. More importantly for drawing the distinction with past watchful eye reforms, dispute resolution–based strategies are more trusting of government employees and interested parties. "Leave them alone to do good," the statutes seem to say. "Liberate them from the hostility imposed by APA, and consensus will follow."

Liberation Management

Liberation management is much more than the opposite of the other three tides. Although it is easiest to define in opposition to scientific management and war on waste, it deserves definition as an administrative philosophy, albeit somewhat confused of late, in its own right (table 1.4).

Liberation management derives much of its current flavor from David Osborne and Ted Gaebler's best-selling book, *Reinventing Government: How the Entrepreneurial Spirit Is Transforming the Public Sector,* which, in turn, draws upon a broad range of private sector best-sellers, most visibly Tom Peters and Richard Waterman's *In Search of Excellence.*[60] Osborne in particular was so important to the NPR that the final report was known as REGO (for *re*inventing *go*vernment) in his honor. Osborne's ideas for making government work were converted into four broad chapter titles for the NPR report:

Table 1.4 Key Characteristics of Liberation Management

Goal	Higher Performance
Key Inputs	Standards, Evaluations
Key Products	Outcomes, Results
Key Participants	Front-Line Employees, Teams, Evaluators
Institutional Champion	The Presidency
Defining Moments	Gore National Performance Review
Defining Statute and	
Most Recent Expression	1993 Government Performance and Results Act
Most Recent Contradictions	1989 Whistleblower Protection Act, 1994
	Independent Counsel Reauthorization
Patron Saints	Richard Nixon, Al Gore
Patron Organization	Alliance for Redesigning Government

(1) "cutting red tape," including streamlining the budget process, decentralizing personnel policy, reorienting the inspectors general, and empowering state and local governments;

(2) "putting customers first," including demanding that service organizations compete and using market mechanisms to solve problems;

(3) "empowering employees to get results," including decentralizing decision-making power, forming a labor-management partnership, and exerting leadership; and

(4) "cutting back to basics," including eliminating programs, investing in greater productivity, and reengineering programs to cut costs.

Although Osborne and Gore use such modern terms such as *empowerment* and *reengineering*, liberation management is hardly a new idea. Jefferson articulated many of the Osborne principles at one time or another during his long public career. According to the historian Lynton Caldwell, Jefferson believed in harmony among employees (hence would likely support the call for labor-management partnership), simplicity (hence would likely endorse cutting back to basics), and adaptability (hence would likely endorse greater flexibility for agencies). Most importantly, Jefferson clearly believed in decentralization of power, reflecting both a personal preference for local control (or devolution, as the NPR might call it) and what Caldwell labels "a highly subjective distrust of professionalized administration and complex administrative machinery."[61]

Not everything in liberation management can be traced back to Jefferson, of course. Jefferson would certainly be perplexed by the attacks on red tape and congressional interference embedded in chapter 1 of the NPR report, for he rather liked the notion of Congress being somehow involved in the administrative state. He might also wonder whether all the reinventing is not just a smoke screen for creating an even more active federal government, and he might ask just who gets empowered when government converts citizens into customers.[62]

Ironically, if one looks back for someone other than Vice President Al Gore as the patron saint of reinventing, it would be Richard Nixon. Although hardly in favor in a Democratic White House, Nixon sounded the "good people–bad systems" theme in a March 1971 message to Congress proposing a "supercabinet" of four new departments. Read the following paragraphs and guess which comes from which, the Nixon message or the NPR report:

1. The problem is not lazy or incompetent people; it is red tape and regulation so suffocating that they stifle every ounce of creativity. No one offers a drowning man a drink of water. And yet, for more than a decade, we have added red tape to a system already strangling in it.
2. [A]fter a quarter century of observing government from a variety of vantage points, I have concluded that the people who work in government are more often the victims than the villains when government breaks down. Their spirit has usually been willing. It is the structure that has been weak.
3. The federal government is filled with good people trapped in bad systems: budget systems, personnel systems, procurement systems, financial management systems. When we blame the people and impose more controls, we make the systems worse.
4. Good people cannot do good things with bad mechanisms. But bad mechanisms can frustrate even the noblest aims. That is why so many public servants—of both political parties, of high rank and low, in both the legislative and executive branches—are often disenchanted with government these days. That is also why so many voters feel that the results of elections make remarkably little difference in their lives.[63]

In spite of the rhetorical similarities, Nixon and Gore came to very different conclusions on how to remedy the problem. Nixon drew heavily from scientific management in proposing the merger of the domestic departments into a supercabinet and creation of a new Office of Management and Budget to provide even greater coordination from the top, while Gore opted for strategies that pushed greater authority and freedom out to the agencies. Nixon soon grew tired of reorganization and took the easier route toward centralization by concentrating authority in the White House staff, under what the political scientist Richard Nathan has called the "administrative Presidency."[64]

Unlike scientific management, which sees its goal in old-fashioned efficiency, liberation management is unabashedly immodest in pursuit of higher performance. It is through the setting of customer service standards, the establishment of measurable goals, the assessment of actual outcomes that liberation management finds the confidence to free agencies from the burdens of central controls. Its notion is to pull government upward by raising the aspirations of agencies and employees, and by measuring their progress toward success.

Liberation management reached a high tide in the 103d Congress with passage of the Government Performance and Results Act (GPRA) of 1993, a statute that can be traced back to the Program, Planning, and Budgeting System (PPBS) established under Defense Secretary Robert McNamara in the mid-1960s. Although PPBS died when it was expanded to domestic agencies under presidential order, its basic emphasis on strategic planning has never been far from the reform surface, particularly as it related to budget reform. It popped up as part of Ford's Management by Objectives (MBO) in the mid-1970s, and again as part of Jimmy Carter's Zero-Based Budgeting (ZBB) two years later.

What makes the GPRA more an expression of liberation than of scientific management is its explicit link to the deregulation of federal management. By 1999, for example, agencies would be allowed to propose waivers of "administrative procedural requirements and controls, including specification of personnel staffing levels, limitations on compensation or remuneration, and prohibitions or restrictions on funding transfers . . . in return for specific individual or organizational accountability to achieve a performance goal."[65] This quid pro quo is a clear break with past reform practice and reflects an effort to trade performance accountability for rule-based compliance accountability.[66]

Although GPRA was originally sponsored by Senator William Roth (R-Del.) two years before Clinton's inauguration, the Democratic administration endorsed it as "an essential step toward making the Government accountable to the American people by making it clear what the taxpayers are getting for their money and removing some of the red tape that bedevils all of us. As every other enterprise has learned, government officials must manage for results, not just rules and regulations. This accountability both empowers and rewards those who improve performance."[67] In spite of the positives, the final bill carried the standard list of war on waste findings:

(1) waste and inefficiency in Federal programs undermine the confidence of the American people in the Government and reduce the Federal Government's ability to address adequately vital public needs;

(2) Federal managers are seriously disadvantaged in their efforts to improve program efficiency and effectiveness because of insufficient articulation of program goals and inadequate information on program performance; and

(3) congressional policymaking, spending decisions and program oversight are seriously handicapped by insufficient attention to program performance and results.[68]

Whether linked to war on waste or not, the GPRA imagined a very different environment for government. Agencies would first create *strategic plans* comprising mission statements, general goals and objectives for major functions, and descriptions of how those goals and objectives would be achieved. Working off these broad outlines, agencies would then produce *annual performance plans* expressing their missions in "an objective, quantifiable, and measurable form." At the end of each year, those plans would form the basis for *annual performance reports* spelling out how agencies did on each measure so that Congress and the public could hold them accountable.

Liberation management also received a boost from passage of three bills tightly linked to the NPR: (1) the Federal Crop Insurance Reform and Department of Agriculture Act of 1994, (2) Government Management Reform Act of 1994, and (3) the Federal Acquisition Streamlining Act of 1994. Although viewed as a single proposal, the three were first separated as they moved to separate committees and subcommittees, then reunited as three consecutively numbered public laws.

Using the Department of Agriculture as its platform for reinvention, the first proposal was designed to close roughly one thousand field offices (a war on waste subtheme), with a linked commitment to greater freedom for those offices that remained (liberation). The second contained a hodgepodge of NPR proposals, most significantly a "Franchise Fund Pilot Program" promoting greater cross-agency competition in providing administrative services. The third contained a sharp reduction in procurement rules as well as a raised threshold for simplified procurement from $25,000 to $100,000.

The reinventing government package reveals the rather uncomfortable merger of two basic tools of liberation management. One is competition, represented above in the Franchise Fund and elsewhere in the liberation movement by various calls for privatization, public school choice, and vouchers of one kind or another. "Injecting competition and market forces into the delivery of these services will reduce duplication, lower overhead costs, and better serve the American people," said Clinton in signing the Government Management Reform Act.[69]

The other is deregulation, represented above by lowering the small purchase threshold and elsewhere by decentralization of a host of traditional management systems, such as personnel. Led by their customer service standards and performance plans, agencies and their workers are to be released from the onerous paperwork required under the old command-and-control procurement regulations. Although customer service standards can be considered a form of competition in the sense that imaginary customers create imaginary markets, the standards hardly carry the ultimate penalty carried by true market forces.

The two tools are not inherently incompatible, but neither are they perfectly in sync. It is reasonable, for example, to imagine fully deregulated agencies that face absolutely no market discipline and have no real customers. Unless such agencies create absolutely clear performance measures, they are essentially free to set their own course, a rather troubling prospect to some. Such worries are no small part of the NPR's occasional drift back to scientific management—for example, in the call for a single chief operating officer in every agency who would be responsible for "ensuring that the President's and agency head's priorities are implemented" and for "applying principles in transforming the agencies' day-to-day management cultures, for improving performance to achieve agency goals, for reengineering administrative processes, and for implementing other National Performance Review recommendations."[70]

Lacking any tools much beyond exhortation, it is not quite clear just how these chief operating officers can exert their will. And lacking any durable organizational champions, it is not clear how long liberation management can sustain a peak. Federal employee unions represent an external champion of sorts, but they largely restrict their enthusiasm to calls for greater labor-management cooperation. Moreover, the tension between the two tools of liberation may yet split the tide in two, with liberation management focusing more on deregulation and proponents of "market forces" targeting privatization and other public choice efforts. As we have seen, it would not be the first time a tide had split.

In this vein, it is important to note that liberation management is hardly unique to the United States. Much of its flavor comes from reinventing efforts in other nations, most notably Britain, New Zealand, and Australia, a debt acknowledged by the NPR in making a case for bipartisanship. "Throughout the developed world, the needs of information-age societies were colliding with the limits of industrial-era government. Regardless of party, regardless of ideology, these governments were responding. In Great Britain, conservatives led the way. In New Zealand, the Labor Party revolutionized government. In Australia and Sweden, both conservative and liberal parties embraced fundamental change."[71] Whether such bipartisanship can be maintained as liberation management strains against its trusting and distrusting selves is yet to be answered.

The power of tides as the central metaphor for tracking reform is simple: it recognizes that philosophies come and go, clearly overlapping as one comes in and the other goes out. Thus, even the highest tide will inevitably subside; even the lowest tide will eventually rise.

Consider, for example, the ebb and flow of scientific management. Building new agencies could not have been more unpopular in the Republican Congress that was swept into its first majority in four decades with the 1994 election. The dominant question was how to cut, not how to build. Agency after agency came under the ax, sometimes for no apparent reason other than a House staffer's inability to recognize its name. Gone was the Advisory Commission on Intergovernmental Relations; gone, too, was the Administrative Conference on the United States.

Yet even as the new Republican majority mounted its war on waste, the National Academy of Public Administration was launching an effort to write the new principles of public administration. Noting its concern that efforts to reinvent government have been approached "without the benefit of the kind of doctrine or conceptualization" that shaped both the Brownlow Committee and first Hoover Commission, NAPA's Standing Panel on Executive Organization offered twelve draft principles. Among the time-honored ideals is the definition of the president as the head of government, the call for appropriate staff assistance, and the demand that Congress stop meddling in the details of administration.[72]

If the past is prologue, NAPA can expect at least modest success, not necessarily because of some great national consensus on a new set of principles, and most certainly not because of some new proof of their impact. Success will come from the natural ebb and flow of the tides of reform. The decentralization of today will inevitably produce stories of scandal; those stories will renew the call for stronger IGs; presidents will once again see the incentives in tight central control; and Congress will surely reassert itself against the newly liberated employee unions.[73]

Some will find this a deeply troubling conclusion. But at least for now there appears to be no end to the fads and fashions, and no way to stop the tides. The fact is that scholars and reformers alike have yet to develop the empirical understandings needed to know what works when, where, and how by way of reform. Lacking a targeting mechanism, advocates of one philosophy or another are free to assert their claims of future success with virtually no basis for dissent. Since no one knows where scientific management might succeed, how war on waste might deter fraud without inhibiting risk taking, whether watchful eye can produce fairness without inefficiency, and what forms of liberation might be risked under which circumstances, there is no way to change the tides, or even to harness their energy.

Before turning to this argument in detail, however, it is first important to understand much more about the tides themselves. Having sketched out the broad theory and a bit of legislative history on each tide in this first chapter, I shall attempt in Chapter 2 to chart the tides in more detail, then examine the role of trust in government and its employees as the driving force dividing the four tides from each other.

2

Charting the Tides

Americans have long been ambivalent about government bureaucracy. They tend to think the worst about bureaucracy as a whole while believing the best about their Social Security claims representative, air traffic controller, or national forest ranger. Americans may believe that the federal government creates more problems than it solves, wastes the taxpayers' money, and turns even the simplest program into a morass of red tape and inefficiency, but they still think government could be more effective if it were just better managed.[1]

Just as Americans hate Congress as an institution but love their own representative, they are the most forgiving of government when they think of their personal experience. Asked in 1994 how often people *in general* can trust government to do what is right, only 19 percent of respondents said "almost always" or "most of the time." But when the question was how often the respondent *personally* could trust the government to do what is right, the number who said "almost always" or "most of the time" more than doubled, to 39 percent.[2]

The public's ambivalence about when and where to trust government is hardly a surprise. As the public administration scholar Charles Goodsell argues, Americans ask the impossible of bureaucracy, giving it "inconsistent, contradictory, and hence unachievable goals and tasks," demanding that it "achieve results indirectly, through the efforts of others," evaluating it "not by how much it tries to move ahead on an impossible front, but whether or not 'success' is achieved," and "both overselling and underselling what it does."[3] Little wonder that Americans are unsure about when and where to trust government and its employees.[4]

Addressed again in the abstract, Americans routinely criticize public employees for being wasteful and lazy, making little distinction between the political appointees at the top of agencies and the career civil servants far below on the front lines.[5] According to the pollster Celinda Lake, "Voters have a strong sense that government employees are the dregs of the labor force—that 'these are basically people who can't get jobs in private industry.' Voters also believe that most government employees are just as political and self-interested as the politicians and bureaucrats they decry."[6] The 1995 budget crisis, with its furlough of nearly one million "non-essential" employees, doubtless did little to ease such harsh conclusions.

Yet Americans are not quite sure whether employees are the problem or, to paraphrase Nixon and Gore, whether government mostly suffers from good people trapped in bad systems. When asked in a 1995 survey about restoring public trust in government, only 8 percent of Americans said changing *who* the bureaucrats are would make the greatest difference; 30 percent said changing the *way* government bureaucrats operate, and 27 percent said changing the way elected officials do business.[7]

Given their confusion about who is to blame for what goes wrong in government, it is hardly surprising that Americans support just about any suggestion for making government work, whether old-fashioned scientific management or liberation, more war on waste, or greater sunshine. According to a 1995 survey, most Americans believe that government would be more effective if it could fire bad employees more easily (war on waste), if it made better use of electronic and communications technology (scientific management), if it shifted more federal responsibilities down to the states (a mix of war on waste and liberation), if it contracted more of its responsibilities to private firms (war on waste and liberation again), or if it gave front-line federal employees more freedom to do their jobs (liberation).[8] Americans appear perfectly comfortable with adding to the layers of distrust inside government through more war on waste, while at the same time arguing that federal employees should be liberated from internal constraints.

The citizenry is not alone in its readiness to inflict greater distrust on government one moment and liberation the next. When should an agency be given greater freedom to do its job? When should it be tightly controlled? What kinds of jobs merit a watchful eye? What kinds deserve liberation? When do federal employees become self-interested power maximizers? When do they favor the public interest? Lacking solid answers, Congress and the presidency lurch from one fad to another, dipping into the four tides of reform almost at random in search of ideas for making government work.

At the core of the confusion is trust. No one is sure when and where to trust government to do its job, not ordinary Americans, not Congress, not presidents and vice presidents, not public administration and management scholars. As a result, much of what Congress and the presidency do about making government work is driven by the political context in which a given reform effort occurs. It is not surprising, for example, that the NPR might produce a stirring call to reinvention at the start of an activist administration, or that Congress might produce an IG at HEW at the end of an investigation of welfare fraud. It is also not surprising that the tides of reform would ebb and flow with political fortune. As I argue in this chapter, those who have reason to trust government and its employees are far more likely to favor scientific management and liberation management, while those who do not trust tend to support war on waste and watchful eye.

Before returning to trust as the dividing line between the four tides, it is first important to chart the tides themselves in more detail. To what extent, for example, are there differences in how the tides roll in through legislative history? To what extent do the tides break differently in their basic approach to making government work? To what extent do the tides target different parts of the government shoreline? Answering these basic questions should lay the foundation for a more detailed understanding of the role of trust in government as a fundamental dividing line between scientific and liberation management in one cycle and war on waste and watchful eye in the next.

The following pages are based on analysis of the 141 major reform initiatives recorded in Appendix A. As noted in the Introduction, these initiatives were culled from the legislative record of 1945–1994. As shown in Appendix B, there are differences in both the number of initiatives from each tide (scientific management accounts for 44 percent of the 141 initiatives recorded, war on waste 23 percent, watchful eye 18 percent, and liberation management 15 percent) and era (almost 60 percent of the initiatives come from the post-Watergate era, beginning with Nixon's resignation in 1974).

Not every expert will agree with every initiative included in Appendix A. Nor will every expert agree with my judgments in sorting those initiatives by the measures summarized in Appendix B. Ultimately, this analysis is based on my efforts to find the best fit between a given initiative and the broad portraits of the tides discussed in Chapter 1. Readers are cautioned to consider the rest of this book as a rough charting of the tides of reform, not as exact mapping— that is, rather like viewing the tides from 30,000 feet instead of at the water's edge. Something gets lost with the elevation, but the big picture is much clearer. The charts should still be sharp enough to pinpoint the ebb and flow of reform.

THE BASIC CHARTS

The question for the moment is whether and how the four tides of reform differ in six basic areas: (1) legislative history, (2) reform philosophy, (3) change strategy, (4) size and scale of the initiative, (5) implementation, and (6) impacts. (In the next chapter we will survey the role of time in reform.)

It is important to note, however, that the four tides do not need to vary on every measure to be declared separate influences on making government work. That two or more tides share the same legislative history, for example, does not render them the same. Just as all ocean tides share the same water, so, too, do the tides of reform often share the same legislative conditions.

Legislative History

Legislative history can be measured in a number of simple ways. Where did the initiative come from? Was there a blue-ribbon commission involved? Were interest groups interested? Was the legislative history routine or controversial? What was the margin of legislative passage? And was a recorded vote even taken? (Voice votes can be assumed to be unanimous for purposes of this charting effort.) The answers to these questions are summarized for each tide in table 2.1.[9]

The four streams clearly vary by origin of idea. Not surprisingly, given its focus on the president as the one true master of government, scientific management is the tide most likely to originate in the White House. And not surprisingly, given the focus of war on waste and watchful eye on greater access for Congress, those tides are far more likely to come from the other end of Pennsylvania Avenue. Liberation management is a bit confused, a creature of neither Congress nor the presidency. We will give more attention later to the impact of origin on reform. For now, suffice it to note that institutions—and even chambers—have their favorite tides.

With its links to the first Hoover Commission, scientific management has a far greater share of blue-ribbon connections than any other tide. As the politi-

Table 2.1 *Legislative History of Reform (percentages)*

	Scientific Management	War on Waste	Watchful Eye	Liberation Management
Origin of Idea				
President	69	31	6	55
Congress	31	69	94	45
Blue-Ribbon Commission Involved?	24	4	3	10
Interest Groups Involved?	27	19	39	30
Legislative Debate				
Routine	55	62	58	50
Controversial	45	39	42	50
Legislative Passage				
Unanimous	44	65	58	30
Near-Unanimous	26	27	30	35
Strong Majority (60% or more)	23	4	6	30
Close (less than 60%)	8	4	6	5
Recorded Vote Taken?	58	50	64	75

N = 141

cal scientists Harold Seidman and Robert Gilmour write, the Hoover Commission marked the high tide of administrative orthodoxy: "The commission's report on 'General Management of the Executive Branch' represents the most categorical formulation of the orthodox or classic organization doctrine derived largely from business administration and identified with the scientific management movement during the early decades of this century."[10]

There is no question that this orthodoxy crested in the 1950s. According to the U.S. Senate Committee on Expenditures in the Executive Departments, the Hoover Commission accounted for forty-six public laws enacted in the two sessions of the Eighty-First Congress (1949–1950) and the first session of the Eighty-Second (1951), or almost 5 percent of all public laws produced. Interestingly, the Hoover Commission also appears to have produced a name change in the Senate. The Committee on Expenditures in the Executive Departments became the Committee on Government Operations as the Committee and its chairman, John McClellan (D-Ark.) sought to broaden its agenda beyond mere tracking of audits and accounting procedures.

Given Herbert Hoover's efforts to strengthen the presidency as the administrative master of government, it is perhaps ironic that the two commissions bearing his name originated in Congress, not the White House. A new Republican congressional majority launched the first Hoover Commission in 1947 with the expectation that a Republican would be elected president in 1948 to implement what would surely be Hoover's recommendations for government cutbacks. Neither a Republican president nor the recommendations emerged. Under intense lobbying pressure from Hoover himself, another new Republican Congress launched the second Commission in 1953, again in the hope that a new Republican president, this time already sworn in, might use the commission to downsize government. Again that hope was disappointed. Although established by a Republican Congress, the two commissions were unrelentingly proexecutive, a fact lost on neither Truman nor Eisenhower as each took ownership of the Hoover recommendations in one reorganization plan after another.

Blue-ribbon commissions are, of course, versions of a scientific approach themselves. "Certainly those of us who serve in the Congress, and especially those of us who serve on this committee, know better than anyone else of the fantastic growth which has taken place in the executive branch of the Federal Government during the last few decades," said Rep. Clarence Brown (R-Ohio) in explaining his reasons for introducing legislation to create the first Hoover Commission. Since it was impossible for either Congress or the president to devote the needed time and energy to a study of the whole executive branch of government, Brown concluded that what "is needed more than anything else today is to have a commission such as the one provided for in this bill to take an over-all look at our executive branch of the Government—its services, activities, and functions—and furnish the President with its findings of facts, along with its recommendations as to how duplicated efforts, overlapping activities, and similar functions can be simplified, consolidated, or eliminated."[11] Only through study and analysis would the truth reveal itself.

If blue-ribbon commissions are a characteristic tool of scientific management, interest group involvement is most prominent in watchful eye, with the key interest groups being Common Cause and Public Citizen. This is not to suggest that watchful eye reforms like the Government in the Sunshine Act or the Federal Advisory Committee Act, both of which opened the internal workings of government to external inspection, would not have passed without these groups. Nevertheless, the presence of such persistent and aggressive organizations accounts for considerable watchful eye pressure during the early to mid-1970s. Such groups can be seen as populist versions of blue-ribbon commissions, operating to grant legitimacy to the watchful eye reforms.

Regardless of the involvement of blue-ribbon commissions and interest groups—or perhaps because of it—table 2.1 suggests that making government work is a relatively noncontroversial issue on the floor of Congress. *Controversy* is defined here as any committee or floor action that arouses at least some minimal level of challenge. It is not clear, however, what a reasonable baseline for all legislation might be against which to compare the nature of the legislative debate. Congressional scholars have long argued that the vast majority of bills pass with little or no controversy. If that is true, making government work may be more difficult than the limited coverage in the *New York Times* and *Washington Post* might indicate.

So noted, when we look at the actual margin of passage, making government work emerges as even less controversial. War on waste is clearly the most popular of the four tides, achieving unanimous or near-unanimous votes in all but 8 percent of its initiatives. Watchful eye comes in close behind, suggesting the pure popularity of just about any bill that gives Congress greater access to the inner workings of government. Scientific and liberation management provoke closer margins—if 60-plus percent unanimity can be declared "close"—largely, it seems, because both tides tend to strengthen presidential control, and scientific management creates new spending vehicles as well, in the form of new agencies.

As for taking recorded votes, liberation management shows the highest visibility. This result, however, appears to be a result of timing. Liberation management is most active in the post-Watergate period, when recorded votes became much more frequent.[12]

Reform Philosophy

Table 2.2 covers two broad measures of reform philosophy that reflect the four tides: accountability mechanism and general view of government. As the figures suggest, these two measures reveal sharp differences between the tides.

Accountability is measured here as either compliance, capacity, or performance, and pertains strictly to the administrative mechanism chosen to create and/or enforce incentives for desired behavior.[13] A compliance-based system seeks accountability through enforcement. Rules are the primary input into a compliance-based system, supervision and discipline the primary managerial activities, detection and adjustment of errors the primary outputs, and deterrence the ultimate outcome. Compliance accountability usually comes into play after the fact—that is, its operating approach is to catch mistakes after they occur, and, in attacking the source of mistakes, to make an example that will deter future behavior. It places its faith in the ability of Congress, presidents, managers, the press, whistleblowers, and individual citizens to create a "visible odium" of deterrence, as one inspector general once described it.

A performance-based system seeks its impact through incentives. Goals are the primary input into a performance-based system, evaluation/auditing and benchmarking the primary managerial activities, measurable results the outputs, and higher performance the ultimate outcome. Performance accountability seeks its impact both before and after the fact, first by creating goals as a pull toward appropriate behavior, then by providing rewards for actual accomplishment. As such, it puts its faith in efforts to set higher standards for performance and finds its clearest expression in the Government Performance and Results Act.

A performance-based system is not the only alternative to compliance, however. Accountability can also reside in a capacity-based system that seeks its impact by providing government and its employees with the skills, tools, and political support to be effective. Technologies are the primary inputs in building capacity, whether defined as human capital, organizational structure, or systems (personnel, budget, information, and so on), advocacy and stewardship in winning and implementing these technologies are the primary managerial activity, and naturally effective performance the output. As such, capacity-based accountability builds accountability at the front end of the process, whether in the design of a new agency, acquisition of new information technologies, or training initiatives.

Table 2.2 Differences in the Philosophy of Reform (percentages)

	Scientific Management	War on Waste	Watchful Eye	Liberation Management
Accountability Mechanism				
Compliance	11	69	88	10
Capacity	73	19	12	55
Performance	16	12	0	35
General View of Government				
Trusting	79	19	3	65
Distrusting	21	81	97	35

N = 141

In spite of their differences, compliance, capacity, and performance accountability are not mutually exclusive, and sometimes they appear side by side in the same statute. The 1978 Civil Service Reform Act contained a mix of all three, including merit pay (performance), whistleblower protection (compliance), and creation of a Senior Executive Service as a repository for particularly skilled and mobile top-level talent (capacity). As I have argued, the "choice of one strategy does not necessarily exclude the need for a second or third. Compliance accountability, for example, is not inconsistent with performance incentives or capacity building and may be essential for assuring the fairness and equity that sometimes undermine employee confidence in performance systems."[14]

Nevertheless, the mechanisms can be seen as distinct legislative options. Indeed, as noted in Chapter 1, the Government Performance and Results Act imagines an explicit trade-off between the traditional compliance accountability embedded in Office of Management personnel ceilings and the performance accountability that resides in setting clear goals. Under section 5 of the act, agencies are free to request waivers, provided that each agency first "shall quantify the expected improvements in performance resulting from any waiver," then demonstrate that such improvements exceed "the projected level of performance that would be achieved independent of any waiver," and "precisely express the monetary change in compensation or remuneration amounts, such as bonuses or awards, that shall result from meeting, exceeding, or failing to meet performance goals." Even here, OMB used a measure of compliance accountability to give agencies a strong incentive for performance. Only by complying with the OMB waiver regulations can agencies be liberated.

As table 2.2 suggests, the four tides do favor different accountability mechanisms. Given its focus on organizations and systems, scientific management clearly favors capacity accountability. But this does not mean scientific management never adopts alternative accountability mechanisms. The 1989 HUD reforms were clearly driven by a concern for compliance, in part reflecting the role of war on waste as a highly visible secondary feature of the effort to clean up the Reagan-era scandals in the nation's housing program. Moreover, scientific management has long been concerned with making government pay competitive with the private sector, which is also defined as performance accountability.

War on waste and watchful eye both share a strong commitment to compliance. War on waste's percentage would be even higher were it not for the three IG statutes in Appendix A. Although these three statutes were part of the war on waste, they focused on building a basic organizational capacity to wage war and must therefore be considered expressions of a capacity-based accountability. It was through the "technology" of creating offices of inspector general where none had ever existed that these three statutes sought their impact.

Liberation management appears the most divided in its accountability mechanism. It is not quite sure whether liberation means creating capacity, incentives, or the occasional rule. Part of the explanation is timing. During the earlier years covered by Appendix A, liberation management expressed itself through the creation of government-sponsored enterprises and corporations of one kind or another. The Communications Satellite Act of 1962, which created a private, for-profit organization to oversee U.S. commercial satellite development, was clearly about creating a kind of capacity free from the ordinary burdens of government management regulations. It shows up in the liberation management inventory as an expression of capacity-based accountability, as does creation of the U.S. Postal Service and Amtrak. (By definition, all government corporations are expressions of liberation management.)[15]

Table 2.2 shows that the general view of government breaks sharply across the four tides. Watchful eye is clearly the most distrusting toward government and its employees. Its basic assumption is that the more sunshine and openness the better, an assumption based on a dim view of the instincts of bureaucracy and its bureaucrats to confuse, obfuscate, and mislead. War on waste is only slightly less distrusting, again seeing its role as ferreting out the basic tendencies of government to make mistakes, misplace funds, and mislead, to say nothing of the tide's suspicious view of those whom government serves through such benefit programs as Aid to Families with Dependent Children and those who serve government under contract through such programs as Medicaid and Medicare.

Not surprisingly, scientific management is far more trusting. How else to sell statutes designed to house new initiatives like the space program or the campaign to conserve energy? By their nature, proposals to create new structure are almost always sold with enthusiasm and great promise. Although scientific management can take a more distrustful tone, particularly with regard to reorganizations and HUD reforms, it still carries the flag of Woodrow Wilson's positive vision for the public service.

Once again, liberation management appears a bit confused, not quite sure whether it is trusting or distrusting. The distrustful initiatives summarized in table 2.2 generally involve various efforts to introduce competition and/or to free programs from the bounds of traditional civil service sloth. Nixon's block grants for community development and job training both fall into the distrusting category. Although block grants free the affected program from bureaucratic red tape, neither can be considered a statement of confidence in the federal government and its employees.

Change Strategy

Change strategy involves the focus, tactics, and target of each tide. As table 2.3 shows, the four tides have a rather different mix of each. Scientific management is the only tide to focus more on changing the structure of government than its procedures. Indeed, one of the most important products of the first Hoover Commission was a standard organizational chart that continues to this day to thicken the federal hierarchy with management layers.[16]

Under Hoover's ideal organizational chart, chiefs of units were to report to chiefs of sections, who were to report to chiefs of branches, who were to report to chiefs of divisions, and so on up the line to chiefs of bureaus, chiefs of services, administrative assistant secretaries, assistant secretaries, undersecretaries, secretaries, and finally to the president, who would have an administrative vice president to supervise independent agencies, coordinate interdepartmental activities, resolve conflicts among the agencies, and supervise liquidation of old agencies.[17]

As such, the chart reflected five of Hoover's principles: (1) the agencies of government should be grouped into departments by major purposes, (2) bureaus within departments should be grouped into administrations by major purposes, (3) department heads should have full operating responsibility through clear lines of authority down to the very last person in the organization, (4) such operating services as accounting, budgeting, and personnel should be decentralized, while policy guidance on such matters should be centralized, and (5) department heads should have adequate staff to do their jobs.[18]

Although the other three tides put a greater weight on changing the procedures of government than on changing its structure, none is without the occasional focus on structure. Liberation management features a structural focus whenever it proposes a government corporation as an alternative to traditional government agencies, as does war on waste whenever a new agency is added to the ever growing list of offices of inspector general. Even watchful eye has its occasional structural option, most recently the Office of Government Ethics Reauthorization Act of 1988, which granted OGE independence from the Office of Personnel Management.

Conversely, even scientific management has its share of procedural offerings, most of which focus on creating new systems or revising old toward a more rational basis for operations. Hence, the 1950 Budget and Accounting Procedures Act shows up as a defining procedural reform. "There is no formal

Table 2.3 *Differences in the Change Strategy of Reform (percentages)*

	Scientific Management	War on Waste	Watchful Eye	Liberation Management
Focus				
Structure of Government	60	27	18	40
Procedures of Government	34	65	73	60
Both	3	8	9	0
Study Commission	3	0	0	0
Structural Tactic				
Create New Agency	21	15	12	10
Merge Existing Agencies	19	0	0	0
Reorganize Existing Agency	15	4	0	0
Create Public Corporation	0	0	0	30
Abolish Existing Agency	0	15	0	0
Grant Agency Independence	0	0	12	0
Elevate Agency to Higher Rank	3	0	3	0
Combination	5	0	0	0
No Structural Reform in Statute	37	65	73	60
Procedural Tactic				
Establish New System	10	35	43	10
Broaden Existing System	5	23	33	0

Revise Existing System	15	4	0	0
Deregulate/Narrow System	0	4	0	45
Reauthorize System	8	4	6	0
Abolish System	0	4	0	0
Combination	0	0	0	5
No Procedural Reform in Statute	63	27	18	40
Target				
General Organization	65	15	12	40
Procurement/Acquisition	5	31	6	10
Ethics/Standards of Conduct	3	4	33	5
Administrative Process	0	0	27	0
Pay Systems	11	0	0	0
Audit/Investigation	0	23	0	0
Rulemaking Procedures	0	4	9	10
General Personnel/Classification	6	4	0	5
Budget/Financial Management	5	4	3	10
Combination	5	4	0	10
Strategic Planning/Analysis	0	0	6	5
Debt Collection	0	12	0	0
Tort Claims	0	0	3	5

N = 141

accounting plan for the Government as a whole," the first Hoover Commission complained in making the case for reform. "As a consequence there is no place where the complete financial picture of our Government can be sensed. . . . As a result we have not had, to this day, a system of accounting that shows the Government's true revenues and expenses for any year, that provides for property or cost accounting, or for a positive control of assets, liabilities, and appropriations."[19] Fast forward to the present and the complaints about shoddy accounting systems remain virtually unchanged.

Once down to the specifics of structure and procedure, the tides hold mostly to expected patterns. On the structural side of the reform ledger, the largest number of scientific management entries come under creating new agencies and merging and/or reorganizing existing agencies; watchful eye splits its meager number of entries between creating new agencies and granting independence to old ones (for example, elevation of the Office of Government Ethics to independent status); and the largest share for liberation management appears on the government corporation line. As might be expected, war on waste has the only initiatives abolishing existing agencies, the most prominent example being the Synthetic Fuels Corporation Act of 1985.[20]

On the procedural side of the ledger, watchful eye has the greatest number of entries on establishing new systems, whether for monitoring bribery, graft, and corruption in the 1960s, opening the shades of government to the sunshine in the 1970s, or assuring computer security in the 1980s. War on waste also has its share of new systems, particularly related to debt collection and procurement in the 1980s. As expected, liberation has the highest share of deregulation entries, while scientific management splits its relatively small numbers across a mix of new, old, and revised systems.

Expected patterns also hold on the target of each reform initiative in table 2.3. Scientific management emerges as the leading tide for shaping the general organization of government and has the only entries under pay; war on waste has the largest share of entries on procurement/acquisition and the only initiatives on the audit/investigation line; watchful eye stands out as the tide for ethics/standards of conduct and administrative process; and, as also presaged by early discussion, liberation management has entries across the board.

Size and Scale of the Initiative

Table 2.4 offers separate measures of size and scale and a unifying measure of the two. The primary questions asked about a given measure are twofold: (1) is it a new idea or a modification of an existing practice, and (2) is it a large departure from prevailing practice or a relatively smaller adjustment?[21]

Answering both questions involves further judgment calls reflecting my

Table 2.4 *Differences in the Scale of Reform (percentages)*

	Scientific Management	War on Waste	Watchful Eye	Liberation Management
Nature of Idea				
New Approach	47	58	42	85
Modification of Old	53	42	58	15
Scope of Impact				
Large	40	35	39	45
Small	60	65	61	55
Overall Scale				
New/Large	26	23	24	40
New/Small	23	35	18	45
Old/Large	16	12	18	5
Old/Small	36	31	39	10

N = 141

sense of the overall context of reform. Some initiatives are easy to measure. Creation of the Department of Health, Education, and Welfare under Reorganization Plan No. 1 of 1953 is coded as a new and very large idea, even though it mostly involved stitching together existing units of government. So, too, for the Departments of Transportation and Energy, which were mostly collections of old wine in new bottles.

Other initiatives are more difficult to characterize. Although the Department of Veterans Affairs Act created a new department, it was basically old wine in an old bottle with a new label. Nothing new was added, nothing much changed. Therefore, the act is defined as an old/small initiative, a decision that most certainly would be challenged by the veterans lobby, but a decision that appears to fit the facts of the case.

As table 2.4 suggests, making government work is very much a mixture of the new and the small, with liberation management by far the leading source of what might be labeled administrative innovation. It is important to note, however, that liberation management shows up as innovative largely because it so often cuts against the prevailing wisdom, not because it offers stunning examples of novel thinking. Reengineering the Internal Revenue Service's tax processing system or raising the threshold for small purchases from $25,000 to $100,000 is innovative only in comparison with what has come before.

War on waste also has a very large number of new/small initiatives, in large part because of efforts in the early to mid-1980s to give the IGs new tools for ferreting out fraud, waste, and abuse. In contrast, watchful eye is the least innovative. One can even argue that most watchful eye reform is a variant of two core statutes: the Administrative Procedure Act of 1946 and the Bribery, Graft, and Corruption, and Conflicts of Interest recodifications of 1962. The Freedom of Information and Privacy Acts both used the APA as their statutory base, while the Ethics in Government Act and its subsequent amendments used the bribery recodification as theirs.

Implementation

If questions of size and scale call for broad judgments, issues of implementation are much more straightforward. Statutes either allow pilots/experiments or do not; they either have a sunset or they do not; they either affect a single agency or several agencies, or they are implemented governmentwide; and they are subject either to centralized oversight by the president, whether through the assorted units of the Executive Office of the President (EOP) (the White House staff, Office of Management and Budget, Office of Personnel Management), to department and agency heads, or, in the case of the war on waste, to decentralized oversight by Congress, the media, and citizens.

Table 2.5 offers an inventory of these implementation strategies for each of the tides.

Four conclusions emerge from the table. First, there is virtually no impulse, in any of the tides, for allowing experimentation in programs. Of the 141 initiatives recorded in Appendix A, only five can be remotely described as having contained any form of experimentation as either a threshold to full implementation or an end in itself:

1. The 1978 Civil Service Reform Act, which allowed up to ten demonstration projects each year under waivers to the act;
2. The 1986 Federal Debt Recovery Act, which created a three-year experiment allowing private firms to collect debt owed to the government;
3. The 1990 Chief Financial Officers Act, which required six agencies to prepare comprehensive, agencywide financial statements by the end of 1991, after which Congress would (and did) escalate the effort governmentwide;
4. The 1990 Negotiated Rulemaking Act, which encouraged agencies to experiment with reg-neg;
5. The 1993 Government Performance and Results Act, which required ten pilots of a performance measurement system followed by automatic governmentwide implementation.

I will return to the question of why there is so little experimentation in making government work. Suffice it to note here that one reason the public might be confused about when and where to trust government is that reformers have yet to adopt a similar question in designing their initiatives.

Second, making government work involves permanence. Rare indeed is the initiative that carries a sunset. Sunsets are no guarantee that Congress and the president will take a second hard look at reform, but at least they provide an opportunity. Consider as an example the 1995 reauthorization of the 1980 Paperwork Reduction Act, which was originally designed to set yearly targets for reducing the government paperwork burden imposed on private citizens and businesses (through tax forms, surveys, information collections, and so on). The sunset eventually allowed Congress to inject elements of liberation management into what had been a strong war on waste reform. By redefining the term *information resources management* to mean "the process of managing information resources to accomplish agency missions and to improve agency performance, including the reduction of information collection burdens on the public," the reauthorization made a small gesture toward harnessing war on waste to liberation as more than just a selling tactic.[22] Whether the effort can succeed given the statute's original goal of reducing paperwork burdens remains to be seen.

Table 2.5 *Differences in the Implementation of Reform (percentages)*

	Scientific Management	War on Waste	Watchful Eye	Liberation Management
Experimental Approach in Statute?	3	4	0	10
Time Horizon in Statute				
Temporary/Sunset	16	15	12	10
Permanent	84	85	88	90
Scope				
Single Agency	39	31	21	60
Several Agencies	27	8	0	5
Governmentwide	34	62	79	35
Oversight Approach				
Centralized	81	46	24	5
Decentralized	19	54	76	95

N = 141

Third, the tides split in the overall scope of implementation, with war on waste and watchful eye much more frequently implemented governmentwide than either scientific or liberation management. Of particular interest is the frequent adoption of liberation management reforms agency by agency rather than governmentwide. Part of the finding is a simple by-product of liberation management's past focus on creating government corporations, but part reflects the tendency of advocates to view scientific management as their main foil in reform. Consider how the NPR report characterizes its enemy:

> From the 1930s through the 1960s, we built large, top-down, centralized bureau-cracies to do the public's business. They were patterned after the corporate struc-tures of the age: hierarchical bureaucracies in which tasks were broken into simple parts, each the responsibility of a different layer of employees, each defined by specific rules and regulations. . . . Many federal organizations are also monopolies with few incentives to innovate. Employees have virtual lifetime tenure, regardless of their performance. Success offers few rewards; failure, few penalties. And cus-tomers are captive; they can't walk away from the air traffic control system or the In-ternal Revenue Service and sign up with a competitor.[23]

Except for the recommendation to "reorient" the inspectors general and frequent references to burdensome procurement regulations, the NPR does not focus its ire on the products of war on waste or watchful eye. There is nary a word in the entire report on the Freedom of Information Act, Privacy Act, Sunshine in Government Act, Federal Advisory Committee Act, or Computer Security Act, all of which imposed substantial regulatory burdens on federal agencies and their employees. And hard as one might search in the language surrounding NPR's recommendation that agencies reduce internal regula-tions by more than 50 percent, there is no reference to the Administrative Pro-cedure Act or the Paperwork Reduction Act.

By adopting scientific management as its opponent, the NPR avoided tough arguments over watchful eye and its procedural guarantees of equity. Although the NPR did take on the OIGs and the intimidation produced by "gotcha" reviews, it did not challenge the hunt for dollars embedded in such statutes as the Federal Managers' Financial Integrity Act. By mostly leaving the war on waste and watchful eye untouched by its recommendations, the NPR also neglected a sizable share of the governmentwide regulatory burden, and therefore may have oversold the potential gains from an agency-by-agency attack on the products of earlier scientific management.

Finally, the tides vary sharply in the degree to which administrative over-sight is centralized or decentralized. It is hardly surprising that scientific man-agement sees the president and EOP as its source of centralized oversight.

Virtually every document associated with the recent expression of scientific management carries its paean to the president as administrative linchpin. War on waste also shows a high level of centralized oversight, this time to be found in the IGs, which were designed to unify the disparate audit and investigative units spread out through their departments and agencies.

In contrast, watchful eye puts its emphasis on an amorphous mass of decentralized overseers, not the least of which are the American people themselves. It is up to the public, media, interest groups, congressional staffers, and assorted whistleblowers to assure that the watchful eye is maintained. If war on waste reflects a form of what the political scientists Mathew McCubbins and Thomas Schwartz call "police patrol" oversight, watchful eye depends on "fire alarms" to be pulled whenever an interested party sees smoke.[24]

Liberation management prefers decentralized oversight as well, but by a very different set of watchers. Liberation puts its focus on the role of individual civil servants and/or the market to assure its effective implementation. There is no doubt, for example, that the NPR sees federal employees as fully competent to police themselves, provided, of course, that they are given the appropriate capacity to do their jobs. Nevertheless, the NPR also looks to the market for discipline and oversight. Breaking monopolies by "giving citizens a voice and a choice," as NPR calls it, introduces a clear discipline of its own, one that advocates believe can be counted upon to assure dedicated implementation.

Interestingly, war on waste tends to favor decentralized oversight. Although the IGs are, by themselves, expressions of a centralizing impulse, the inspectors general cannot keep track of everything. It is through decentralized implementation of a host of procurement and acquisition rules that war on waste must seek its ultimate impact. Even though those rules are subject to sporadic inspection by the OIGs, the war on waste must ultimately rely on a widely decentralized deterrence to assure effective implementation.

The Paperwork Reduction Act, for example, seeks its yearly reductions in paperwork burden by requiring a federal control number on every information collection request, from tax forms to hazardous waste tracking surveys. If such a document does not carry such a number, recipients are free to disregard the request in what is very much decentralized oversight: taxpayers do not have to fill out the form, polluters do not have to track their waste. It is in the effort to get that number that agencies must pay attention to the yearly targets.

In a similar vein, the False Claims Act Amendments of 1986 created new incentives for individual citizens to join the war against government contract fraud. Under a *qui tam* claim, individuals can collect up to 30 percent of the total penalties assessed and collected in successful fraud cases.[25] Although the *qui tam* provision had existed for well over one hundred years under the original statute, which was signed into law under Abraham Lincoln in 1863, the amendments revitalized the concept by injecting a much larger incentive. As such, the amendments reflected an effort to widen the base of overseers by creating a voluntary force of fraud hunters.[26]

Impact

Charting the likely impacts of reform moves this discussion back to highly subjective answers to a range of broad questions. Does a given initiative shift shared powers toward the president or Congress? Increase or decrease the cost of government? Expand or contract the role of government? Thicken or thin the federal hierarchy? Increase or decrease administrative speed? Enhance or reduce interest-group access? Enhance or reduce public access? Improve or impair government morale? And strengthen line (delivery) or staff (advisory) units? A set of admittedly speculative answers based on a reading of historical judgments is recorded in table 2.6.

As noted in the Introduction, some questions are impossible to answer; these are shunted into a special category called "not clear/no impact discernible" in table 2.6. Others are governed by simple rules. For example, all pay increases are automatically declared an improvement in government morale, and all department and agency creations are automatically defined as both a shift of power to the president and an expansion of the role of government. Still others are relatively easy to answer by inspecting the statute itself. It is relatively easy, for example, to spot the thickening of the federal hierarchy. The creation of the Synfuels Corporation in 1980 added a new unit to government (thickening); its abolishment in 1985 subtracted similarly (thinning). The 1978 IG Act added new units to twelve departments and agencies; thus far, none has been abolished.[27]

Even with these rules, charting impacts is a risky endeavor at best. It is attempted here mostly in the spirit of trying to force critical debate about the need for baselines against which to measure the ultimate consequences of reform, a debate that will be engaged more directly in Chapter 5. For the time being, however, readers are asked to consider the figures in table 2.6 as broad illustrations of impacts, not as absolute proofs.

Caveat noted, there are relatively few surprises in the figures. As expected, given its links to the principles of administration and the first Hoover Commission, scientific management emerges as the tide most favoring presidents and most likely to cost money, expand the role of government, thicken the hierarchy, and strengthen line units. Liberation management also emerges as a gen-

Table 2.6 Differences in the Impact of Reform (percentages)

	Scientific Management	War on Waste	Watchful Eye	Liberation Management
Shift in Shared Powers				
Toward President	82	31	0	40
Toward Congress	8	12	73	35
Not Clear/No Shift Discernible	10	58	27	25
Impact on Cost of Government				
Increase	42	0	9	35
Decrease	2	27	0	20
Not Clear/No Impact Discernible	57	73	91	45
Impact on Role of Government				
Expand	57	4	3	25
Contract	3	31	0	25
Not Clear/No Impact Discernible	40	65	97	50
Impact on Shape of Government				
Thicken Hierarchy	66	35	79	30
Thin Hierarchy	5	35	0	50
Not Clear/No Impact Discernible	29	31	21	20

Impact on Administrative Speed				
Accelerate	40	31	9	75
Slow Down	5	35	75	0
Not Clear/No Impact Discernible	55	35	15	25
Impact on Interest Group Access				
Enhance	10	12	24	35
Reduce	19	19	46	10
Not Clear/No Impact Discernible	71	69	30	55
Impact on Public Access				
Enhance	8	4	55	10
Reduce	5	8	0	25
Not Clear/No Impact Discernible	87	89	46	65
Impact on Government Morale				
Improve	27	8	31	35
Reduce	0	8	3	0
Not Clear/No Impact Discernible	73	85	67	65
Impact on Bureaucratic Balance				
Strengthen Line Units	77	4	12	65
Strengthen Staff Units	19	77	79	20
Not Clear/No Impact Discernible	3	19	9	15

N = 141

eral aid to the president—albeit one that also contains six statutes creating government corporations, which are defined as shifting power toward Congress (the notion here being that government corporations tend to weaken presidential control in favor of Congress).[28] Liberation is first among the tides in increasing administrative speed, first in improving government morale, and a source of strengthening for line units. At least in terms of these broad impacts, liberation management is, indeed, liberating.

Also not surprisingly, given its origins in the demand for access to information, watchful eye is the source of the greatest shift of power toward Congress. Yet watchful eye also emerges as the tide most likely to thicken government, largely through the addition of senior-level staff to monitor compliance with the assorted reform initiatives, which may ultimately weaken Congress's vision. Interestingly, watchful eye shows virtually no impact one way or the other on either the cost or role of government, in part because it is nearly impossible to estimate the direct costs of such statutes as Sunshine in Government. Finally, watchful eye also leads the tides in slowing down the administrative process, which is precisely what many of its initiatives are designed to do. The APA, for example, was designed not to accelerate the process but to make it far more predictable and most certainly more deliberate.

In fact, it was the potential for delay that attracted business interests to the cause.[29] They understood fully that APA could become a central tool for delaying, if not completely frustrating an activist government. So, too, for the Paperwork Reduction Act of 1980. By creating an entirely new process for approving information collections, the act was certain to slow the administrative system, as it most surely has. Part of the slowing comes from greater public access, which watchful eye clearly promotes (see table 2.6); part comes from the simple layering that arises from the new rules that emerge almost automatically from watchful eye.

War on waste leads four categories in table 2.6: reducing the cost of government, contracting the role of government, reducing government morale, and strengthening the staff units of government. War on waste also tends to decrease administrative speed by imposing additional rules on already cumbersome internal systems. Cutting costs, abolishing programs, and creating the "visible odium" of deterrence may all help save money but can undermine employee morale in the process. Although this book counts the three IG acts in Appendix A as having no discernible effect on government morale, a strong case could be made for declaring all three as negatives. The OIGs have not earned a reputation for "gotcha" audits and investigations for nothing. At least during the 1980s, many sought that reputation as part of their overall effort to inject fear into their departments and agencies.[30]

Given its primary selling point, war on waste does not have a particularly significant impact on lowering the cost of government. It is nearly impossible to know just how much the war on waste has actually saved. My analysis of OIG effectiveness suggests more questions than answers about dollars saved and funds put to better use. Setting aside the rather significant yearly records for funds put to better use—which are, after all, funds not saved but redirected—the OIGs would be hard pressed to demonstrate more than a few billion in total recoveries over the decades. On an OIG-by-OIG basis, the savings are mostly insignificant compared to total agency expenditures.[31]

Moreover, to the extent resources that are invested in the OIGs subtract from resources available elsewhere in an agency, the OIGs may actually weaken overall efficiency, thereby contributing to the very waste they seek to reduce. "To the extent that the IGs discover fraud, for example, they plug a hole in the leaky bucket of federal programs," I have argued. "However, if Congress and the president allow IG growth at the expense of basic program delivery capacity, a greater potential for errors is created. The hole is filled even as a large number of small holes are being drilled."[32]

The Kinship of Reform

Before returning to the general view of government as a defining undertow running through all four tides, it is useful to note the relative purity of the four tides. As mentioned earlier, roughly 30 percent of the 141 initiatives carry expressions of more than one tide.

Although these riders are always secondary or even tertiary to the main thrust of an initiative, they have enough moment to merit notice nonetheless. In this regard, management reform is not much different from other legislative issues in attracting extra freight. The question in table 2.7 is just what kinds of extra freight each tide attracts.

The answer is threefold. First, watchful eye is by far the purest tide in its reluctance to carry expressions of the other reform philosophies. When it does carry other expressions, it does so exclusively with war on waste. Watchful eye advocates appear steadfast in their unwillingness either to accept new structure through scientific management or to give government greater freedom to act unfettered through liberation management.

Second, liberation management has a noticeable tendency to accept war on waste as a secondary or tertiary theme. Although such scholars as Donald Kettl have criticized the NPR in particular on this issue, liberation has often sold itself through promises of dollar savings. This is certainly how the Postal Service and Amtrak conversions to government corporations were sold, just as it is how employee buyouts were packaged in 1994. It may be, as Osborne argues

Table 2.7. *Kinship and Reform* (*percentages*)

	Scientific Management	War on Waste	Watchful Eye	Liberation Management
Purity of Statute				
No Other Tides Found	63	73	91	62
One Other Tide Found	37	27	9	40
Two Other Tides Found	10	12	0	0
Other Tides Found in Statute				
Scientific Management	—	12	0	0
War on Waste	16	—	16	30
Watchful Eye	11	8	—	10
Liberation Management	10	8	0	—
No Tides in Support	63	73	91	60
Appearances in Secondary Positions[a]				
Never Found in Other Statute	96	83	90	93
Found in Other Statutes	4	17	10	7

N = 141

[a]Figures are calculated by dividing the number of appearances as a secondary rider by the number of opportunities to appear as a secondary tide—that is, number of appearances as secondary/(141 minus number of appearances as primary).

in defense of the NPR, that the case for liberation management simply cannot be made without some proof of dollar savings. Lacking credible proof that liberation will produce greater efficiency in and of itself, dollar savings may be the only way to sell Congress on the need for less regulation.

Third, scientific management carries a large amount of freight but is almost never found in a secondary or tertiary position in other reform statutes. It is very much the tide that carries but does not ride. This finding may be a simple by-product of the relative dominance of scientific management in the 1940s and 1950s. Other reforms may have simply attached themselves to a sure thing.

The Civil Service Reform Act of 1978 is an example of just such free riding. It is the only initiative in Appendix A to contain expressions of all four tides of reform: a Senior Executive Service (SES) to strengthen the presidential chain of command (scientific management), a cap on total federal employment to save money (war on waste), whistleblower protection to assure truth telling from the inside (watchful eye), and pay for performance to reward employees for doing something more than just show up for work (liberation management).

Toward these ends, the bill combined structural and procedural reforms, creating both an Office of Personnel Management to help the president administer the system and new procedures for giving members of the SES sabbaticals, while establishing the Merit Systems Protection Board as a structural guarantor of watchfulness and creating new procedures for firing incompetent employees. It also used a mix of accountability mechanisms: compliance for whistleblower protection, capacity in the SES, and performance in new pay bonuses.

This mix of reform philosophies is clear in the language used to justify the complex bill. As the Senate Governmental Affairs Committee explained the need for reform, "Both the public and those in government have a right to the most effective possible civil service; that is, one in which employees are hired and removed on the basis of merit and one which is accountable to the public through its elected leaders. . . . Assaults on the merit system have taken place despite, and in some instances because of, the complicated rules and procedures that have developed over the last century. The welter of inflexible strictures that have developed over the years threatens to asphyxiate the merit principle itself."[33]

The language echoed President Jimmy Carter's Personnel Management Project, which was created to design the reform package. "It is the public which suffers from a system which neither permits managers to manage nor which provides assurance against political abuse," the project argued in a blend of liberation and war on waste rhetoric. "Valuable resources are lost to the public service by a system increasingly too cumbersome to compete for talent. The opportunity for more effective service to the public is denied by a system so tortuous that managers regard it as almost impossible to remove those who are not performing."[34]

The question for kinship is how the final bill attracted such a mix of trust and distrust. One answer is simply that the first top-to-bottom reform of the civil service system in a century was bound to be complex, attracting ideas in good currency from around the government. The President's Personnel Project canvassed widely, hoping to build a constituency for a reform that was not likely to generate much congressional interest. "It was an unknown," a White House legislative liaison staffer explained. "No bill had been put up there like it. There wasn't an identifiable constituency. You couldn't look at previous votes and see how somebody would vote on the thing."[35] Thus, some of the war on waste expressions helped the bill pass political muster on Capitol Hill, while some of the liberation expressions were designed to assuage federal employee unions, whose support would be essential on the House Civil Service and Post Office Committee.

A second answer is that Carter desperately needed a legislative victory and was willing to accept whatever cargo was needed to assure passage. The civil service proposal began to take shape late in his first year, a year that had been characterized by a string of legislative disasters. "We'd rather have a Christmas tree than a dead bush," one administration aide argued.[36] The House was clearly hungry for more war on waste, particularly as it moved ahead on the 1978 Inspector General Act, while the Senate was pushing for more watchful eye, particularly as it shaped the 1978 Ethics in Government Act. As the bill evolved, both chambers added and subtracted accordingly from the Carter proposal.

In the House, for example, James Leach (R-Iowa) added an amendment to establish a four-year employment ceiling for the federal government. Under the amendment, the total number of employees on January 20, 1981, could not exceed the number on September 30, 1977. Senator John Heinz (R-Pa.) had tried to get just such a ceiling in the Senate but had been rebuffed by his colleagues on the Governmental Affairs Committee. As Heinz explained his reasoning in an "additional views" section to the final Governmental Affairs legislative report, "The Committee may have overlooked what should be one of the most fundamental principles of any substantive reform and what is one of the chief causes of citizen concern and complaint about government. That problem, simply, is size, and the principle—equally simple—is that a responsible reform designed to streamline the bureaucracy and make it more efficient should necessarily make it smaller."[37] Apparently, the House found the war on waste argument more compelling and persevered in spite of White House opposition.

Back in the Senate, Muriel Humphrey (D-Minn.) added an amendment to toughen whistleblower protection by expanding the definition of protected activities. In contrast to the original Carter proposal, which had offered protection only to employees who blow the whistle on other employees, the Humphrey amendment provided shelter for employees who reveal waste or mismanagement more broadly or who disclose a specific danger to the public health or safety. "Protecting employees who disclose government illegality, waste, and corruption is a major step toward a more effective civil service," the Senate Governmental Affairs Committee explained. "In the vast Federal bureaucracy it is not difficult to conceal wrongdoing provided that no one summons the courage to disclose the truth."[38]

Nearly two decades later, it is not clear that the compromises were worth making. Many of the more trusting pieces of the reform were never implemented, while most of the distrusting pieces remain alive and active. Congress has never appropriated money for the SES sabbaticals, for example, and merit pay has been more mirage than reality. By allowing war on waste and watchful eye to board the reform effort, advocates may have undermined their case for a new civil service based on trust and performance.

DIVIDING THE TIDES

As the basic charts presented above strongly suggest, making government work involves tactical choices on a host of issues. Will the initiative attempt to change structure or process? New agencies and systems or old? Will it target procurement or pay, ethics or budget? Will it be something entirely new or a modification of the old? Will it involve centralization or decentralization, sunset or permanence, one agency or all of government?

Such tactical questions involve a much deeper strategic question about when and where to trust government and its employees. Can they be mostly trusted to do their jobs or should they be mostly distrusted? Are they driven mostly by commitment to mission and a sense of service or by power aggrandizement and self-interest? Are they basically altruistic or utility maximizing?

Back to the Founding

The general view of government as trustworthy or untrustworthy has been a dividing line in making government work ever since the constitutional debates between the Federalists, who supported ratification, and the Anti-Federalists.

Although the Federalists never trusted government to operate completely un-fettered, they shared a broader confidence in the ultimate effectiveness of en-ergetic agencies than their Anti-Federalist opponents.

Consider as an example Hamilton's call for energy in the executive branch in *Federalist Paper 70:* "A feeble Executive implies a feeble execution of the government. A feeble execution is but another phrase for a bad execution; and a government ill executed, whatever it may be in theory, must be in practice a bad government."[39] Hamilton proceeds with a broad defense of the "one true master" principle of administration: "That unity is conducive to energy will not be disputed. Decision, activity, secrecy, and dispatch will generally character-ize the proceedings of one man in a much more eminent degree than the pro-ceeding of any greater number; and in proportion as the number is increased, these qualities will be diminished."[40]

The Federalists most certainly did not believe in the perfectibility of human nature, however. As James Madison wrote in *Federalist Paper 51,* "If men were angels, no government would be necessary. If angels were to govern men, neither external nor internal controls would be necessary."[41] How could the public govern, wrote Madison in *Federalist Paper 63,* when "there are par-ticular moments in public affairs when the people, stimulated by some irregu-lar passion, or some illicit advantage, or misled by the artful misrepresenta-tions of interested men, may call for measures which they themselves will afterwards be the most ready to lament and condemn"?[42]

Surely, such a public could never be allowed to govern directly. Not only was opinion subject to "every sudden breeze of passion, or to every transient impulse," wrote Hamilton in further defense of an energetic executive in *Fed-eralist Paper 71,* it was also prone to making mistakes, presumably because it lacked the education to do otherwise.

The Federalists also saw the public as prone to nearly constant bickering and conflict, a harsh view of human nature rooted in the writings of the En-glish philosopher Thomas Hobbes and many of his contemporaries. Hobbes clearly saw human beings as deeply flawed, driven by a "perpetual and restless desire of Power after power, that ceaseth only in death."[43] In this "War of everyone against every one," life was nothing more than "solitary, poor, nasty, brutish, and short."[44] The Federalists agreed that the state of humans in na-ture was one of division and self-interest: the one above the many.[45]

Hobbes's stark view of human nature clearly influenced the Federalists. "So strong is this propensity of mankind to fall into mutual animosities," wrote Madison in *Federalist 10,* "that when no substantial occasion presents itself, the most frivolous and fanciful distinctions have been sufficient to kindle their unfriendly passions and excise their most violent conflicts." Having concluded that the seeds of faction were "sown in the nature of man," Madison dismissed the history of pure democracies as "spectacles of turbulence and contention."[46]

These tendencies did not apply equally to all human beings, however. Even as Madison worried about the "degree of depravity in mankind," he celebrated the potential for virtue among America's future leaders. The problem of division and self-interest could be solved in part, he wrote, by passing public opinion "through the medium of a chosen body of citizens, whose wisdom may discern the true interest of the country, and whose patriotism and love of justice, will be least likely to sacrifice it to temporary or partial considerations."[47] Only by straining human nature through the filter of enlightened leadership could the government act on the public's behalf. Government could somehow be hoped to stay above it all, not fully trustworthy by any means, but deserving of great confidence under the skilled guidance of an energetic executive led by what would later become scientific management.

The Anti-Federalists drew a very different portrait of the public and government. It was not the public but government, especially big government, that could scarcely be trusted, and it was government leaders and bureaucrats, not individual citizens, who would act in pure self-interest. The potential for abuse lay in the very nature of a large republic.

Consider the argument made by "Brutus" in response to the *Federalist Papers* as an example. "In so extensive a republic, the great officers of government would soon become above the countroul of the people, and abuse their power to the purpose of aggrandizing themselves, and oppressing them," writes Brutus in prefacing an inventory of the powers conferred on the new government. "When these are attended with great honor and emolument, as they always will be in large states, so as greatly to interest men to pursue them, and to be proper objects for ambitious and designing men, such men will be ever restless in their pursuit after them. They will use the power, when they have acquired it, to the purposes of gratifying their own interest and ambition, and it is scarcely possible, in a very large republic, to call them to account for their misconduct, or to prevent their abuse of power."[48] A similar view of bureaucratic abuse can be found in both the war on waste and watchful eye, as well as in the contemporary writings of public choice political scientists and economists.[49]

This basic debate about the nature of government and its employees continues to influence reform today, perhaps stated in less elegant terms and less carefully reasoned, but often in evidence nonetheless. As the public administration scholar John Rohr argues convincingly, the contest between trust and distrust was evident in the debates over the Administrative Procedure Act in the late 1930s.[50]

On one side were advocates of full judicial review of all rules, a position repeated in the 1994 Republican Contract with America. These advocates believed that the public, not expert administrators, should have the final say on the merits of a given rule. Launched by Roscoe Pound's attack on power-hungry bureaucrats, the effort to impose full judicial review on rulemaking carried the unmistakable mark of the original Anti-Federalist critique.

On the other, more trusting side of the debate were the advocates of an energetic executive, represented by the majority authors of the Attorney General's Report (AGR) on *Administrative Procedure in Government Agencies*. As Rohr argues, the AGR linked a "strange silence" on the danger of industry capture of agency rulemaking with a strong emphasis on the good character of administrators as the essence of effectiveness: "If these two points are linked, we might conclude that the AGR did not worry about agencies being captured, because the sort of men and women whom it envisioned in such agencies would not allow themselves to be captured. The same conclusion might explain why the AGR is quite chary of regulating administrative behavior by law; the report prefers to rely on the good sense and good character of the administrators, along with the periodic studies and recommendations of the proposed Office of Federal Administrative Procedure."[51]

It is important to note, as Rohr rightly does, that the Federalists did not believe good character alone was sufficient to assure effective administration. Hence, they would likely disagree with the AGR's broad confidence in exhorting good behavior. The Federalists did not expect administrators to be virtuous purely because they heard the call of public service. They were to be led by an energetic executive, who, in turn, would be constrained by constitutional checks and balances that would insulate government from public passions.

The General View from the Tides

As already noted in table 2.2, the general view of government creates a sharp break within the tides. Scientific management and liberation management emerge as much more trusting than either war on waste or watchful eye. As such, general trust may operate as the immutable force that explains the ebb and flow of the four tides. What one believes about the basic nature of government and its employees clearly influences the preferred tide of reform.

Deciding whether a given initiative is trusting or distrusting is yet another one of the many judgment calls made in the course of this project. The best one can do is read the legislative history, inspect the statute itself, and try to reach a conclusion on the basic thrust. Luckily, many reform proposals are prefaced with congressional findings that make the decisions easier, while others are introduced with precise statements of trust or distrust. Nevertheless, it remains best to take the percentages discussed more as a general illustration than as absolute proof. Caveat again noted, table 2.8 shows the simple relationship between general view of government and the other measures discussed in this book.

The table contains few surprises. With regard to legislative history, presidents are much more likely to be the source of trusting initiatives than Congress, in large part because trusting initiatives tend to shift authority from Capitol Hill toward the White House. Trusting initiatives are also more likely to come from blue-ribbon commissions, in part because commissions provide the political cover needed to pass initiatives that so clearly counter the public's longstanding distrust. Finally, trusting initiatives have a slightly lower probability to generate unanimous or near-unanimous passage.

Trust finds its most comfortable philosophical fit in the scientific management tide, which is both an artifact of the very large number of scientific initiatives recorded in Appendix A and a confirmation of the basic confidence in the potential for effectiveness once expressed by the Federalists. Note that only 8 percent of trusting initiatives fall under war on waste and watchful eye. As already noted in the comparison of the four tides, trust puts its faith in capacity and performance accountability, distrust in compliance and the capacity to create and enforce deterrence.

Trust expresses a preference for structural reforms, distrust for procedure. When trust goes procedural, it does so mostly to revise and deregulate; when distrust goes structural, it does so to build organizations to enforce compliance. Distrust finds its most frequent targets in procurement/acquisition, ethics/standards of conduct, and administrative process, all tightly linked to a compliance accountability.

Regarding scale, distrust shows up more frequently as a new idea, primarily because it has found so many new issues to tackle during the past fifty years. Similarly, distrust tends to arise in much larger initiatives, such as the Ethics in Government Act. Putting the two together, distrust finds its expression more in new/large initiatives than in old/small. As such, distrust allows Congress and the president to claim a break with "politics as usual," thereby creating even more incentive for passage.

Distrust finds a comfortable niche in implementation by governmentwide initiatives. Except for the OIGs and occasional efforts to address fraud in a specific setting, such as HUD, distrust is very much about governmentwide reform, again allowing Congress and the president to claim broad impacts.

Table 2.8 General View of Government (percentages)

	Trusting	Distrusting
Legislative History		
Origin of Idea		
President	66	24
Congress	34	74
Blue-Ribbon Commission Involved?	19	8
Interest Groups Involved?	25	33
Legislative Debate		
Routine	59	55
Controversial	41	45
Legislative Passage		
Unanimous	43	55
Near-Unanimous	27	30
Strong Majority (60 or more)	24	10
Close (less than 60)	7	6
Recorded Vote Taken?	62	59
Philosophy		
Tide		
Scientific Management	72	18
War on Waste	7	29
Watchful Eye	2	44
Liberation Management	19	10
Purity of Statute		
No Other Tides Found in Statute	79	63
One Other Tide Found	18	27
Two Other Tides Found	3	10
Primary Accountability Mechanism		
Compliance	13	64
Capacity	66	27
Performance	21	8
Change Strategy		
Focus		
Structure of Government	57	26
Procedures of Government	43	62
Both	0	10
Create a Study Commission	0	3
Structural Tactic		
Create New Agency	19	14
Merge Existing Agencies	18	0
Reorganize Existing Agency	10	4
Create Public Corporation	4	4

Table 2.8 (Continued)

	Trusting	Distrusting
Abolish Existing Agency	0	6
Grant Agency Independence	0	6
Elevate Agency to Higher Status	4	0
Combination	2	3
No Structural Reform in Statute	43	64
Procedural Tactic		
Establish New System	6	37
Broaden System	6	22
Revise System	12	3
Deregulate/Narrow System	10	4
Reauthorize System	7	4
Abolish System	0	1
Combination	2	0
No Procedural Reform in Statute	57	29
Target		
General Organization of Govt.	59	22
Procurement/Acquisition	7	12
Ethics/Standards of Conduct	4	18
Administrative Process	0	12
Pay Systems	9	1
Audit/Investigation	3	6
Rulemaking Procedures	3	6
General Personnel/Classification	4	4
Budget/Financial Management	3	7
Combination	4	4
Strategic Planning/Analysis	0	4
Debt Collection	2	3
Tort Claims	2	1
Scale		
Nature of Idea		
New Approach	56	51
Modification of Old	44	49
Scope of Impact		
Large	32	47
Small	68	53
Overall Scale of Reform		
New/Large	24	30
New/Small	34	21
Old/Large	10	18
Old/Small	32	32

Table 2.8 (Continued)

	Trusting	Distrusting
Implementation		
Experimental Approach in Statute?	2	3
Time Horizon in Statute		
Temporary/Sunset	9	15
Permanent	91	85
Scope		
Single Agency	43	30
Several Agencies	22	7
Governmentwide	35	63
Oversight Approach		
Centralized	59	43
Decentralized	41	58
Impact		
Shift in Shared Powers		
Toward President	71	26
Toward Congress	10	44
Not Clear/No Shift Discernible	19	30
Impact on Cost of Government		
Increase	44	8
Decrease	4	12
Not Clear/No Impact Discernible	52	80
Impact on Role of Government		
Expand	54	7
Contract	4	16
Not Clear/No Impact Discernible	41	77
Impact on Shape of Government		
Thicken Hierarchy	54	62
Thin Hierarchy	10	21
Not Clear/No Impact Discernible	35	18
Impact on Administrative Speed		
Accelerate	44	29
Slow Down	2	49
Not Clear/No Impact Discernible	54	22
Impact on Interest Group Access		
Enhance	16	18
Reduce	10	37
Not Clear/No Impact Discernible	74	45
Impact on Public Access		
Enhance	4	32
Reduce	6	8
Not Clear/No Impact Discernible	90	60

Table 2.8 (Continued)

	Trusting	Distrusting
Impact on Government Morale		
Improve	24	27
Reduce	0	4
Not Clear/No Impact Discernible	77	69
Impact on Bureaucratic Balance		
Strengthen Line Units	80	16
Strengthen Staff Units	15	71
Not Clear/No Impact Discernible	6	12

$N = 141$

Distrust also expresses itself in decentralized oversight, perhaps placing its faith more in the public than in the government. Although this analysis does not address the general view of the public embedded in each statute, it is worth noting that such views both exist and merge with a general attitude toward government into rather provocative portraits of the four tides. War on waste, for example, tends to be distrusting of government and the people, particularly beneficiaries, while liberation management tends to be trusting of both. By putting its faith in customers and the front line, even as war on waste puts its faith in neither, liberation management might be characterized as either the most hopeful or the most naive of the reform tides. Scientific management and watchful eye have perhaps more balanced views. Scientific management puts its trust in government as the source of expertise, leaving the public with a minimal role at best, while watchful eye sees the public as an active participant in a government filled with sunshine.

Trust is also linked to impacts that favor the presidency, increased costs, an expanded role for government, administrative speed, and line units, while distrust favors Congress, administration deceleration, less access for interest groups but more for the public, and greater confidence in staff units. Interestingly, both views of government favor thickening. Ever was it thus, or so it seems, that the hierarchy is the pure beneficiary of either view. Reformers create hierarchy to express both confidence and suspicion.

By itself, general view of government exerts an undeniable pull on the tides. However, it is in combination with three other measurements that general view separates the four tides from each other: (1) accountability mechanism, (2) reform focus, and (3) oversight approach. The combinations are summarized in table 2.9.

How the general view merges with these three administrative choices proves essential in drawing the final chart for each tide. Start with accountabil-

Table 2.9 *Dividing the Tides: General View of Government*

	Trusting	Distrusting
Accountability Mechanism		
Compliance	5% of all Scientific Management fit here	7% of all Scientific Management
	15% of all War on Waste	54% of all War on Waste
	0% of all Watchful Eye	88% of all Watchful Eye
	10% of all Liberation Management	0% of all Liberation Management
Capacity	60% of all Scientific Management	13% of all Scientific Management
	0% of all War on Waste	19% of all War on Waste
	3% of all Watchful Eye	9% of all Watchful Eye
	35% of all Liberation Management	20% of all Liberation Management
Performance	15% of all Scientific Management	2% of all Scientific Management
	4% of all War on Waste	8% of all War on Waste
	0% of all Watchful Eye	0% of all Watchful Eye
	20% of all Liberation Management	15% of all Liberation Management
Focus of Reform		
Structures	57% of all Scientific Management	7% of all Scientific Management
	0% of all War on Waste	29% of all War on Waste
	3% of all Watchful Eye	17% of all Watchful Eye
	25% of all Liberation Management	15% of all Liberation Management

Procedures	28% of all Scientific Management	9% of all Scientific Management
	21% of all War on Waste	50% of all War on Waste
	0% of all Watchful Eye	80% of all Watchful Eye
	40% of all Liberation Management	20% of all Liberation Management
Oversight Approach		
Centralized	61% of all Scientific Management	19% of all Scientific Management
	4% of all War on Waste	42% of all War on Waste
	3% of all Watchful Eye	21% of all Watchful Eye
	0% of all Liberation Management	5% of all Liberation Management
Decentralized	18% of all Scientific Management	2% of all Scientific Management
	15% of all War on Waste	39% of all War on Waste
	0% of all Watchful Eye	76% of all Watchful Eye
	65% of all Liberation Management	30% of all Liberation Management

N = 141

ity mechanism, which is a particularly useful combination for distinguishing scientific management, war on waste, and watchful eye. Scientific management fits well into the capacity/trusting cell, while war on waste and watchful eye find a strong fit within the compliance/distrusting cell. Of those three tides, watchful eye fits the most tightly within its cell, with nearly nine out of ten initiatives in one niche. Liberation management, however, is mostly lost in the combinations. It does not quite know what it is. The largest concentration is 33 percent in the capacity/trusting cell, with spotty representation in all but the compliance/distrusting cell.

Next turn to the focus of reform. Once again, three of the four tides are well sorted by the combination with general view. Scientific management locates well in the structure/trusting cell, while war on waste and watchful eye claim the procedures/distrusting cell. As with accountability mechanism, watchful eye nests the most tightly in its cell. And liberation management gets lost. It spreads across all four cells, with a plurality under the combination of procedures and trusting.

Turn last to the oversight approach. Here, scientific management, watchful eye, and liberation management also nest well. Liberation management, lost in the previous combinations, does quite well in the decentralized/trusting cell, while watchful eye again fits well into its decentralized/distrusting home. Because of its mixed oversight approach, war on waste has an uncomfortable break between the centralized and decentralized expressions of distrust.

Of particular note in this last combination is the better fit for liberation management. This tide might not know whether it is about compliance, capacity, or performance and might not know whether it is concerned mostly with structure or procedures, but it holds a strong line on decentralization. As we have seen, it is unabashedly willing to place its faith in an assortment of decentralized overseers, whether the market, the customer, or the individual manager.

Although liberation management finds a better fit under oversight approach, there is enough confusion to suggest that the tide is still evolving. As noted in Chapter 1, liberation management involves two very different tools of reform, competition and deregulation. In spite of the generally trusting nature of liberation management, competition often carries a more distrusting edge. The notion is that government and its employees cannot get better on their own without the discipline and ultimate penalty imposed by the market. Liberation management may yet split in two, producing a new "market forces" tide composed of assorted competition and privatization approaches. This new tide is described in table 2.10. It is too early to tell whether the market forces philosophy will produce enough initiatives to create more than a ripple in the ocean of reform described throughout this book.

Table 2.10   Characteristics of Market Forces

Goal	Lowest Cost
Key Input	Competition
Key Product	Survival of the Fittest
Key Participants	The Market, Organizational Engineers
Institutional Champion	The Presidency
Defining Moments	Reagan A-76 Process, Gore National Performance Review
Defining Statute	1984 Competition in Contracting Act
Most Recent Expressions	Not Clear
Most Recent Contradiction	1994 Federal Acquisitions and Streamlining Act?
Patron Saints	Ronald Reagan, Al Gore
Patron Organization	Not Yet Clear

At the same time, there is no question that liberation management remains unresolved on its general view of government. Faced with similar tensions during the Progressive Era, scientific management eventually split in two, as watchful eye and war on waste eventually claimed enough momentum to be recorded here as separate philosophies in their own right. The NPR may see no problem with putting market forces and deregulation back to back in its final report as parts of a unified package, but the tension exists nonetheless. Sooner or later, each tide of reform seeks purity, whether because one set of advocates eventually seeks dominance or because Congress can tolerate only so much dissonance in a given call for change.

Should such a break in liberation management occur, it will have Ronald Reagan to thank. Reagan was the first president to articulate a clear agenda for privatization, and he supported a range of efforts to introduce more competition into the federal procurement process, thereby adding some of the acquisition rules from which the NPR would later seek relief. Under the 1984 Competition in Contracting Act, for example, Congress lowered the dollar thresholds for awarding contracts on a basis other than competitive bids, thereby narrowing the use of single-source, noncompetitive arrangements that sometimes ease procurement paperwork. Reagan also pressured agencies to put more of their internal operations up for outside bid under Budget Circular A-76, which can be considered a form of indirect privatization. Under A-76, agencies were required to prepare an inventory of all activities that might be performed by private contractors, bid those activities out through a competitive process, and accept any bid that was at least 10 percent lower than the government's current personnel costs. "To the Reagan administration, A-76 was a keystone of its broader privatization movement," writes Donald

Kettl. "To many federal employees, employee unions, and members of Congress who represented them, however, A-76 loomed as a huge threat."[52]

The fact that A-76 created enormous political resistance in return for relatively low savings suggests the problems with sustaining a market forces tide in the future. Americans may say they want a government that works better and costs less, but may balk when they discover that private contractors are making large profits delivering what were once basic government services.

Given the patterns charted in this chapter, it seems reasonable to conclude that there are, indeed, four distinct tides of reform for making government work. Scientific management and watchful eye appear to be mutually juxtaposed. The former clearly puts its faith in structure and capacity in an effort to fulfill Hamilton's promise of an energetic executive sketched more than two hundred years ago, while the latter puts its focus on procedure and compliance to create the checks needed to balance that energetic executive with an equally strong legislature and well informed public.

Because saving money is a strong selling point in an era of impossibly tight budgets and angry citizens, war on waste is perhaps more flexible in terms of structure and procedures. With the OIGs as its structural deterrent and antifraud rules as its procedural hammer, war on waste may be the most distinctive of the four tides in its singular distrust of government and the public. Paradoxically, one of the best ways to sell liberation management, with its nearly opposite trust in front-line employees and their customers, is to take war on waste as a secondary theme. Thus did the NPR offer itself as a way to create not only a government that works better, but one that costs $108 billion less.[53]

Having both charted the tides in greater detail and defined trust in government and its employees as a key dividing force in distinguishing the four tides against one another, the question is "so what?" To what extent does the existence of four competing images of reform matter to making government work?

One answer is to be found in the simple fact that the four tides often contradict each other. It hardly makes sense to liberate government's managers in one statute only to impose new watchfulness in another; to create structure as a source of efficiency in one statute only to fill it with endless red tape in another. The result is a government filled with cross-pressures and layer upon layer of conflicting aims. Not only do Americans give government inconsistent, contradictory, and hence unachievable goals and tasks, they also give government administrators inconsistent, contradictory, and hence often *unusable* tools for implementing those goals and tasks.

Advocates often push for governmentwide implementation because they lack solid research on just where and when each of the reform philosophies might be most appropriate—no research to justify using liberation in one circumstance and watchfulness in another, no research to suggest more structure for one program aim and less for another, and certainly no research to tell when a war on waste is doomed to be an endless quagmire rather than a surgical success.

I shall return in Chapter 6 to this theme and its associated call for a greater commitment to careful experiments in making government work. But in the intervening chapters, we shall examine the timing, origins, and consequences of reform in more detail. Knowing a bit more about how the tides have ebbed and flowed over the past fifty years, which party and branch of government has championed each approach, and what explains the controversies and impacts associated with each tide might help future advocates resist the temptation that led King Canute to order the tides to cease lo these many centuries ago.

3

The Climate of Reform

Using the tides of the ocean as a metaphor for a book about federal management reform creates an inevitable image not just of ebb and flow but of predictability. After all, nothing is as steady as the tides.

Yet, just because tides can be predicted does not mean they are regular. As with the tides of the ocean, which come and go with changes in climate and the relative positions of the sun and moon, the tides of reform also ebb and flow with changes in the political and budgetary climate and with the relative position of Congress and the presidency and other "heavenly" bodies.

There can be little doubt that the tides of reform rise and fall with public trust in government, for example. As we shall see shortly, the oceans of reform have been buffeted by a "low pressure" zone for the better part of three decades, bringing war on waste and watchful eye to a crest while pushing scientific management ever farther from shore. And with little new money to invest in building new agencies, supporters of a positive administrative state have been led toward liberation management as a way to rebuild public confidence, or at least customer satisfaction, in government.

The long-term decline in public confidence is hardly restricted to government, however. Virtually every social institution—from churches to big business, colleges to foundations—has lost ground with the public. It is a decline easily spotted by looking back at books atop the *New York Times* best-sellers lists over the past fifty years.[1] Back in the 1940s and 1950s, the number-one books on management, if indeed they can even be called books on management, were essentially hopeful, uplifting volumes. Dale Carnegie's *How to Stop Worrying and Start Living* hit the list in August 1948 and stayed at the top for three months. Norman Vincent Peale's *The Power of Positive Thinking* reached number one in May 1953 and stayed there for an unprecedented ninety-eight weeks.

During the same period, histories were equally optimistic. John Gunther's *Inside U.S.A.* served as an essential fact book on a newly emerged superpower in 1947, while Dwight Eisenhower reprised his *Crusade in Europe* for three months at number one in 1948 as a precursor to his run to the presidency four years later. (Colin Powell is not the only best-selling former general to ride the *New York Times* best-seller list to national speculation.) The closest the list of number ones offered by way of controversy was Thor Heyerdahl's grand adventure *Kon-Tiki*, which proved that South Americans could, indeed, have sailed across the Pacific in a reed and papyrus raft.

Page forward through the number ones to the end of the 1950s and the rising tide of distrust is unmistakable. Vance Packard's two best-sellers, *The Hidden Persuaders* in 1957 and *The Waste Makers* in 1960, heralded a long decade of suspicion, detailing the abuse of social science research by the advertising industry and decrying America's throwaway society.

The 1960s were not without their glowing histories, but the two most notable number-one bestsellers, one by Theodore Sorenson and the other by Arthur Schlesinger Jr., reached the list largely because they profiled a martyred president. The other number ones were equally somber or antiestablishment, from Rachel Carson's *Silent Spring* in 1962, about environmental pollution, to Mark Lane's attack on the investigation into Kennedy's assassination, *Rush to Judgment* in 1967, to Laurence Peter and Raymond Hall's *The Peter Principle* in 1969, to Robert Townsend's *Up the Organization* in 1970. These latter two number ones set a tone for much of the management literature in the 1970s, with Peter and Hall arguing that individuals are invariably promoted to their precise level of incompetence and Townsend recommending that the only way to succeed in modern organizations was to attack the prevailing traditions. Management did not reach the number-one spot again until Tom Peters and Robert Waterman's *In Search of Excellence*, an essentially uplifting account of how corporations could become successful by sticking to their knitting. It was a rare moment of hopefulness in an otherwise dispiriting decade of number-one best-sellers on takeovers, insider trading, and the loss of American competitiveness.

As for politics, all pretense of hopefulness was gone from the number-one best-seller list by the late 1970s. Carl Bernstein and Bob Woodward hit number one with *All the President's Men* in 1974, spawning a cottage industry in Watergate books that included CBS anchor Dan Rather and Gary Paul Gates's *The Palace Guard,* Bernstein and Woodward's *The Final Days,* and White House schemer H. R. Haldeman's *The End of Power.*

The selling power of distrust can also be spotted on the list of fiction best-sellers. No thrillers reached the best-seller lists in the 1940s and just one in the 1950s, but there were eleven such best-sellers in the 1970s and forty-six in the 1980s. Led by Stephen King, horror novels produced thirteen number ones during the Reagan decade, spy novels twelve, mysteries fifteen, and high-tech thrillers six. As for ordinary drama, stories about one person's ordeal increased from six top best-sellers in the 1940s to twelve in the 1980s.[2]

This inventory of best-sellers is not meant to suggest that the *New York Times* has somehow become the ultimate arbiter of social climate, but it suggests the ebb and flow of ideas in recent U.S. history. As the best-seller list changed to reflect broad markets for distrust and horror, perhaps so, too, did the inventory of reform change to reflect broad markets for war on waste and watchful eye. Thus, the tides of reform may not ebb and flow with watchlike predictability, but they certainly do ebb and flow. As I suggest in this chapter, the ebb and flow in recent years has been dominated in part by a sustained lack of confidence in government, a climate that favors war on waste and watchful eye over scientific management.

SEVEN HURRICANES OF REFORM

Like the tides of the ocean, the tides of reform often generate their greatest impacts in great waves of legislation driven ashore by hurricanes of activity that occur only once or twice a decade. These hurricanes can be spawned in national crises like Vietnam or Watergate, in periods of legislative activism like the Great Society or the Reagan Revolution, even by blue-ribbon commissions led by a former president of the United States like Herbert Hoover or a savvy vice president like Al Gore. But whatever the spawning ground, such hurricanes leave long-term impacts on the administrative coastline.

In all, there have been seven such hurricanes over the period covered by this book. Together, the seven account for almost half of all reforms recorded in Appendix A and help record the changing climate for making government work. The first two hurricanes were products of a hopeful climate in which scientific management flourished; the next two reflected a shift in the weather toward increasing distrust; and the last three, starting with the 93d Congress, which followed Watergate, have involved an unmistakable shift toward war on waste and watchful eye.

The 79th Congress (1945–1946)

As Appendix A shows, the 79th Congress produced just six statutes for the list. But what statutes they were. In 1945, the Federal Employees Pay Act provided the first pay raise in fifteen years, the Government Corporation Act imposed order on the growing list of wholly owned government enterprises, and reauthorization of the Reorganization Act signaled Congress's willingness to receive proposals from the executive once again, albeit with tight restrictions on the president's ability to abolish, merge, or rename any department or agency.

In 1946, Congress enacted two great watchful eye statutes, both reflecting years of debate: the Administrative Procedure Act (APA), which established clear requirements governing the rulemaking process, and the Federal Tort Claims Act, which subjected government to liability for injury, loss of property, or death due to the negligent or wrongful acts or omissions of federal employees acting within the scope of their employment.

Both statutes had been put on hold during World War II, only to emerge phoenixlike at the war's end. The two bills were driven forward by the growing unpopularity of Franklin Roosevelt's successor, Harry Truman, who fell from an 87 percent approval rating in July 1945 to 63 percent by February 1946 and just 32 percent seven months later.[3] Whatever brief honeymoon Truman had enjoyed after the war had disappeared in short order as the economy experienced a predictable postwar slowdown.

In contrast to its prewar history of controversy and veto, the APA sailed through the 79th Congress by voice vote in both chambers, heralded by one senator as "a bill of rights for the hundreds of thousands of Americans whose affairs are controlled or regulated in one way or another by agencies of the Federal government."[4] This is not to suggest that the APA passed unnoticed. The public administration scholars Frederick Blachly and Miriam Oatman ridiculed the new legislation in the Winter 1946 *Public Administration Review,* hoping that "when Congress understands the act and its implications, as certainly was not the case when it passed the bill without hearings, it will either repeal the law or make drastic amendments. It should be the function of political scientists, students of public administration, and all persons interested in sound administration to see that Congress is urged to take such action."[5]

With the nation mired in a postwar recession, such pressure was never to materialize. Instead, Republicans recaptured the House and Senate under a campaign, as Republican National Committee chairman B. Carroll Reece of Tennessee called it, to restore "orderly, capable and honest government in Washington and replace controls, confusion, corruption and communism."[6] It was a call that combined war on waste with watchful eye, resulting in the red scare of the late 1940s and early 1950s that, in turn, lifted a young congressman named Richard Nixon into the vice presidency.

Not all of the management bills in the 79th Congress were distrusting, however. Even as Congress worked its will on administrative procedure and tort claims, there was a growing realization that government was not put together correctly. Having swelled to giant proportions during the war, the federal government clearly had to shrink in the postwar years. The question was not whether but how.

Much as Congress wanted a say in the restructuring, in particular through efforts to protect favored agencies, it simply did not have the capacity to weigh in on administrative reorganization. The Bureau of the Budget (BoB) had the only credible administrative expertise for such efforts. "From the standpoint of the reformers who proposed it and the top officials of the Bureau of the Budget at the time," writes Frederick Mosher, "the most significant development in the late thirties was the birth and growth of the Division of Administrative Management. . . . By the close of World War II, administrative management in the BoB was a sizable (more than one hundred persons), widely respected, going concern."[7] When it came time to staff the first Hoover Commission in 1947, for example, it was the Division of Administrative Management that supplied the bodies. No other institution had the capacity.

As I shall argue, the decline of the Division of Administrative Management during the 1970s and 1980s is akin to the erosion of a tidal wall. As the unit was slowly disbanded, the tides of reform began to wash in with greater force and confusion. As Mosher argues, its "decline was probably due as much to the changing nature and interests of BoB's top leadership as to its internal organization. Eisenhower's budget directors—bankers and accountants—were certainly more concerned with dollars than they were with the sticky problems of general administration. And in a much different way, the same was true of the economists appointed by Kennedy and Johnson."[8]

This is not to argue that the division stood against all reform. Quite the contrary. Created in the same push that produced the Executive Office of the President, the division was unabashedly pro–scientific management. Its reform philosophy is obvious in the reports of the first Hoover Commission, particularly in the call for greater presidential authority. And its impact is unmistakable in the reorganization plans that sailed through Congress in 1949 and 1950, two years that constitute the modern high point of scientific reform.

It is important to note that the 1946 Legislative Reorganization Act is not included in Appendix A, only because the legislation focused exclusively on Congress and thereby escaped the list of major reforms. Nevertheless, the act confirms the rising influence of both scientific management and watchful eye. The two tides washed ashore on both ends of Pennsylvania Avenue.

The Legislative Reorganization Act reflected a congressional endorsement of scientific management. Its long list of goals embodied a familiar set of scientific principles: streamline and simplify the committee structure, eliminate the use of special or select committees, end duplication and overlap, standardize committee procedures, reduce the overall workload, and professionalize the staff system.[9] (Prior to the act, for example, most congressional committees borrowed staff from executive agencies.[10]) "Modernization of the standing committee system," wrote George Galloway, staff director of the Joint Committee on the Organization of Congress for the 79th Congress, "was the first objective of the Act and the keystone of the arch of congressional reform."[11] The principles of administration were all there: unity of command, agencies grouped by major purpose, staff assistance, even the one true institutional master in each chamber (the Senate majority leader and the speaker of the house).

At the same time, the Legislative Reorganization Act also established a significant watchful eye precedent in lobbying reform. Under Title III of the act, which was labeled the Federal Regulation of Lobbying Act, all lobbyists were required to register with the clerk of the House or the secretary of the Senate and report the amount of money raised and spent on lobbying. As the House explained, the key to lobbying control was disclosure: "The availability of information regarding organized groups and full knowledge of their expenditures for influencing legislation, their membership and the source of contributions to them of large amounts of money, would prove helpful to Congress in evaluating their representations without impairing the rights of any individual or group freely to express its opinion to Congress."[12]

Passage of the lobbying act is less important for its impact in curbing interest group influence—which it did not do—than for its expression of a watchful eye theme that would return again and again over the next fifty years. Although the act is generally viewed as a failure, Congress clearly expressed a longstanding preference for sunshine as a cure for hidden influence.

The 81st Congress (1949–1950)

Virtually every initiative that passed in the 81st Congress came from the first Hoover Commission, which called for greater efficiency and smaller government. After signing the Reorganization Act of 1949, which provided a needed reauthorization of presidential authority, this time without the 1945 restrictions, Truman immediately forwarded eight reorganization plans to Congress. Only one of the eight, Reorganization Plan No. 1 to create a Department of Health, Education, and Welfare, was rejected.

At roughly the same time, Congress was putting the final touches on separate statutes that created a General Services Agency to coordinate governmentwide procurement; a Department of Defense, National Security Council, and Joint Chiefs of Staff; and a new classification and pay schedule for government. The reform onslaught continued into 1950 with another twenty-seven reorganization plans and culminated with passage of the Budget and Accounting Procedures Act late in the year. Seven of Truman's plans were rejected, including a second try for a Department of HEW.

Hoover became a tireless campaigner in favor of his recommendations, creating the Citizens Committee for the Hoover Report as a lobbying agent. Established in time to support Truman's 1950 reorganization plans, the committee issued a monthly newsletter called *Reorganization News* and had a full-time staff to work the halls of Congress. Unlike the Hoover Commission, which never attached a savings figure to its recommendations, the committee readily accused "vested interests" of being "more anxious to 'save their own skins' than they are to save the taxpayer a possible quarter of a billion dollars."[13]

This is not to suggest that Hoover thought the savings issue unimportant. He clearly believed that his recommendations would reduce the size and cost of government, which he characterized as "the most gigantic business on earth." He also seemed to believe that his recommendations would reduce the national debt, which he noted had increased from "about $500 to $7,500" per average family during the twenty years since he had left office.[14] Nevertheless, Hoover himself never put a dollar total on his report, leaving that task to his paid lobbyists. Hoover also readily admitted that some of his recommendations would have cost government more, including pay increases at the top of government, where salaries, according to the Commission, remained "pitifully low."[15]

Of the long list of statutes that emerged from the 81st Congress, none is more important in this ebb and flow of reform than the Classification Act. Although primarily designed to flatten the federal grade structure used to hire and pay employees, the statute was a true breakthrough in scientific management. It collapsed the then-current system of thirty-one grades into eighteen and completely restructured the position descriptions and pay scales within each grade. It also created a new set of supergrades at levels 16, 17, and 18 to help agencies attract and retain high-level managers, thereby addressing the need for better pay at the top. It made a gesture to war on waste by eliminating the connection between supervisor pay and unit size and even carried a bit of liberation in its use of longevity pay increases as a way to reward long service without having to promote employees to higher grades.[16]

Age takes its toll on even the boldest reform, however, and the Classification Act is no different. Twenty-five years later, for example, Congress and the president took another run at reforming the personnel system in the Civil Service Reform Act, replacing the supergrades with a Senior Executive Service and attempting to create more incentives for performance. Fifteen years after that, the NPR recommended abolishing the 10,000-page *Federal Personnel Manual* and all agency implementing directives governing the system, as well as a complete decentralization of all hiring and firing authority to agencies. "Costs to the taxpayer for this personnel quagmire are enormous," the final report of the NPR argued in making the case for abandoning the system created under the Classification Act. "In total, 54,000 personnel work in federal personnel positions. We spend billions of dollars for these staff to classify each employee within a highly complex of some 459 job series, 15 grades and 10 steps within each grade. Does this elaborate system work? No."[17]

Although it is impossible to estimate just how long a reform can endure before being washed away by a new tide of reform, the Classification Act has proven a durable, perhaps even rocklike reform. Even as it erodes slightly with time, there are only so many ways to hire and fire employees without abandoning the merit system enacted in 1883.

That the reform philosophy peaked in the early 1950s is unmistakable. "In retrospect," writes public administration scholar Ronald Moe, "the intellectual influence of the two Hoover Commissions appears to have lasted just over a decade. . . . By the mid-1960s, the philosophy that had guided the two Hoover Commissions was undergoing rapid erosion. Not only was the constituency calling for a smaller government in retreat, but the dominant academic position was clearly in favor of a larger public sector and more government involvement in all aspects of national life."[18] So noted, there are still strong advocates of the Hoover philosophy, most notably those who call for a third Hoover Commission to somehow place things back in proper order.[19]

The 89th Congress (1965–1967)

In spite of occasional squalls of reform in the mid-1950s and early 1960s, there were no hurricanes until the 89th Congress in 1965, when lawmakers and the president added two new departments to government, Transportation and Housing and Urban Development, while establishing key precedents in both the war on waste and watchful eye. In many ways, the 89th Congress shared the Hoover Commission's passion for department building, even as it contained harbingers of future challenges to the president's administrative authority.

The Hoover Commission would have endorsed the basic rationale for the new departments. "When the President seeks to coordinate related governmental functions by assigning a leadership role to one or another agency," the House Government Operations Committee argued in making a rational case for HUD, "he is more effectively served if that agency has departmental status. In order to perform such a role most effectively, the agency should have status at least equal to that of the other agencies whose activities it is charged with coordinating."

Because the Housing and Home Finance Agency, which already contained many of government's housing programs, did not have such authority, it only made sense to the committee to elevate it. As the committee concluded, "a Cabinet-level unit is necessary to provide maximum assistance to the President in coordinating the many complex federal programs relating to housing and urban development and to provide a focal point in the Federal Government for guidance and assistance to the efforts of State, county, and municipal governments and private enterprise to improve the Nation's Communities."[20] It was a rationale similar to the Hoover Commission's call for a Department of HEW ten years before, and one that would be copied in legislation to establish the Departments of Energy and Education ten years later.

The 89th Congress was willing to challenge presidential authority, however, and pushed forward on its watchful eye agenda with 1966 Freedom of Information Act (FOIA), which threatened the president's prerogatives as the one true master of government. Although Lyndon Johnson's political decline obviously was connected to the continued escalation of the Vietnam War, passage of FOIA came near the beginning of the period that ended with Johnson's withdrawal from the 1968 presidential campaign.

This is not to suggest that the Johnson administration campaigned hard against passage. Johnson signed the statute into law on July 4, 1966, picking the day for its special significance. "This legislation," he announced, "springs from one of our most essential principles: a democracy works best when the people have all the information that the security of the Nation permits. No one should be able to pull curtains of secrecy around decisions which can be revealed without injury to the public interest."[21] His attorney general, Ramsey Clark, also endorsed the act in instructing agencies on implementation:

> Public Law 89-487 is the product of prolonged deliberation. It reflects the balancing of competing principles within our democratic order. It is not a mere recodification of existing practices in records management and in providing individual access

to Government documents. Nor is it a mere statement of objectives or an expression of intent.

Rather this statute imposes on the executive branch an affirmative obligation to adopt new standards and practices for publication and availability of information. It leaves no doubt that disclosure is a transcendent goal, yielding only to such compelling considerations as those provided for in the exemptions of the act.[22]

These endorsements notwithstanding, FOIA carried a clear congressional demand for greater access to executive information, whether through citizen-initiated petitions or through more aggressive oversight. Johnson may have signed the bill and Clark may have written a stirring implementation memo, but the administration had been unenthusiastic at best regarding passage. Like the 1978 Inspector General Act, virtually every agency about to be affected was opposed.

As for the attorney general's later embrace, his assistant attorney general had initially labeled the original Senate proposal both "unwise" and "unconstitutional," prompting a representative of newspaper editorial writers to declare the administration's opposition "an invitation to you gentlemen to pass a strong bill and put a powerful, headstrong bureaucracy in its place."[23] As a young member of Congress and future White House staffer named Donald Rumsfeld (R-Ill.) declared in the key floor debate preceding passage, "Our democratic society is not based on the vested interests of Government employees. It is based upon the participation of the public who must have full access to the facts of Government to select intelligently their representatives to serve in Congress and in the White House."[24]

Contrary to conventional wisdom, this growing demand for information did not begin with Vietnam and Watergate. Rather, it emerged during the 1950s in a series of high-profile investigations of executive branch withholding. Indeed, the precursor to the 1966 act was a barely noticed one-line statute clarifying the meaning of a 1789 housekeeping statute that had given agencies authority to establish filing systems for their records.

Under the 1958 reform, which is one of the 141 initiatives covered in this book, that housekeeping statute was amended as follows: "This section does not authorize withholding information from the public or limiting the availability of records to the public."[25] This one-line bill, which is arguably the shortest major reform bill ever to pass, was the product of three years of hearings, including a compilation of hundreds of examples of congressional requests that had been denied by uncooperative agencies. (Recall that a similar compilation under the authorship of Senate Judiciary Committee chairman Sam Ervin played a central role in the 1974 FOIA amendments.)

The rise of public choice economics as a distinctive intellectual enterprise in the mid-1960s also helped shape the future tides of reform. Led by Gordon Tullock, the new field offered a broad indictment of the trusting imagery underpinning traditional scientific management. The critique of the principles of administration was much sharper than Herbert Simon's clever attack on what he called the "proverbs of administration" in the late 1940s, and harked back to language familiar in the Anti-Federal debates.

Simply put, Tullock and his colleagues disparaged all hope of motivating government employees through calls to altruism and public good. Efficiency is so elusive in modern government agencies, writes Tullock in *The Politics of Bureaucracy*, that "the higher ranks of most governmental bureaus are made up of people who are less interested in the ostensible objectives of the organization than in their own personal well-being." Since it is always difficult to distinguish between "what is good for me" and "what is good," and even more so in the kind of towering hierarchies characterized by government, a "man with no morals will possess a marked advantage over the moral man who is willing to sacrifice career objectives. From this it follows that the man who tends to ignore moral considerations and chooses courses of action designed to advance his own personal status will be the man likely to advance in the hierarchy. The general 'moral level' of those bureaucrats who have reached the top layers in such a structure will tend to be relatively low."[26]

The importance of Tullock and his followers is not in their immediate influence over the tides of reform, for they had little immediate impact. Rather, it is in their long-term persuasiveness on the core problems of government monopolies. Much as the basic argument can be traced back in time to both Publius (in Madison's effort to counteract ambition with ambition) and Brutus, the 1960s produced a bevy of new thinkers who argued the basic case against bureaucracy. Over time, the argument found fertile ground and was reflected in both the Reagan administration's push for privatization and the NPR's commitment to market forces. And, as I suggested in Chapter 2, Tullock's work may yet account for a new tide of reform.

The 91st Congress (1969–1971)

Only the second session of the 91st Congress in 1970 produced major initiatives for this book. The slow start was undoubtedly due to Nixon's newness to the White House and his preoccupation with the Vietnam War. Nixon spent much of his first year assembling his staff and building a domestic agenda, relegating management reform to 1970 at the earliest. So noted, the reforms were among the most important in recent history, including products of scientific management, war on waste, and liberation management.

Chief among the reforms was the creation of an Office of Management and Budget (OMB) as a replacement for what was seen as a tired Bureau of the Budget. Recognizing his thin victory margin in 1968 and his lack of congressional support, Nixon turned to a time-honored device for drafting the key proposal: a blue-ribbon commission. Having recruited the head of Litton Industries, Roy Ash, as its chair, Nixon appointed the President's Advisory Council on Executive Organization Management in March 1969.

The Ash Council's first recommendation was to create OMB, its second to create a White House Domestic Council as a new source of policy leadership. "The Domestic Council will be primarily concerned with *what* we do," Nixon said in forwarding the needed reorganization plan to Congress in March 1970, "the Office of Management and Budget will be primarily concerned with *how* we do it, and *how well* we do it."[27] (Note the similarity to the NPR's focus not on what government does, but on how it does it.)

The plan was hardly met with enthusiasm on Capitol Hill. Indeed, the House subcommittee on Executive and Legislation Reorganization actually voted to reject the plan, only to be reversed by the full committee. The subcommittee's concern was that the centralization of power in a more malleable OMB reflected a heightened politicization of the budget process. Harbingers of the 1974 Budget and Impoundment Act can be found in the debate as Congress struggled with the potential loss of another source of needed information.[28]

Even as Nixon tightened budgetary control, he elected to jettison one of the nation's oldest cabinet departments and create a new structure for administering the government's dwindling railroad subsidies. The decision to convert the postal and rail subsidies into two new government corporations, the U.S. Postal Service and Amtrak, reflected a clear preference for liberating certain kinds of government programs from the federal management system. In putting both programs on a "businesslike basis," the proposals reflected a rising tide of liberation management. As the House Post Office and Civil Service Committee explained the U.S. Postal Service, a government corporation would eliminate "serious handicaps that are now imposed on the postal service by certain legislative, budgetary, financial, and personnel policies that are outmoded, unnecessary, and inconsistent with the modern management and business practices that must be available if the American public to is to enjoy efficient and economical postal service."[29]

Much as the proposals reflected this liberating impulse, neither corporation could have passed administration muster if not for the promise of significant budget savings. Indeed, the administration's original proposal for a government corporation called Railpax was actually rejected by the White House on budgetary grounds. At the same time, however, both statutes contained the seeds for expanded federal support. Thus, Congress used the Postal Reorganization Act to increase pay for postal employees and the Rail Passenger Service Act to "prevent the complete abandonment of intercity rail passenger service and to preserve a minimum of such service along specific corridors."[30]

As if to further complicate a year of already complicated reform, Congress produced a major reform of the federal pay-setting process. Frustrated by its own inability to raise pay, Congress enacted the Federal Salary Comparability Act, creating a permanent device for linking private and public pay rates. It was an effort clearly influenced by the Postal Reorganization Act, which had provided an 8 percent increase for postal employees.

Given public resistance to pay increases, it is hardly surprising that the final salary act was a baffle of advisory committees and councils, all of which would somehow work together to keep federal pay competitive with comparable private sector jobs. Driven by pay surveys conducted by the Bureau of Labor Statistics, which would be filtered first through a Federal Employees Pay Council and next through an Advisory Committee on Federal Pay, the act gave the president final authority to adjust pay accordingly, provided that a national emergency or economic conditions made the raise inappropriate, in which case the president was to submit an alternative plan to Congress, which, in turn, would be subject to a one-house legislative veto. Alas, even with such a complicated process, pay increases still carried the kind of public visibility that makes Congress and presidents wince. It is safe to say that the comparability statute never worked. Pay increases remained rare, and the gap between private and public salaries continued to grow.

The 93d Congress (1973–1975)

Despite his success in the 91st Congress, Nixon was unsatisfied with the pace of administrative reform. Failure to win congressional support for a host of domestic priorities, most prominently welfare reform, prompted an even greater effort to centralize administrative control early in his second term. With the legislative path foreclosed by strong Democratic majorities in both chambers, Nixon turned to the only tools he controlled: appointments, executive orders, the budget, and regulations. The grand imagery of good people caught in bad systems that had flavored his call for department reorganization gave way to a new imagery of appointees "gone native" and civil servants as saboteurs.[31]

Gone were the days, for example, when the White House would let cabinet secretaries pick their key lieutenants; gone, too, were the days when the departments would have the edge in the annual budget process. Nixon vowed not to repeat the mistakes of his first term, a vow that formed the basis for his administrative Presidency. "Getting control over these processes was the aim of the President's strategy for domestic government in his second term," writes Richard Nathan of Nixon's centralizing impulse. "Judged against the lack of legislative success on domestic issues in the first term, there are grounds for concluding that this was a rational decision."[32]

Whatever the wisdom of the approach, Nixon was almost immediately stymied by the Watergate investigation. The result was the most active year recorded in Appendix A. In all, thirteen management initiatives passed in 1974, creating a medley of reform, from the Congressional Budget and Impoundment Act, which established a new budget process and placed sharp limits on executive discretion, to the Freedom of Information Act Amendments, which further opened government to public inspection, and the Privacy Act, which guaranteed protection against arbitrary release of information.

The year also produced a patchwork of smaller but still important reforms, including use of a government corporation to save the legal services program, a block grant to pass the first housing bill since 1968, and new agencies for protecting employee pensions, enhancing energy research and development, and assuring transportation safety. It also produced the Office of Federal Procurement Policy as a platform for future procurement reform. Alongside the major reforms cited, which reflected a peak for watchful eye, these lesser reforms suggests the continued presence of the other tides. Even a hurricane such as Watergate could not completely disrupt the flow of scientific management and the occasional expression of liberation management.

Nevertheless, Watergate clearly changed the flow of the tides. As table 3.1 suggests, 1974 produced a sea change in the way Congress and the president approach making government work.

Of particular note in table 3.1 is the changing origin of reform. Before 1974, the president was by far the most frequent source of reform ideas. Whether operating through blue-ribbon commissions, informal task forces (for example, Eisenhower's Advisory Committee on Government Organization, Johnson's Task Force on Government Organization, and Nixon's Ash Council), or the old Division of Administrative Management, presidents introduced roughly three quarters of the management reforms recorded in Appendix A.[33] In the years since 1974, Congress is the dominant source of ideas, accounting for almost three quarters of the reforms.

At least in terms of the origin of ideas, 1974 is the watershed year. Ten of the thirteen reform initiatives passed that year came from Congress, including all but two of the ten initiatives signed into law by Gerald Ford. That Ford did not have much impact as an originator of ideas in 1974 is hardly surprising. He was

Table 3.1 *The Watergate Divide (percentages)*

	Pre-1974	Post-1974
Legislative History		
Origin of Idea		
President	71	27
Congress	29	73
Blue-Ribbon Commission Involved?	25	5
Interest Groups Involved?	22	34
Legislative Debate		
Routine	59	55
Controversial	41	45
Legislative Passage		
Unanimous	46	51
Near-Unanimous	22	33
Strong Majority (60 or more)	29	7
Close (less than 60)	3	9
Recorded Vote Taken?	58	62
Philosophy		
Tide		
Scientific Management	71	24
War on Waste	5	28
Watchful Eye	12	32
Liberation Management	12	16
Purity of Statute		
No Other Tides Found in Statute	73	70
One Other Tide Found	24	22
Two Other Tides Found	10	9
Primary Accountability Mechanism		
Compliance	24	51
Capacity	66	32
Performance	3	17
General View of Government		
Trusting	71	31
Distrusting	29	69
Change Strategy		
Focus		
Structure of Government	58	29
Procedures of Government	39	62
Both	0	9
Create a Study Commission	3	0
Structural Tactic		
Create New Agency	17	16

Table 3.1 (Continued)

	Pre-1974	Post-1974
Merge Existing Agencies	15	4
Reorganize Existing Agency	12	4
Create Public Corporation	7	2
Abolish Existing Agency	0	5
Grant Agency Independence	0	5
Elevate Agency to Higher Status	2	2
Combination	5	0
No Structural Reform in Statute	42	62
Procedural Tactic		
Establish New System	14	28
Broaden System	7	20
Revise System	10	6
Deregulate/Narrow System	3	10
Reauthorize System	5	5
Abolish System	0	1
Combination	0	1
No Procedural Reform in Statute	61	29
Target		
General Organization of Government	59	26
Procurement/Acquisition	3	16
Ethics/Standards of Conduct	7	13
Administrative Process	3	9
Pay Systems	7	4
Audit/Investigation	0	7
Rulemaking Procedures	2	6
General Personnel/Classification	2	6
Budget/Financial Management	5	5
Combination	7	2
Strategic Planning/Analysis	2	2
Debt Collection	2	2
Tort Claims		
Scale		
Nature of Idea		
New Approach	53	54
Modification of Old	48	46
Scope of Impact		
Large	44	37
Small	56	63
Overall Scale of Reform		
New/Large	31	24

Table 3.1 (Continued)

	Pre-1974	Post-1974
New/Small	24	29
Old/Large	15	13
Old/Small	31	33
Implementation		
Experimental Approach in Statute?	0	4
Time Horizon in Statute		
Temporary/Sunset	9	15
Permanent	91	85
Scope		
Single Agency	41	33
Several Agencies	22	9
Governmentwide	37	58
Oversight Approach		
Centralized	61	43
Decentralized	39	57
Impact		
Shift in Shared Powers		
Toward President	66	38
Toward Congress	24	28
Not Clear/No Shift Discernible	10	34
Impact on Cost of Government		
Increase	42	13
Decrease	9	9
Not Clear/No Impact Discernible	49	78
Impact on Role of Government		
Expand	54	12
Contract	5	15
Not Clear/No Impact Discernible	41	73
Impact on Shape of Government		
Thicken Hierarchy	68	51
Thin Hierarchy	12	18
Not Clear/No Impact Discernible	20	31
Impact on Administrative Speed		
Accelerate	44	31
Slow Down	15	34
Not Clear/No Impact Discernible	31	35
Impact on Interest Group Access		
Enhance	15	18
Reduce	24	24
Not Clear/No Impact Discernible	61	57

Table 3.1 (Continued)

	Pre-1974	Post-1974
Impact on Public Access		
Enhance	15	21
Reduce	12	4
Not Clear/No Impact Discernible	73	75
Impact on Government Morale		
Improve	15	33
Reduce	2	2
Not Clear/No Impact Discernible	83	65
Impact on Bureaucratic Balance		
Strengthen Line Units	68	32
Strengthen Staff Units	29	55
Not Clear/No Impact Discernible	3	13

N = 141

too late to the office to have any real influence on the legislative agenda, and he was preoccupied with other issues, not the least of which was the Nixon pardon. Moreover, that Congress produced so much legislation of its own making in 1974 reflects legislative developments clearly under way before Nixon resigned. Legislation does not spring full blown from Congress with only a week or two of notice any more than hurricanes come ashore with no warning. Many of the signal bills that emerged in 1974 had been years in the making.

Other than origin of idea and the involvement of the occasional blue-ribbon commission, table 3.1 shows few other meaningful differences in legislative history between pre- and post-1974. The debate is a bit less routine after Watergate, perhaps, and passage quite a bit more likely to be unanimous, but the legislative concentration on management reform seems mostly unchanged.

It is in reform philosophy where strong differences emerge. Here, compliance accountability finds a dramatic rise in the post-1974 period, in large measure due to a rising tide of statutes that imposed new rules on administrative behavior, many of which came from the war on waste and watchful eye tides. As noted in Chapter 2, however, many of these new rules involve efforts to constrain administrative conduct, a point that is evident later in table 3.1, with increased numbers of procurement/acquisition, ethics/standards of conduct, and administrative process targets. As Congress became more involved—or so I shall argue in the next chapter—reform became more focused on compliance. Reform also became much less trusting. If there had been any remnants of Wilson's public service vision left in the late 1950s and 1960s, it appears mostly gone by the mid-1970s.

Equally important is the clear change in preference toward procedural reforms. Except for the addition of two new departments in the late 1970s, the creation of the occasional new agency such as the Synfuels Corporation, and the elevation of the Veterans Administration to cabinet status in 1988, there is precious little structure in the post-1974 period.

Part of the reason is the simple exhaustion of the broad supply of agency-building ideas. Other than undoing what the Hoover Commission had assembled, which explains the Department of Education and independence for the Social Security Administration, or trying once again to fix what the Hoover Commission originally tried to fix, which explains yet another attempt at Defense Department reorganization in the mid-1980s, most of today's structure had been built by the mid-1970s. All that was left were the sort of small structural adjustments that I noted in *Thickening Government*—that is, the addition of a new assistant secretary here and there, the creation of a drug czar, or the elevation of a buried unit.[34]

Part of the reason, as I shall discuss in Chapter 6, is the erosion of the Division of Administrative Management at OMB. The steady weakening of the division staff produced an exhaustion of ideas of a different sort. Lacking staff to flesh out scientific proposals, OMB slowly faded as a significant participant in management reform, while Congress's own management agency, the General Accounting Office, slowly grew. The result was a dramatic increase in the number of financial management reforms during the 1980s, many of which originated in the hallways of GAO, particularly the Accounting and Financial Management Division.

Once the supply of structural ideas played out, it simply made sense to turn to the procedural. In an administrative version of *Field of Dreams,* if the federal government builds it, the procedures will come. Short of either abolishing an agency or converting it to a corporation, the only path to reform is through procedures. It is clearly a path taken more frequently in the post-1974 period.

Table 3.1 reveals other noteworthy differences in the two eras. There is a clear increase, for example, in the number of experimental initiatives, led by a growing Senate interest in trying major reforms in pilots first. At the same time, however, there is a parallel growth in the number of governmentwide reforms, mostly as a consequence of the rising number of war on waste and watchful eye initiatives during the period. Finally, there is a clear shift away from initiatives that strengthen the president, increase the cost and role of government, and strengthen line units of government.

Interestingly, the number of initiatives that improve government morale actually goes up, in large measure because of efforts both to confront the continuing pay problems and to liberate all agencies from the kind of burdensome rules criticized in the Postal Reorganization Act back in 1970.

The 95th Congress (1977–1979)

Many of these post-1974 trends continued, indeed accelerated, into the 95th Congress. Setting aside the 94th Congress as a holding action while Ford exercised his veto pen with extraordinary vigor, the 95th presented the first opportunity to cement the gains made immediately after Watergate. Combined in the same ocean of reform, the two Congresses account for more than a fifth of all initiatives recorded in Appendix A.

Acknowledging the continuity, the 95th Congress has to be accorded its own status as a separate storm of reform. According to the staff director of the Senate Governmental Affairs Committee at the time, Richard Wegman, it was a heady time. "There was a sense that we had a narrow window of opportunity to move legislation that was pretty significant. And I think the window of opportunity was created by the fact that you did have a president who was committed to a number of these reforms and you had a reform-minded Congress." Wegman's committee had arguably the strongest collection of members in recent history. The Democrats had Abraham Ribicoff (Conn.) as chairman, Henry "Scoop" Jackson (Wash.), Ed Muskie (Maine), Thomas Eagleton (Mo.), Lawton Chiles (Fla.), Sam Nunn (Ga.), and John Glenn (Ohio) among others, five of whom had or would be involved in future presidential campaigns, while the Republicans had Charles Percy (Ill.) as ranking member, Jacob Javits (N.Y.), William Roth (Del.), Ted Stevens (Alaska), Charles "Mac" Mathias (Md.), John Danforth (Mo.), and John Heinz (Pa.). As Wegman argues: "You had senior members on the committee with a great deal of experience and integrity, and who wanted to move an agenda. You also had the sense of common purpose in the Senate that, unfortunately, doesn't exist today. It started breaking down several years after 1978 and I think we were aware, at the time that this group of members was up there, that we had just these few precious years to make a difference."[35]

- There can be little doubt that the committee and the rest of the 95th Congress made a difference: yet another effort to create a stable pay-setting process (the 1970 comparable pay system had failed to produce an increase in eight years), a cabinet department to wage war on the energy crisis, a massive civil service reform, expansion of the inspector general concept across government, airline deregulation, and the massive Ethics in Government Act.

Not all of the legislation came from the Senate or from the Congress as a whole, of course. Having run on a platform to create a government as good as the people, Jimmy Carter was a key player in several reforms, most visibly the creation of the Department of Energy and the Civil Service Reform Act.

In keeping with his reputation for sweating the details, Carter actually wrote several key provisions of the civil service act. Facing a Senate impasse over an obscure provision on presidential authority to appoint members of the new Senior Executive Service, Carter called members and staff together at the White House in July 1978. "There wasn't much time left to get the legislation through in the Senate," Wegman remembers, "so a meeting was put together at 4 o'clock one afternoon with the senators in the Oval Office and staff waiting just outside in the Cabinet Room. Carter met with the senators for five or ten minutes, then stepped out of the Oval Office to meet with the staff." What happened next is classic Carter:

> Carter had the civil service legislation under his arm and open[ed] it up to the key issue. "Now as I understand it, the problem is in Section such and such of the bill," he said. "You know, I was thinking maybe if we added a couple of sentences along these lines this might take care of the problem." And he penciled in some words in the margin of the legislation, and I remember saying to him, "Mr. President, I think that will solve part of the problem, but we have to add another sentence here." And so he said, "Yes, I can do that." So he wrote in another sentence, turned to the two staffers who represented the Republicans, and said, "Well, can your senators live with that?" We sat there looking open-mouthed, not quite sure what to say. Then he said, "Well, Rosalyn and I have a tennis date on the court and we are going to go off and play, but we'll be back in about a half hour in case you need some more help." We worked on the bill for another half hour or so and the next day had a deal that could pass the Senate.

Nevertheless, even the president's top priorities were reshaped by Congress. Consider the Department of Energy Act. Carter's original proposal was drafted along the scientific management ideal—that is, a strong secretary, nearly invincible regulatory power, a set of assistant secretaryships to be defined by the secretary, and a clear chain of command leading directly to the president and the president alone. The department that finally emerged was anything but clear. It contained an inspector general, however, and a much weaker secretary. "The legislation was significantly modified so that the Secretary of Energy didn't hold all of those power strings," Wegman recounts. "We created a Federal Energy Regulatory Commission, which was a new kind of administrative mechanism, a quasi-independent regulatory agency, multi-member, housed within a cabinet department. The administration wasn't happy with this agreement but ultimately accepted the compromise."

Beyond altering presidential priorities, the 95th Congress also produced three massive contributions to the history of management reform: (1) the In-spector General Act, which represented a defining statute in the war on waste, (2) the Ethics in Government Act, which accelerated watchful eye, and (3) the Civil Service Reform Act, which actually combined elements of all four tides within what was a primarily scientific management reform. I discussed the IG Act in Chapter 1, and the Civil Service Reform Act will be tackled in greater detail in Chapter 4, so we shall review the Ethics in Government Act here.

Bluntly put, the Ethics in Government Act did what the majority support-ers of the attorney general's *Report on Administrative Procedure in Govern-ment Agencies* said in 1941 should not be done: it wrote a code of ethics and created an administrative infrastructure for assuring compliance. The statute was pure watchful eye, bringing a general distrust to bear on the problem of hidden influence. Using the public's right to know as its input and raw informa-tion as its product, the act used disclosure to assure compliance with what was a broad inventory of both implied and explicit rules for behavior.

The general view of government embedded in the act is unmistakable in the Senate Governmental Affairs Committee legislative report. After drawing two conclusions about the state of government corruption—the first being that the Department of Justice had not allocated sufficient resources to the cause, the second that the department has particular difficulty investigating high-level corruption—the committee argued its case as follows: "The solu-tion to these problems is not merely the enactment of more criminal laws. It is essential that the President, the Attorney General and other top officials in the Department of Justice be men of unquestioned integrity. However, it is also essential that we have a system of controls and institutions which make the misuse and abuse of power difficult, if not impossible."[36] As if to reinforce its point, the very next sentence drew upon Madison's famous statement from *Federalist Paper No. 51:* "If men were angels, no government would be neces-sary. If angels were to govern men, neither external nor internal controls on government would be necessary."

Toward providing those internal controls, the Ethics in Government Act created the Office of Government Ethics (OGE) within the Office of Person-nel Management (OPM), which had been created under the Civil Service Re-form Act just weeks before. Although the Senate had originally called for an Office of Government Crimes within the Justice Department, the give-and-take of legislative compromise produced a somewhat more optimistic name and a more comfortable, perhaps encouraging home. (Congress later broke OGE out of OPM as a freestanding independent agency.)

As we have noted, OGE was responsible for overseeing two different codes of conduct. For an implied code of conduct, the Ethics in Government Act erected a series of disclosure requirements governing all executive branch employees at grade 16 and above. Each would have to file a detailed annual disclosure report on the source, type, and amount of unearned income. Each would also have to report any gifts (other than transportation, lodging, food, or entertainment) worth at least $100 from any one source other than a relative during a year, as well as identify any interest in property held in a trade or business, or for investment or the production of income, with a fair-market value of more than $1,000. Although the totals would be summarized in six broad categories—for example, under $1,000, over $100,000—the disclosure would be precise enough to establish a kind of tracking between the source of money and its likely impact.

Disclosure would work its will only by being public. As Senator Paul Douglas (D-Ill.) had observed in making the case for a code of conduct back in 1952, "Sunlight is a powerful disinfectant. This is as true of the moral life as it is of bacteria."[37] The 95th Congress appeared to agree. All financial disclosure documents would be made available to the public and the media, thereby creating at least some incentive against taking things of value that might eventually wind their way into a headline or campaign issue. The Governmental Affairs Committee argued that disclosure would simultaneously increase public confidence in government by making financial interests visible; demonstrate "the high level of integrity of the vast majority of government officials"; prevent conflicts of interest from arising in the first place, not by telling an official what to do about outside interest, but simply by assuring that what he or she does will be subject to scrutiny; deter some "persons who should not be entering public service from doing so"; and "better enable the public to judge the performance of public officials."[38]

For an explicit code of conduct, the act zeroed in on what it labeled "post-employment conflict of interest"—that is, jobs taken after leaving government that might involve indirect payoffs for having helped old friends. Former executive branch employees would be permanently barred from representing anyone before their agencies on issues in which they had personally and substantially participated while in government and would face additional one- and two-year bans on matters that had been pending or under their general supervision. As the Governmental Affairs Committee explained Title V of the statute, "The fundamental character of the men and women who serve in Federal office is, as it should be, a matter of greater importance to the American public; and conflict of interest statutes are a reflection of that interest and concern.... Title V is an attempt to prevent corruption and other official misconduct before it occurs, as well as penalizing it once it is uncovered."[39]

Finally, and most controversially, the act created an entirely new mechanism as an ultimate deterrent to corruption: the special prosecutor. Appointed by the U.S. Court of Appeals for the District of Columbia on the basis of an attorney general's investigation and request, a special prosecutor would have enormous latitude to further investigate and prosecute a violation of the act independent of the Department of Justice.

Together, these provisions challenged the personal morality of the public service. Even though the authors argued that only a "small fraction of a percent of all government officials have ever been charged with professional impropriety," the provisions applied to all. In essence, the act substituted broad regulation for self-restraint, and, in doing so, ended the pretense that government and its employees can be trusted to do good on their own.

Whatever the Senate's estimate of the number of public servants who could not be trusted, the act owes a debt not just to the Watergate scandal but to the Anti-Federalist statements of Brutus and his latter-day colleagues. "Too great a reliance on legal regulation can have side effects, like a drug too frequently used," argues public law expert Robert Vaughn, in a statement reminiscent of the AGR majority critique of codes of conduct. "By converting ethical problems into legal ones, the law becomes the sole judge of propriety. What can be done becomes what should done. If what is legal continues to seem improper, additional conduct is made illegal, reinforcing the perception that what is legal constitutes what is proper."[40]

The 100th Congress (1987–1989)

The 100th Congress is included in the list of seven reform Congresses not just for its sheer number of initiatives (eleven) or its significant legislative achievements (reauthorization of the special prosecutor provisions of the 1978 Ethics in Government Act, expansion of the 1978 IG Act, establishment of a military base closure commission, and the first major revision of the Federal Tort Claims Act since its initial passage in 1946), not even for the fact that I was a staffer for the Senate Governmental Affairs Committee at the time, and therefore have some self-interest in promoting the 100th Congress as one of the most productive.

It is also included because it produced at least one initiative from each of the four tides. Although war on waste and watchful eye predominate, scientific and liberation management both show up in the 100th Congress. Led in part by a fresh congressional majority that eagerly awaited the nearly inevitable (or so it seemed) election of a Democrat to the White House, the 100th Congress celebrated the bicentennial of the Constitution with a long list of major and not-quite-so-major reforms, all designed to make government work.

For supporters of the war on waste, the 100th Congress produced five reforms, ranging from the creation of new crime deterrents to better enforcement. The Major Fraud Act, for example, declared contractor fraud to be a new criminal offense punishable by up to a $1 million fine and/or ten years in prison, while amendments to the Office of Federal Procurement Policy Act provided new authority to oversee the awarding of contracts, and the Base Closure and Realignment Act created a blue-ribbon commission as a device for closing obsolete military bases. All three statutes were designed to reduce fraud, waste, or abuse, the first by enhancing deterrence, the second by strengthening centralized oversight, and the third by providing political cover for a nearly impossible legislative task.

Alongside these notable reforms, Congress expanded the IG concept to two new departments and a host of small and large agencies, including everything from the Panama Canal Commission to the U.S. Postal Service. In passing the bill, Congress finally established OIGs at the Departments of Justice and Treasury. Justice was the ultimate breakthrough, for it had fought off the concept for the better part of a decade on constitutional and operational grounds. Justice had campaigned against the 1978 act as a clear breach of the Constitution's "take care" clause.

Arguing, for one example, that the reporting relationship between the IGs and Congress violated "the President's power to control and supervise all replies and comments from the Executive Branch to Congress," Justice concluded that "the bill is not a proper legislative function but is rather a serious distortion of our constitutional system."[41] As the House Government Operations Committee noted in rejecting the arguments again ten years later, "The constitutional issues raised by the Justice Department are aimed at provisions contained in the 1978 act and the acts which established inspectors general in the then–Department of Health, Education, and Welfare, and in the Department of Energy. These arguments were presented to the Congress prior to passage of those laws, but were not accepted. Moreover, the President signed the laws containing the questioned provisions and the committee knows of no effort to overturn them in the courts."[42]

For supporters of watchful eye, the 100th Congress produced four major reforms, from a reauthorization of the provisions in the 1978 Ethics in Government Act pertaining to the special prosecutor (now called independent counsel) to an act granting independence to the Office of Government Ethics. Both initiatives paled in importance, however, when compared to the Computer Matching and Privacy Act, a bill in the making since the early 1980s and the first of several Privacy Act extensions.

The act, drafted by Senators William Cohen (R-Maine) and Carl Levin (D-

Mich.), reflected Senate discomfort with the war on waste, which had been pressing for broader authority to conduct computer matches of benefit programs with tax records to locate an assortment of payee fraud.[43] There was no question that such matches were on the rise during the 1980s. The Office of Technology Assistance (which was abolished by Congress in 1995) estimated that the number of computer matches had tripled between 1980 and 1984. As Cohen argued in making the case for reform before the Senate Subcommittee on Government Management, "The subcommittee's investigation and past hearings have revealed tremendous potential for abuse in computer matching, because there are no mandatory rules for agencies to follow when performing matches, little protection for the person whose records are matched, and inadequate oversight of how these programs are being conducted."[44]

This was not the time to simply abolish all matches, however, if only because they offered such promise in ferreting out fraud. Thus, even though the act required agencies to provide detailed justifications for each matching activity and to notify individuals that their records were being matched, it did not guarantee an individual right to privacy. As the political scientist Priscilla Regan shows in her history of privacy legislation, the act countered the war on waste only in providing new guarantees of procedural fairness. In doing so, matching actually became more permissible, provided that the records were clean and the individuals notified.

Although war on waste and watchful eye reached a crest in the 100th Congress, there was a small gesture to liberation management in passage of the Federal Employees Liability and Tort Compensation Act, perhaps presaging the high tide that would come in the first two years of the Clinton administration. The legislation was provoked by a Supreme Court decision in *Westfall v. Erwin* that held federal employees liable for negligence even if they were acting within the scope of employment.[45] Under the Federal Employees Liability Reform and Tort Compensation Act, which was also known as the Westfall Act, the federal government would be the sole defendant in such cases, liberating individual employees to do their jobs without fear of personal liability.

The 100th Congress even produced a gesture to scientific management in passage of the Presidential Transitions Effectiveness Act. The act represented the first effort since 1963 to strengthen the president-elect's transition support. Although the new act increased moving expenses for the outgoing president, its primary purpose was to increase the expense allowance for the incoming president, thereby assuring adequate staff support, a key feature of scientific management. The Senate version of the bill also contained funds to support preelection transition planning by the two national parties, also reflecting, perhaps, a strengthening of the president's leadership prospects once in office. (The provision was dropped in conference with the House.)

Even here, however, watchful eye attempted to regulate the role of private money and volunteers in the transition. Under the act, presidents-elect would have to report the source, amount, and expenditure of all private money raised for the transition, as well as the names, most recent employment, and source of funding for all full- or part-time transition employees. The Senate explained the need for private money regulation in classic sunshine terms:

> After its own study of past transition records, the Committee concluded that private money has grown increasingly important to presidential transitions. Presidents Nixon, Carter, and Reagan all raised private funds for their transitions. . . . The Committee noted with concern the complete absence of regulations covering private funding for presidential transitions, whether during the pre-election period or following the general election. . . . The lack of disclosure in the pre-election period undermines the efficacy of the Federal election rules, providing a loophole for money that might otherwise have to be disclosed in the campaign. The absence of disclosure in the post-election period creates the appearance of potential conflicts of interest during a very sensitive period in the policymaking and personnel process.[46]

Having written the legislative report for the Presidential Transition Effectiveness Act, I can testify that none of the act's sponsors thought to ask whether the disclosure requirements were in conflict with the broader aim of helping the president-elect into office. Quite the contrary. Disclosure was seen as a way to lead transitions not into temptation, as well as a way to sell the broader goal of preelection planning by the national parties. In retrospect, it seems clear that the disclosure requirements created an extra burden on the transition that might actually disrupt the president-elect's focus. Filling out forms, while hardly onerous, added an additional duty during a profoundly stressful period and clearly thickened the transition hierarchy with a new set of overseers, cross-checkers, and auditors.

In a similar vein, perhaps, elevation of the Veterans Administration to cabinet status is defined as an expression not of scientific management but of watchful eye. There was almost nothing in the bill that fits the principles of administration. Indeed, representatives of the National Academy of Public Administration were among the few to testify against the bill.[47] Viewed again from my personal experience, elevation reflected a desire among veterans and their representatives to move an already well-protected organization to a much more visible and therefore inspectable position within the executive branch. The hope was that having a seat at the cabinet table would make the secretary both more influential and watchable in winning the inevitable budget battles that would arise as the population of veterans dwindled over the years.

THE CHANGING CLIMATE OF REFORM

Studying the hurricanes of reform is one way to see the changing movement of the tides over time. War on waste and watchful eye have clearly grown more visible over the years, as have procedural approaches to making government work. Whereas half of all the scientific management statutes recorded in Appendix A had passed by 1965, liberation management reached the halfway mark only in 1980 (an early mark that reflects the popularity of government corporations during the Nixon administration), watchful eye in 1981 (largely because of Watergate), and war on waste in 1984 (a product of the Reagan administration's singular commitment to the cause).

Studying hurricanes is not the only way to chart the changing climate of reform, however. Tide watchers can also study the climate decade by decade, searching for highs and lows in the tides as one product of what may be a permanent zone of low confidence that assures continued conflict between advocates of liberation and continued war and watchfulness.

Decades of Reform

Because there are too few statutes passed in any given year to provide meaningful percentages, it is best to look for broad trends across four spans of roughly a decade each. The first, "Glory Days," covers the Truman and Eisenhower administrations and suggests the broad consensus on scientific management as the key to making government work. The second, "Great Society," covers the Kennedy and Johnson terms. The third, "Reassessment," covers the Nixon, Ford, and Carter years and suggests the growing preference for alternatives to scientific management, from both a trusting and distrusting general view. The fourth, "The New Proceduralism," covers the Reagan, Bush, and Clinton administrations and reflects what readers will shortly see as the rise of procedural fixes as the preferred method for making government work regardless of the tide involved. The relation between these four periods and the other measures used in this book are summarized in table 3.2.

The movement of the tides over time occurs in every category of the table, confirming many of the divisions already noted in the Watergate divide. With regard to legislative history, the president remains the source of ideas for management reform in the first two periods, even more so before 1960 than after. This may be a product of Eisenhower's willingness to defer slightly more to

Table 3.2 Decades and the Tides (percentages)

	Glory Days (1945–1960)	Great Society (1961–1968)	Reassessment (1969–1980)	The New Proceduralism (1981–1994)
Legislative History				
Origin of Idea				
President	63	89	47	18
Congress	37	11	53	82
Blue-Ribbon Commission Involved?	41	6	11	4
Interest Groups Involved?	19	28	38	27
Legislative Debate				
Routine	59	56	51	61
Controversial	41	44	49	39
Legislative Passage				
Unanimous	59	33	34	63
Near-Unanimous	15	22	47	20
Strong Majority (60 or more)	22	44	9	10
Close (less than 60)	4	0	11	6
Recorded Vote Taken?	44	72	70	55
Philosophy				
Tide				
Scientific Management	82	72	40	16
War on Waste	7	6	11	37
Watchful Eye	11	11	28	31
Liberation Management	0	11	21	16

Purity of Statute				
No Other Tides Found in Statute	69	66	89	70
One Other Tide Found	20	30	6	26
Two Other Tides Found	10	4	6	4
Primary Accountability Mechanism				
Compliance	57	34	17	33
Capacity	25	51	72	59
Performance	18	15	11	7
Change Strategy				
Focus				
Structure of Government	20	49	61	52
Procedures of Government	74	43	39	41
Both	6	9	0	0
Create a Study Commission	0	0	0	7
Structural Tactic				
Create New Agency	10	19	28	15
Merge Existing Agencies	0	15	11	11
Reorganize Existing Agency	2	9	11	11
Create Public Corporation	2	6	11	0
Abolish Existing Agency	6	2	0	0
Grant Agency Independence	4	4	0	0
Elevate Agency to Higher Status	2	2	0	4
Combination	0	0	0	11
No Structural Reform in Statute	74	43	39	48

Table 3.2 (Continued)

	Glory Days (1945–1960)	Great Society (1961–1968)	Reassessment (1969–1980)	The New Proceduralism (1981–1994)
Procedural Tactic				
Establish New System	15	11	23	29
Broaden System	7	11	6	27
Revise System	11	11	6	4
Deregulate/Narrow System	0	0	13	8
Reauthorize System	7	6	2	8
Abolish System	0	0	0	2
Combination	0	0	0	2
No Procedural Reform in Statute	59	61	49	20
Target				
General Organization of Government	56	61	45	18
Procurement/Acquisition	7	0	6	20
Ethics/Standards of Conduct	4	11	6	18
Administrative Process	4	6	9	6
Pay Systems	4	11	6	2
Audit/Investigation	0	0	4	8
Rulemaking Procedures	4	0	6	4
General Personnel/Classification	4	0	6	4
Budget/Financial Management	7	0	6	4
Combination	7	6	2	4
Strategic Planning/Analysis	0	0	2	4

Debt Collection	0	6	0	4
Tort Claims	4	0	2	2
Scale				
Nature of Idea				
New Approach	44	55	60	51
Modification of Old	56	45	40	49
Scope of Impact				
Large	48	44	43	31
Small	52	56	57	69
Overall Scale of Reform				
New/Large	30	39	30	18
New/Small	15	22	30	33
Old/Large	19	11	13	14
Old/Small	37	28	28	35
Implementation				
Experimental Approach in Statute?	0	0	0	10
Time Horizon in Statute				
Temporary/Sunset	15	6	6	18
Permanent	85	94	94	82
Scope				
Single Agency	33	44	47	25
Several Agencies	19	22	17	6
Governmentwide	48	33	36	69
Oversight Approach				
Centralized	78	56	45	39
Decentralized	22	44	55	61

Table 3.2 (Continued)

Impact	Glory Days (1945–1960)	Great Society (1961–1968)	Reassessment (1969–1980)	The New Proceduralism (1981–1994)
Impact				
Shift in Shared Powers				
Toward President	74	61	49	27
Toward Congress	11	28	38	27
Not Clear/No Shift Discernible	15	11	13	47
Impact on Cost of Government				
Increase	41	56	28	4
Decrease	4	0	11	12
Not Clear/No Impact Discernible	56	44	62	84
Impact on Role of Government				
Expand	63	61	26	4
Contract	0	0	15	16
Not Clear/No Impact Discernible	37	39	60	80
Impact on Shape of Government				
Thicken Hierarchy	74	67	64	41
Thin Hierarchy	4	6	23	18
Not Clear/No Impact Discernible	22	28	13	41

Impact on Administrative Speed				
Accelerate	52	17	40	31
Slow Down	19	11	28	35
Not Clear/No Impact Discernible	30	72	32	35
Impact on Interest Group Access				
Enhance	15	17	21	14
Reduce	15	22	23	31
Not Clear/No Impact Discernible	70	61	55	55
Impact on Public Access				
Enhance	11	17	26	16
Reduce	7	11	6	6
Not Clear/No Impact Discernible	82	72	68	78
Impact on Government Morale				
Improve	15	22	19	39
Reduce	4	0	0	4
Not Clear/No Impact Discernible	82	78	81	57
Impact on Bureaucratic Balance				
Strengthen Line Units	59	83	55	18
Strengthen Staff Units	41	17	32	67
Not Clear/No Impact Discernible	0	0	13	14

$N = 141$

Congress on accounting and budget procedures, as well as to the set of watchful eye statutes that emerged from the 79th Congress in 1946. It is also due, of course, to the enormous support for Johnson's Great Society in the mid-1960s, a time when the president's persuasiveness was at a postwar high.

Interestingly, the middle two decades emerge as the most contentious for management reform. Vote margins are tighter and recorded votes on management reform much more frequent. Part of the explanation involves the Great Society again and the disagreements over the new administrative infrastructure of civil rights and the war on poverty. Part also can be attributed to the divisions prompted by the post-Watergate reforms, divisions that reflected sharp constitutional disagreements of the kind hinted at in the Justice Department's stance on the 1978 IG Act.

Table 3.2 clearly shows the break in the four tides regarding reform philosophy. Just as a high tide eventually moves out to sea, scientific management has steadily dwindled as a source of reform ideas. Cutting, not building, has become the fashion of the day. Table 3.2 also shows the steady rise in war on waste, rising from an occasional item on the agenda to a plurality. Watchful eye doubles over time to a stable level, while liberation moves up, then slightly down. War on waste is clearly at its crest in the 1980s and 1990s, an inevitable consequence of the pressure for budget savings and the "body count" mentality that prevails in modern politics. Being able to show yearly records in cutting budgets, fighting fraud, and eliminating employees produces the defining energy underpinning efforts to make government work. Increasingly rare is the statute that does not carry some gesture to war on waste.

As would be expected, given the changing tides, the primary accountability mechanism used to improve government shifts over time to favor compliance. Contrary to the impulses of the Government Performance and Results Act and NPR, the dominant notion is that more rules of behavior will assure better performance. The failure of the NPR to address the growing inventory of watchful eye rules suggests that the rules will continue to pile up. Nevertheless, as table 3.2 also shows, performance accountability is clearly growing as an accountability mechanism, suggesting a perhaps inevitable confrontation with those who see compliance as the path to impact.

The passage of time reveals a steady decline in structure as a change strategy, falling from a high point during the Great Society to a low in the era of new proceduralism. Creating new agencies becomes passé, as does merging and reorganizing, while abolishing makes its first appearance in the 1970s and grows in the 1980s. Even a cursory inventory of the cuts in the 104th Congress led by the new Republican majority suggests that abolishing agencies is a growth industry, as is creating new systems of one kind or another for regulating what government and its employees do. As for targets, the growth of procurement/acquisitions and ethics/standards of conduct as topics of reform has eclipsed the organization of government as topics of fascination for reformers, both obvious consequences of the war on waste and watchful eye.

It is important to note that the rising popularity of procedural reform has affected all four tides. As table 3.3 suggests, even scientific management has become more procedural in tone, hence the label "new proceduralism" to describe the Reagan-Bush-Clinton years.

Scientific management became more procedural during the 1980s, no doubt reflecting the unfriendly climate for building new agencies. Changing the federal retirement system (which also carries a dose of war on waste), augmenting presidential transition support, rebuilding HUD, and creating a new pay-setting process based on local cost of employment are all examples of this movement. It is useful to note, however, that similar initiatives have existed over the decades, meaning that the rising level of procedural focus in scientific management is primarily the result of a *lack* of structure. As scientific management accounts for fewer and fewer reform ideas, it is procedure, not structure, that is most likely to survive.

Ironically, given its distaste for bureaucracy, watchful eye becomes more structural over time, reflecting an awareness that structure can be essential to procedural success. Elevation of the Office of Government Ethics to an independent perch, for example, provided an institutional base for both overseeing and advocating full compliance with the 1978 Ethics in Government Act and its later amendments. In a different variation on the theme, war on waste started with structure in the 1970s, creating the IGs as an enforcement base for future procedural reforms. Having an enforcement mechanism handy allowed Congress to ladle on additional responsibilities over the years, including OIG oversight of the Federal Manager's Financial Integrity Act and Chief Financial Officers Act.

Liberation management also starts out heavily invested in structure, largely reflecting the preference for government corporations as an escape device for specific agencies. Thus did the Postal Service break free of the ordinary bounds of federal agencies. Having exhausted most, but not all of these breakout opportunities (the NPR proposed a government corporation for air traffic control), liberation management began to turn its attention to governmentwide regulations dealing with personnel, budget, and procurement. As we have seen, however, liberation has yet to turn its focus to the watchful eye and war on waste regulations that came with administrative procedure, freedom of information, or paperwork reduction. And, given the political popularity of such regulations, liberation management likely never will.

Table 3.3 *The New Proceduralism (percentages)*

	Glory Days (1945–1960)	Great Society (1961–1968)	Reassessment (1969–1980)	The New Proceduralism (1981–1994)
Tide and Focus				
Scientific Management				
Structure	65	70	72	29
Procedure	35	30	28	71
War on Waste				
Structure	50	0	60	19
Procedure	50	100	40	81
Watchful Eye				
Structure	0	0	20	29
Procedure	100	100	80	71
Liberation Management				
Structure	0	100	50	11
Procedure	0	0	50	89

N = 132

Note: table does not include study commissions or combinations of structure and procedure.

In fact, liberation management appears to be turning back to structure. Drawing upon the British experience, U.S. liberation advocates have invented a new administrative structure called a performance based organization. Like the government corporations of the 1960s and 1970s, a PBO is designed to liberate an agency from governmentwide personnel and procurement regulations. Unlike a traditional corporation, which is usually completely independent of government and allowed to raise its own revenue through sales of service, a PBO remains closely linked to its parent department and continues to receive annual legislative appropriations. It gets its freedom through a performance contract with its parent department. If a PBO hits its performance targets, its management and staff can reap substantial financial bonuses.

Having reached an impasse in 1995 with the new Republican Congress on further governmentwide liberation, the NPR began proposing PBOs in March 1996. Among the proposed conversions were the Patent and Trademark Office (5,200 employees) and the Defense Commissary Agency (17,600).[48] Although Congress was unenthusiastic about the eight proposed conversions, the PBOs clearly represent a move away from governmentwide deregulation and toward agency-by-agency liberation through administrative structure. If not quite yet a harbinger of the "new structuralism," the PBOs do suggest the adaptation that occurs as the tides work their will.

Returning to impact of the four spans on issues of scale, table 3.2 shows a clear trend over time toward new/small ideas. This finding fits well with both the rise of the three newer tides and the budgetary pressures restricting new/large ideas. By reversing the gains made under scientific management in the 1940s and 1950s, new/small ideas challenge the prevailing wisdom on making government work and gain at least some extra legislative support simply because of their newness. In this sense, then, scientific management may someday be the new tide in town, offering entrepreneurial politicians the chance to be different. The preference for smallness may also reflect the political difficulty of achieving any policy success in an increasingly unfriendly legislative setting, let alone success in a policy arena as naturally unattractive as federal management reform.

With regard to implementation, the number of experimental reforms has grown ever so slightly in recent decades (one in the 1970s, one in the 1980s, and three more in the 1990s), and sunsets have become more popular. Although the Senate Governmental Affairs Committee was unable to persuade the rest of the Senate or the House to pass its Sunset Act of 1977, the basic premise that there should be more sunsets appears to have taken hold, albeit at a level just a bit higher than during the glory days of scientific management.

A far more impressive change has been the rise in governmentwide reforms. This may be yet another manifestation of the *Field of Dreams* phenomenon. Agencies and departments typically get built one by one, but they get reformed in groups (domestic, economic, international) or en masse.

Equally impressive in table 3.2 is the clear tendency toward decentralized implementation. Gone are the days when the president would be trusted to faithfully execute the management reforms. Congress is not the only branch to favor decentralization, however. President Clinton has been converted to customer standards, too, endorsing his vice president's call for empowering those served by the government as the arbiters of reform.

Not surprisingly, given the broad decade-by-decade changes inventoried above, the impacts of reform change over time, too. Shifts of institutional power toward the president have dropped dramatically, as have initiatives affecting the cost and role of government. Although there are fewer thickening statutes, I have argued elsewhere that government is quite some distance from becoming svelte. Efforts to thin government have increased slightly, but they largely involve abolishment of specific agencies, not wholesale diets throughout the federal hierarchy.[49] At the same time, the rise of war on waste and watchful eye have tended to slow government down over time, producing a Catch-22 for managers who are told to take risks and move fast, all the while honoring existing law. Woe to the manager or employee who decides that a computer match just might be a good idea no matter what the law says. The "permission slips" that circulated throughout government at the height of the reinventing government fervor in 1993–1994 have no standing in a court of law or on Capitol Hill.

As for interest group and public access, both show slight declines over time. It is hard to tell, however, just who was served by the watchful eye reforms of the 1970s. No doubt the public gained greater access than ever before, access that continues to this day. No doubt interest groups were driven into the sunshine. However, interest groups have a vast array of alternative channels into the administrative arena, not the least of which are campaign spending and independent advocacy campaigns. Efforts to close interest groups out through ethics and lobbying reform do not always close the door elsewhere. And, as already noted, such legislation does little by way of creating aspirations for ethical conduct. Watchful eye has done very well in establishing the floor for behavior but has devoted far less energy to raising the ceiling.

Contrary to conventional wisdom of the battered civil service, there has actually been a considerable increase in statutes that would tend to raise government morale, most notably in statutes designed to solve the continuing pay problem. The Federal Employees Pay Comparability Act, which creates cost-of-employment adjustments in particularly high-cost cities (federal employees in Boston, New York, Los Angeles, and San Francisco were among the first covered), was a major achievement in narrowing the pay gap between private and public jobs. So noted, these statutes may have been overwhelmed by the parallel increase in antigovernment rhetoric from both parties and the "bureaucrat bashing" that so characterizes modern political campaigns.

The fact that so many war on waste and watchful eye initiatives show no discernible effect on morale does not mean that they are value neutral, however. Although recent efforts to raise federal pay address a significant cause of dissatisfaction, the bureaucrat bashing that so often accompanies war on waste and watchful eye may explain why some believe that government morale continues to drift downward. Indeed, the argument can be made that the rising tides of war on waste and watchful eye are inherently negative—that is, that the two tides leave a residue of ill will regardless of their best intentions. Although that is not an argument used in coding the initiatives in Appendix A, it is perhaps supported in the final cells of table 3.2 nonetheless. When most management reform strengthens staff, not line, employees may have good reason to wonder whether they are getting all the help they need.

Permanent Low Pressure?

The rising tides of war on waste and watchful eye confirm the impact of growing public distrust on the climate of reform. As confidence in government has plummeted over the past three decades, the rewards for adopting a distrusting stance toward reform have also grown.

Recall, for example, that war on waste is often attached to scientific and liberation management as a way to sell these more trusting reforms. One out of three liberation reforms carry war on waste as a companion, as do one sixth of scientific management and watchful eye. And even though watchful eye has remained the purest of tides—rarely attaching in secondary or tertiary position and rarely accepting attachments—its often intensely distrusting rhetoric clearly influences the legislative process. Employees are to be empowered, trained, liberated, and renewed not as a public good in and of itself but as a way to save money or tame the unaccountable administrative state.

Elements of distrust have been evident in many reform efforts, of course, dating all the way back to Andrew Jackson's efforts to unseat an entrenched bureaucracy. Even the Hoover Commission, that bastion of scientific reform, was quite willing to apply war on waste rhetoric to its cause.

Yet to argue that economy and efficiency have often been linked in the past is not to deny the enormous animus toward government today. The figures are startling. Pollsters seem to be unable to ask a question that might prompt a favorable view of government. According to a 1996 survey by the Pew Research Center for the People and the Press, 61 percent of Americans believe the federal government is almost always wasteful and inefficient, while just 21 percent say the federal government often does a better job than people give it credit for.[50]

Although there is an occasional positive in the negatives, particularly in how Americans view their personal relationship with government, rare is the candidate who stands ready to defend bureaucracy to a broadly distrusting electorate, let alone create a positive vision of the administrative state. Once in office, these candidates rarely become champions of a more trusting stance toward making government work.[51]

The United States is not the only nation experiencing low pressure, however. Making government work has become a theme all across the world, with a mix of liberation management and war on waste dominant. As Donald Kettl writes, "This revolution spread quickly around the world. Although the Westminster countries (notably New Zealand, Australia, and the United Kingdom) typically receive credit for starting first and pushing farthest, the reform movement has been remarkably global: in developed and developing nations, the urge to shrink the size of the state and improve its performance spread in a world-wide tidal wave."[52]

Driven by a negative or distrusting theory of the state, the climate sucked ideas for improving performance from every sector. Whereas national governments around the globe had once been the primary source of reform ideas, the private sector moved to the fore, injecting customer satisfaction as a central goal of improvement. Unfortunately, no one knows just how or why this international tidal wave began. Was it a broad decline in trust fueled by global competition? Was it media cynicism? Was it a desperate rescue attempt by the professional civil service and activist leaders such as Clinton and Gore? The answers remain for future research.

Whatever the source, there is no question that the reform wave is not over. Liberation management remains sharply divided between its trusting and distrusting pulls. As noted earlier, market forces may yet break free as a mostly conservative response to public dissatisfaction, leaving those who would "let the managers manage" to create a more convincing rationale for a trusting view of government and its employees.

Forgotten in the long list of legislative successes in Appendix A is the much larger list of legislative failures. The history of making government work is littered with failed proposals, not the least of which are the dozens of proposals over the years for lobbying reform. Congress came close to passing lobbying reform in the 95th Congress but simply could not inflict tighter controls upon itself. A decade later, in 1988, it actually sent a lobbying reform bill to President Reagan, only to encounter a pocket veto. Almost a decade later still, Congress and the president finally agreed on a comprehensive lobbying bill, almost fifty years after passage of the 1946 Federal Regulation of Lobbying Act.

Thus, a tide's inactivity for one year or one decade does not mean it has disappeared completely. The tides seem to have their greatest strength in propelling their respective reforms toward passage, not in suffocating competing proposals from other tides. In fact, one of the problems with the tides is precisely that Congress and the president feel perfectly comfortable dipping into the four tides virtually at random. Simply put, the tides are always out there waiting for the next hurricane.

During the past two decades, for example, Congress considered but did not pass dozens of proposals for new cabinet departments, focusing variously on peace, aging, women, international trade, children, arts and humanities, science and technology, environment, food, agriculture, and renewable resources. The 100th Congress came remarkably close to approving a Department of Industry and Technology; the 101st and 103d flirted with a Department of the Environment. That none of the proposals passed is a sign of the relative weakness of scientific management, not the lack of flotsam just below the legislative surface.

As I have argued in the chapter, part of what propels such proposals is the climate of reform, a climate that has turned distinctly distrusting over the past three decades. Whether this climate can or will change in coming years remains very much in doubt. Much as liberation management sees one outcome as higher customer satisfaction, the public distrust is so tightly linked to anger over campaign finance, special interests, legislative gridlock, and concerns about whether the nation is headed in the right direction that government management reform may have little or nothing to do with changing public attitudes.

Climate is not the only explanation for the impact of the tides, however. The next chapter will turn to the gravitational pulls created by individual presidents, the two political parties, and Congress and the presidency. As the House, Senate, and presidency rise and fall in influence over making government work, so, perhaps, do the tides. It may well be, for example, that the House has always been enamored of the war on waste but that it has only recently been in a position to do something about it. It may well also be that the

Senate has always favored a watchful eye but that it has only recently had the excuse (Vietnam, Watergate, and the continued petty scandals that have plagued all recent administrations) to act. If each institution has its own favorite tide, perhaps it is just a matter of time before that tide will roll in, and just a matter of time before it will roll out again.

4

The Gravitational Pulls of Reform

Making government work is one of the easiest promises a candidate can make. The public's confidence in government is so low, and readiness to believe the horror stories about $600 toilet seats so high, that the phrase "making government work" has joined mom, apple pie, and the American flag as a staple of campaign imagery.

Once past broad promises about *Creating a Government That Works Better and Costs Less* (the title of the first NPR report) or *Common Sense Government* (the title of the third), presidents and Congress, Democrats and Republicans quickly bog down in very different images of what the reforms should look like.[1] As with so many issues in the legislative ocean, the devil is in the details.

As already noted, the two ends of Pennsylvania Avenue have very different views about when and where to trust government and its employees, and, as might be guessed, so do Democrats and Republicans. In many ways, *where* a reform comes from can be just as important as *what* it proposes. Driven by different political winds and riding different tides, reforms will rise and fall with institutional and political fortunes. And when a particularly large reform is sailing toward inevitable passage, it invariably attracts a great deal of loose cargo.

Neither the tides of the ocean nor the tides of reform are self-propelled. Absent the gravitational pull of the sun and the moon, there would be no neap or spring tides, nor any tides at all for that matter. Waves would still come ashore, driven by wind and storm, but sea levels would be constant. In a similar vein, the tides of federal management reform might not exist but for the pulls of three sources of gravity: (1) the individual presidents who come into office with very different philosophies of reform, (2) the two political parties that struggle for control of the reform agenda, and (3) Congress and the presidency.

THE PULL OF THE PRESIDENTS

It should not be surprising that different presidents have held very different convictions about making government work. As we have seen, Lyndon Johnson was a department and agency builder, viewing the creation of the Equal Employment Opportunity Commission (EEOC), Office of Economic Opportunity (OEO), and the Department of Housing and Urban Development as one way to shelter the hard-fought gains of his Great Society war on poverty. In doing so, he defined a decade of reform as his own.

According to table 4.1, however, LBJ was hardly the most distinctive president among the ten who served in the period covered by this book. Quite the contrary, LBJ joins Harry Truman and Jimmy Carter as being the three presidents most likely to fall toward the midpoint of the various measures summarized in the table. It is Dwight Eisenhower, Ronald Reagan, and Bill Clinton who stand out as the trendsetters of their respective decades: Eisenhower for his commitment to scientific management, Reagan for war on waste, and Clinton for liberation management.

Start with legislative history. Nine out of Johnson's ten government reform initiatives came from the White House. Only the Freedom of Information Act originated on Capitol Hill. Not all the credit goes to Johnson, however. Two reforms were well under way before he became president, and one, the Presidential Transition Act, was designed to help Jacqueline Kennedy move home after her husband's assassination. It is useful to note, however, that LBJ's dominance is mostly an artifact of the small number of total initiatives during his term. Johnson accounts for just 7 percent of the 141 items enrolled in Appendix A, tying him with Eisenhower for seventh on the list of ten presidents covered; only John F. Kennedy, who served less than three years, and Clinton, who served only two during the period covered here, accounted for fewer.

The origin of idea and the nature of the legislative debate both show the impact of the Watergate divide. Gerald Ford, Reagan, and George Bush all show very low totals in the origin of ideas, confirming the rising importance of Congress after 1974. And although Clinton's share of origins rises with Democratic control of both branches, his percentage is nowhere near the high points established in the 1950s and 1960s and is well below Carter's mark in the late 1970s. Richard Nixon marks the watershed. Seventy percent of the initiatives passed during Nixon's first term came from the White House, compared with just 50 percent in 1973. As the Watergate crisis heated up, the president was rendered increasingly irrelevant to the debate about government reform.

Interestingly, Reagan sets the ten-president high in the percentage of routine legislative debate. Part of the explanation rests in the fact that 90 percent of the thirty-one legislative initiatives recorded during his two terms in office came from Congress. As I shall argue soon, Congress tends to go easy on itself when its own legislative proposals are on the docket. However, as I observed in Chapter 2, legislative debate is also likely to be routine when war on waste is involved.

With regard to philosophy of reform, time also shows its mark on each tide. Scientific management drifts steadily from its high in the 1960s to zero percent in the first two years of the Clinton administration. Clinton's one gesture to structure—creation of an organization to house his national service program—involved an explicit rejection of traditional department/agency structure.

Even though the proposed Corporation for National and Community Service would have little call to operate in a businesslike fashion—its transactions were to be little more than cash transfers to individuals and nonprofit organizations—a corporate structure was deemed more attractive to a reluctant Congress. Anything but an organization that reminded Congress of the Comprehensive Employment and Training Act (CETA), or so the designers argued. As if to punctuate its complete rejection of science, the new corporation would also house ACTION, which had been created as one of several shelters for LBJ's war on poverty.[2] The national service corporation was more a statement about what it was *not* organizationally than a scientifically designed instrument for administering what would be, after all was said and done, a traditional transfer program.

Yet the mere passage of time is hardly the only device for predicting the ebb

Table 4.1 Individual Presidents and Reform (percentages, except for presidential status)

	HST	DDE	JFK	LBJ	RMN	GRF	JC	RR	GB	WJC
Time										
Era										
Pre-1974	✓	✓	✓	✓	✓	—	—	—	—	—
Post-1974	—	—	—	—	—	✓	✓	✓	✓	✓
Decade										
Glory Days	✓	✓	—	—	—	—	—	—	—	—
Great Society	—	—	✓	✓	—	—	—	—	—	—
Reassessment	—	—	—	—	✓	✓	✓	—	—	—
New Proceduralism	—	—	—	—	—	—	—	✓	✓	✓
Legislative History										
President's Party										
Democratic	✓	—	✓	✓	—	—	✓	—	—	✓
Republican	—	✓	—	—	✓	✓	—	✓	✓	—
Congressional Party										
Democratic	82	60	100	100	100	100	100	39	100	100
Republican	18	40	0	0	0	0	0	0	0	0
Divided Between Chambers	0	0	0	0	0	0	0	61	0	0
Party Control of Government										
Unified	53	40	100	100	0	0	100	0	0	100
Divided	47	60	0	0	100	100	0	100	100	0
Origin of Idea										
President	65	60	88	90	59	15	59	10	27	43
Congress	35	40	13	10	41	85	41	90	73	57

Blue-Ribbon Commission Involved?	41	40	13	0	18	15	0	3	9	0
Interest Groups Involved?	12	30	13	40	18	62	41	26	18	43
Legislative Debate										
Routine	59	60	63	50	53	46	53	68	55	43
Controversial	41	40	37	50	47	54	47	32	45	57
Legislative Passage										
Unanimous	59	60	25	40	29	31	41	74	55	29
Near-Unanimous	18	10	25	20	41	54	47	19	27	14
Strong Majority (60 or more)	18	30	50	40	24	0	0	3	9	43
Close (less than 60)	6	0	0	0	6	15	12	3	9	14
Recorded Vote Taken?	47	40	75	70	71	77	65	45	64	86

Philosophy

Tide										
Scientific Management	77	90	75	70	47	31	41	13	36	0
War on Waste	12	0	0	0	0	8	24	55	9	0
Watchful Eye	12	10	13	13	18	46	24	29	36	29
Liberation Management	0	0	13	13	35	15	12	3	18	71
Purity of Statute										
No Other Tides Found in Statute	71	70	75	100	59	77	65	74	64	57
One Other Tide Found	29	20	13	0	41	23	24	16	18	43
Two Other Tides Found	0	10	13	0	0	0	12	10	18	0
Primary Accountability Mechanism										
Compliance	35	30	13	20	18	46	41	68	46	29
Capacity	53	70	75	70	71	39	41	19	18	57
Performance	12	0	13	10	12	15	18	13	36	14
General View of Government										
Trusting	65	70	75	90	59	39	41	16	36	43
Distrusting	35	30	25	10	49	61	59	84	64	57

Table 4.1 (Continued)

	HST	DDE	JFK	LBJ	RMN	GRF	JC	RR	GB	WJC
Change Strategy										
Focus										
Structure of Government	41	70	63	60	65	46	35	19	18	29
Procedures of Government	53	20	38	40	29	46	53	74	73	71
Both	0	0	0	0	6	8	12	7	9	0
Create a Study Commission	5	5	0	0	0	0	0	0	0	0
Structural Tactic										
Create New Agency	6	30	38	20	12	31	18	7	27	0
Merge Existing Agencies	12	10	0	20	29	8	6	0	0	0
Reorganize Existing Agency	12	10	13	10	12	0	12	3	0	0
Create Public Corporation	0	0	13	10	19	0	0	4	0	14
Abolish Existing Agency	0	0	0	0	0	0	6	10	0	0
Grant Agency Independence	0	0	0	0	0	15	0	3	0	14
Elevate Agency to Higher Status	6	0	0	0	0	0	6	3	0	0
Combination	6	20	0	0	0	0	0	0	0	0
No Structural Reform in Statute	59	30	36	40	29	46	52	60	73	72
Procedural Tactic										
Establish New System	18	10	13	10	18	23	29	32	18	29
Broaden System	12	0	13	10	0	8	12	36	18	0
Revise System	12	10	0	20	6	8	6	3	18	0
Deregulate/Narrow System	0	0	0	0	12	15	12	3	18	14
Reauthorize System	12	0	13	0	0	0	6	6	9	14
Abolish System	0	0	0	0	0	0	0	3	0	0
Combination	0	0	0	0	0	0	0	0	0	14

	47	80	63	60	65	46	35	19	18	29
No Procedural Reform in Statute	47	80	63	60	65	46	35	19	18	29
Target										
General Organization of Government	47	70	63	60	68	31	35	19	9	29
Procurement/Acquisition	12	0	0	0	0	15	6	26	9	0
Ethics/Standards of Conduct	6	0	13	10	6	8	6	13	27	29
Administrative Process	0	10	0	10	0	23	6	10	0	0
Pay Systems	6	0	13	0	6	8	6	0	9	0
Audit/Investigation	0	0	0	0	0	8	6	13	9	0
Rulemaking Procedures	6	0	0	0	0	0	18	0	18	0
General Personnel/Classification	6	0	0	0	0	0	18	3	0	14
Budget/Financial Management	6	10	0	0	12	8	0	3	0	0
Combination	6	10	13	0	6	0	0	3	0	14
Strategic Planning/Analysis	0	0	0	0	6	0	0	0	9	14
Debt Collection	0	0	0	10	0	0	0	7	0	0
Tort Claims	6	0	0	0	0	0	0	3	0	0
Scale										
Nature of Idea										
New Approach	35	60	50	60	65	69	47	48	46	71
Modification of Old	64	40	50	40	35	31	33	52	54	29
Scope of Impact										
Large	53	40	38	50	35	46	47	23	36	57
Small	47	60	62	50	65	54	53	77	64	43
Overall Scale of Reform										
New/Large	24	40	25	50	24	39	29	13	18	43
New/Small	12	20	25	20	41	31	18	36	27	29
Old/Large	29	0	13	10	12	8	18	10	27	14
Old/Small	35	40	38	20	24	23	35	42	27	14

Table 4.1 (Continued)

	HST	DDE	JFK	LBJ	RMN	GRF	JC	RR	GB	WJC
Implementation										
Experimental Approach in Statute?	0	0	0	0	0	0	6	3	18	14
Time Horizon in Statute										
Temporary/Sunset	18	10	13	0	6	0	12	19	9	29
Permanent	82	90	88	100	94	100	88	81	91	71
Scope										
Single Agency	24	50	38	50	53	54	35	23	27	29
Several Agencies	18	20	25	20	24	8	18	3	9	14
Governmentwide	59	30	38	30	24	38	47	74	64	57
Oversight Approach										
Centralized	82	70	63	50	41	39	53	42	36	29
Decentralized	17	30	38	50	59	62	47	58	64	71
Impact										
Shift in Shared Powers										
Toward President	71	80	75	50	59	39	47	23	46	14
Toward Congress	12	10	25	30	41	54	24	23	27	43
Not Clear/No Shift Discernible	18	10	0	20	0	8	29	55	27	43
Impact on Cost of Government										
Increase	29	60	63	50	29	31	24	0	0	29
Decrease	6	0	0	0	24	0	6	16	0	14
Not Clear/No Impact Discernible	65	40	38	50	47	69	71	84	100	57
Impact on Role of Government										
Expand	53	80	75	50	29	15	29	3	0	14

Contract	0	0	0	0	18	8	18	16	9	29
Not Clear/No Impact Discernible	47	20	25	50	53	77	53	81	91	57
Impact on Shape of Government										
Thicken Hierarchy	71	80	63	70	59	77	59	36	46	57
Thin Hierarchy	0	10	13	0	35	15	18	23	0	29
Not Clear/No Impact Discernible	29	10	25	30	6	8	24	42	55	14
Impact on Administrative Speed										
Accelerate	53	50	13	20	65	23	29	32	27	29
Slow Down	18	20	13	10	12	39	35	42	27	14
Not Clear/No Impact Discernible	29	30	75	70	24	39	35	26	46	57
Impact on Interest Group Access										
Enhance	12	20	13	20	18	0	41	13	18	14
Reduce	18	10	25	20	35	31	6	29	36	29
Not Clear/No Impact Discernible	71	70	63	60	47	69	53	58	46	57
Impact on Public Access										
Enhance	12	10	13	20	18	31	29	7	36	29
Reduce	6	10	13	10	18	0	0	10	0	0
Not Clear/No Impact Discernible	82	80	75	70	65	69	71	84	64	71
Impact on Government Morale										
Improve	18	10	25	20	6	23	29	26	55	71
Reduce	6	0	0	0	0	0	0	7	0	0
Not Clear/No Impact Discernible	77	90	75	80	94	77	71	68	45	29
Impact on Bureaucratic Balance										
Strengthen Line Units	53	70	88	80	65	62	41	10	27	43
Strengthen Staff Units	47	30	13	20	24	31	41	74	64	43
Not Clear/No Impact Discernible	0	0	0	0	12	8	18	16	9	14

N = 141

and flow of the tides. Given that the sun and the moon of politics can and do change positions, the question is what might have happened beneath the cover of time to change the tides. Was it an individual president who rode a specific tide to power? Was it the rise and fall of the two parties? Was it a change in the relative influence of Congress and the presidency? The answer is "yes" to all of the above. Individual presidents, political party, and institutional origins all show some predictive power on the rise and fall of the tides. However, that power is not uniform across all tides, nor across all time periods. Presidents can pull the tides either by developing proposals of their own or by supporting ideas that originate elsewhere. Clinton's influence over liberation management is clearly an example of the former, while Eisenhower's influence on scientific management and Reagan's on war on waste are more appropriately described as the latter.

Eisenhower's impact is the easiest to explain. He merely picked up the scientific management cause where Truman left it. Entering office with a substantial popular vote margin but a razor-thin Republican congressional majority, Eisenhower signed one Hoover Commission recommendation after another—some that he adopted as his own, such as further tightening at the Department of Defense, others that came from Congress, such as creation of the second Hoover Commission. Whether Eisenhower actually cared much about making government work is in some dispute, however. Although the political scientist Fred Greenstein finds ample evidence of Eisenhower's hidden hand at work throughout the presidency, there is perhaps less administrative activism in the eight years than one might otherwise expect.[3] Indeed, adjusting for years in office, Eisenhower emerges as the least active of all ten presidents covered by this analysis.

Conversely, Reagan's influence is the most difficult to explain. After all, he counts as the originator of just three out of the thirty-one initiatives recorded during his administration. Two of those three, the 1981 budget cuts and the abolishment of the Synfuels Corporation, were war on waste, while one, reauthorization of the Reorganization Act, was scientific management. How then could he be credited with changing the tides? The answer is that Reagan changed the climate governing reform.

It will hardly come as a surprise that the war on waste reached its peak during 1981–1986, when Republicans controlled the Senate. Of the seventeen war on waste enactments during the Reagan years, thirteen (76 percent) emerged between 1981 and 1987. It is a remarkable and sustained high tide. In contrast, of the nine watchful eye statutes during the same eight years, only three were passed before the Democrats returned to the Senate majority in 1987.

Nevertheless, party control of Congress is not the only explanation for what occurred under Reagan. He might not have been the author of each war on waste initiative, and almost certainly did not know the intimate details of such statutes as the Federal Managers' Financial Integrity Act, but Reagan most certainly set the rhetorical tone for the war on waste. His constant attacks on bloat in government, as well as his support for the Grace Commission survey of waste in government, lent needed aid and comfort to the congressional advocates of reform.

Similarly, Reagan invited the watchful eye backlash that followed late in his administration. Congress was already deeply troubled by ethical lapses in the Reagan administration long before the Democrats recaptured the Senate majority in 1986. The HUD scandal was well under way by then, Attorney General Ed Meese had been eased out of the administration, and the Iran-Contra arms-for-hostages deal had been sealed. Just as Reagan set a tone that encouraged war on waste, so, too, did he create an atmosphere that invited watchful eye.

Reagan's place as the champion of war on waste is well supported by history. As I have argued, for example, the eight Reagan years can justifiably be labeled the "glory days" of the inspector general concept. Although Reagan entered office promising $195 billion in savings from a full-scale war on waste and soon recognized the value of the IGs in waging such a war, he started his term by firing every last IG appointed under Carter, informing Congress, "It is vital that I have the fullest confidence in the ability, integrity and commitment of each appointee to the position of Inspector General."[4]

Most of the Carter IGs survived, in part aided by the congressional backlash against the firings. By the end of Reagan's first term, the IGs had entered an alliance with the Office of Management and Budget, thus gaining new resources and independence as they set yearly records in the war on waste. As long as the saving totals went up, I have noted, "Congress and the president were encouraged to promote the idea that the war was being won. And as long as the totals went up, the IGs could do no wrong. Their budgets were given special director's review to assure proper staffing, and their offices secured a remarkable amount of self-determination. First, the IGs won the right to investigate their wayward colleagues, then they were given an unprecedented role in selecting their successors."[5]

The tide of watchful eye reform was also whipped forward during the Reagan administration, albeit in an entirely different way. This was not a case of the president providing voice to an already robust congressional concern. Rather, the rise of watchful eye reflected the impact in part of the Ethics in Government Act of 1978 and its creation of a "culture of mistrust in American politics," as Suzanne Garment characterizes the changing environment surrounding politics in the 1980s. It is a culture that produced a tenfold increase in the number of federal prosecutions of public officials within its first decade, an increase driven in large measure by a growing inventory of war on waste and watchful eye statutes and the enforcement staffs to go with them. As Garment writes, "Since Watergate, despite the growth in our efforts, the number of our political scandals has continued to increase. The post-Watergate scandals did not simply proliferate while corruption was being exposed and then abate as politicians began complying with today's new, more rigorous standards. Instead, the scandals have continued at their high levels for more than 15 years, with the recent savings and loan debacle the biggest of all. In other words, the attack on corruption seems to have had few of the cleansing effects that such efforts are supposed to bring in their wake."[6]

Six years after Garment's pessimistic assessment, however, there appears to have been at least some decrease in anticorruption legislation. Indeed, the inventory in Appendix A suggests that the watchful eye tide may have peaked at just about the point that Garment's book went to press, with implementation of the 1989 Ethics Reform Act. Would that every author could claim such success. This is not to suggest that the anticorruption tide was little more than a passing response to Reagan-era revelations and to memories of Watergate. Calls for independent prosecutors still resonate in Washington, as do proposals for creation of new IGs in just about every corner of government, including the White House.[7] Moreover, Congress continues to tighten internal controls on itself, not the least of which involved the 1995 gift ban and lobbying reform.

Nevertheless, the statutory tide may have reached its peak. It is not clear, for example, just how much more Congress could do to strengthen the 1989 Ethics in Government Act. This general trend is partially confirmed in table 4.1, which shows the steady rise and subsequent decline of compliance accountability following Watergate. Although the Lobbying Disclosure Act of 1995 would make any list of major government management reforms, the new Republican Congress swept into office in 1994 seemed dedicated to a more traditional war on waste than a vast expansion of watchful eye. Indeed, as I shall shortly suggest, watchful eye is far more likely to emerge when a Democratic Congress is the originator of ideas than under any other circumstance. Democrats, not Republicans, have been the congressional party of decentralized distrust, especially when juxtaposed against a sitting Republican president. Not surprisingly, therefore, the high point of distrust in table 4.1 is under Reagan, the low point under LBJ at the height of the Great Society.

Table 4.1 confirms the general historical trends regarding change strategy that were highlighted in Chapter 3. Even with Democratic majorities in Congress, neither Carter or Clinton come close to the level of structure as their Democratic predecessors in the 1940s or 1960s. Although Truman sets a thirty-year high point for procedures in the 1940s, the Hoover Commission orthodoxy appears to have lasted a bit longer than a decade. The notion that building structure is the answer to making government work still held considerable influence until Reagan.

Although table 4.1 suggests a comeback for creating new agencies under Bush, the effect is illusory. Creation of the Resolution Trust Corporation, which had a seven-year sunset, establishment of chief financial officers in every department, and creation of an independent regulator over the Federal National Mortgage Association and Federal Home Loan Mortgage Corporation do not quite fit the grand structural designs of the Hoover Commission. Indeed, an independent regulator for government-sponsored enterprises might well offend the Hoover Commission, for it generally believed the way to solve the growing power of such independent agencies was to bring them under tighter presidential control.

Turning to the target of reform, table 4.1 confirms the suggestion above regarding the peak of ethics in government. Although the next ethics reform may be just awaiting the next scandal, it may take some time for the most recent batch of reforms to generate momentum for further expansion. Of those reforms, the Hatch Act revisions hold the greatest potential for such action. As stories begin to filter in from the 1996 presidential campaign about how federal employees and their unions sought to influence this campaign or that, Congress will likely take up the cause again. Such a review would have been even more likely had Republicans recaptured the White House alongside their continued congressional majority.

Scale of reform yields both expected and unexpected patterns in the overall scale of ideas. As expected, LBJ emerges as the president most likely to produce new/large ideas, a conclusion that fits well with his Great Society leadership. Surprisingly, Ford also emerges with a rather high number of new/large ideas, not because of his own forcefulness, but because the post-Watergate Democratic Congress took control of the reform agenda. Recall that 85 percent of the initiatives passed under Ford came from Congress.

Clinton emerges with the second-highest percentage of new/large and new/small reforms. As with LBJ, less than a third of the initiatives considered during Clinton's first two years fall into the old/large or old/small categories. Although these percentages are clearly distorted by the very small total number of reforms involved in the period covered by this book, Clinton did stake himself to a remarkable list of precedent-breaking reforms, whether in advocating his vice president's reinvention package or supporting the Social Security Independence and Improvement Act. That Clinton endorsed the latter in the hopes of a favorable Senate hearing on his health care initiative does not make the legislation any less offensive to the Hoover ideal.

Perhaps the most interesting finding regarding the overall scale of reform involves Nixon's very high percentage of new/small initiatives. Nixon appears to have been very much a small-scale innovator in both the substance and management of domestic policy. As I have documented elsewhere, 43 percent of Nixon's domestic agenda was composed of new/small ideas, compared with 17 percent each for Kennedy and Johnson, 13 percent for Ford, and 22 percent for Carter: "In order to make an impact on federal policy, Nixon had to concentrate on fundamental departures from past programs. Johnson's success with the Great Society forced Nixon toward an agenda composed of new programs. . . . Nixon had little choice but to present new initiatives. To adopt modifications of old Democratic programs would have been contrary to his political goals."[8]

It is important to note, however, that Nixon's new/small administrative agenda was not entirely of his own making. Four of the seven new/small reforms that emerged during his tenure in office originated in Congress, including the Federal Advisory Committee Act, which was a classic government-in-the-sunshine initiative. So noted, all three of Nixon's new/small ideas involved structural reforms of one kind or another. So, too, for his new/large agenda. Although few of his administrative reforms, small or large, challenged the status quo in the same way that Nixon's proposed supercabinet would have done, his management reforms have proven more durable than the rest of his policy efforts. Although challenged from time to time over the years, OMB, EPA, and NOAA are still standing almost a quarter century after Nixon left office in disgrace.

Reagan, too, shows a high concentration of new/small requests, also not by his own hand. Ten of the eleven new/small initiatives that emerged during Reagan's term in office came from Congress. It may be that Democratic or divided Congresses matched with Republican presidents produce a higher share of small-scale innovations, in part because nothing much larger can pass. It is a point supported at least in part by the high percentage of old/small initiatives under Reagan, a pattern not found under Nixon.

The general trends of implementation strategy established in Chapter 3 still hold. Carter, Reagan, Bush, and Clinton are much more alike than different in the implementation of reform and clearly must be set apart from the earlier presidents. Yet within these broad patterns, table 4.1 suggests a slight wave effect in oversight approach, with a clear low point in decentralization under Truman, rising to a near high point under LBJ, then falling to a low under Carter, then starting back up toward Clinton. Admittedly, LBJ's high point in decentralization involved passage of the Freedom of Information Act and the creation of several agencies (EEOC, OEO, the Public Broadcasting Corporation) that widened the government's span of control, while Clinton's involved a somewhat different mix of tides. Moreover, small numbers in several of the administrations, including both LBJ and Clinton, make such a wave highly speculative.

Nevertheless, what comes around in the form of oversight mechanism—or, for that matter, accountability mechanism—may go around. The notion of an ebb and flow in making government work fits well with the notion of a national mood described by the political scientist John Kingdon: "People in and around government sense a national mood. They are comfortable describing its content, and believe they know when the mood shifts. The idea goes by different names—the national mood, the climate in the country, changes in public opinion, or broad social movements. But common to all of these labels is the notion that a rather large number of people out in the country are thinking along certain common lines, that this national mood changes from one time to another in discernible ways, and that these changes in mood or climate have important impacts on policy agenda and policy outcomes."[9]

It seems reasonable to add "making government work" to Kingdon's list of policy outcomes. There are times when the public and its representatives in Congress and the presidency appear willing to accept new structure and times when the call is for cutting government. Such moods are surely part of the explanation for the movement of the figures in table 4.1.

Finally, turning to the impact of reform, the ten presidents show a variety of highs and lows. The early presidents are highest in the shift of power toward the executive, a finding easily related to the strength of scientific management during the period. They are also highest on initiatives that increase the cost and role of government, again confirming the broad impact of time on reform. There are few surprises until the figures on government morale, where Bush and Clinton set remarkable highs in impact.

The figures reflect an assortment of statutes that either fixed glaring problems inside government (the Resolution Trust legislation, HUD reforms), improved public images of government by trying to close the revolving door between political appointments and lobbying firms (Ethics in Government), granted new freedoms (Administrative Dispute Resolution Act, Negotiated Rulemaking Act, Hatch Act reform), or offered a relaxation of compliance systems in return for greater performance accountability (Government Performance and Results Act). Certainly, the general tone of the first round of reinventing government, which is often labeled REGO I, had to help government morale. Even with its occasional descent into war on waste rhetoric, the overall tone of Vice President Gore's message was resoundingly positive.

Ironically, government morale appeared to plummet even as these legislative accomplishments took effect.[10] At least during the early to mid-1990s, procurement reform, agency-by-agency repairs, and efforts to raise the overall quality of government performance were no match for continuing budget battles, two long furloughs of "nonessential" personnel, a cut of 272,900 federal employees, and rising tensions between Congress and the president over the proper role of government.

THE PULL OF THE PARTIES

Although this book covers half a century and five presidencies from each party, untangling the influence of party control on the tides of reform presents a special challenge. At 1600 Pennsylvania Avenue, it is always difficult to separate a president's individual influence from party history. Was Reagan's impact on the war on waste attributable to his unique commitment to the effort or a natural consequence of his long history as a Goldwater Republican? Was Clinton's impact on liberation management due to his vice president's unique understanding of organizational reform or to the difficulties in electing a traditional Democrat to the White House in the 1990s? There is also a predictable overlap between the analysis of the individual presidents presented above and the discussion of presidential party below.

At the other end of the avenue, the Republican Party controlled both houses of Congress for but the tiniest slice of time, just long enough to produce two initiatives in the 80th Congress (1947–1949) and another four in the 83d (1953–1955). It would be thirty years before Republicans would recapture the Senate and forty before they would win back the House. Although Republicans did hold the Senate majority from 1981 to 1987, a period that produced nineteen initiatives, there are too few cases to compare Republican Congresses with divided Congresses and Democratic Congresses. The best one can do is lump the two Republican periods together under a "Republican/ Divided" banner and hope that the combination yields at least some understanding of how such a condition might predict the rise or fall of a given tide.

Notwithstanding these assorted methodological challenges, party has long been imagined an important force in shaping the tides. And, as table 4.2 suggests, changes in presidential and congressional party over the years appear

Table 4.2 Party Control (percentages)

	Presidency		Congress		Government	
	Democratic	Republican	Democratic	Republican/ Divided	Unified	Divided
Time						
Era						
Pre-1974	59	29	46	24	61	28
Post-1974	41	71	54	76	39	73
Decade						
Glory Days	29	12	18	24	31	10
Great Society	31	0	16	0	30	0
Reassessment	29	37	41	0	28	38
New Proceduralism	12	51	26	76	12	53
Legislative History						
President's Party						
Democratic	N/A	N/A	49	8	93	3
Republican			51	92	7	98
Congressional Party						
Democratic	97	72	N/A	N/A	93	74
Republican	3	5			7	3
Divided Between Chambers	0	23			0	24
Party Control Government						
Unified	86	5	49	16	N/A	N/A
Divided	14	95	51	84	N/A	N/A

Table 4.2 (Continued)

	Presidency		Congress		Government	
	Democratic	Republican	Democratic	Republican/Divided	Unified	Divided
Origin of Idea						
President	68	29	50	24	67	29
Congress	32	10	50	76	33	71
Blue-Ribbon Commission Involved?	14	13	15	16	18	10
Interest Groups Involved?	29	29	28	32	31	28
Legislative Debate						
Routine	54	59	55	64	56	58
Controversial	46	41	45	36	44	43
Legislative Passage						
Unanimous	42	54	44	72	41	55
Near-Unanimous	27	29	32	12	26	30
Strong Majority (60 or more)	24	11	17	12	26	9
Close (less than 60)	7	6	7	4	7	6
Recorded Vote Taken?	64	57	64	44	66	56
Philosophy						
Tide						
Scientific Management	56	35	46	36	57	34
War on Waste	12	23	11	52	12	24
Watchful Eye	17	28	26	12	16	29
Liberation Management	15	13	17	0	15	14

Purity of Statute						
No Other Tides Found in Statute	73	70	72	64	72	70
One Other Tide Found	22	23	22	28	23	23
Two Other Tides Found	5	7	6	8	5	8
Primary Accountability Mechanism						
Compliance	31	46	38	48	30	48
Capacity	56	39	47	40	57	38
Performance	14	15	15	12	13	15
General View of Government						
Trusting	61	38	53	24	62	38
Distrusting	39	62	47	76	38	63
Change Strategy						
Focus						
Structure of Government	44	39	45	24	46	38
Procedures of Government	51	54	51	60	49	55
Both	3	6	4	8	3	6
Create a Study Commission	2	1	0	8	2	1
Structural Tactic						
Create New Agency	15	17	19	4	15	17
Merge Existing Agencies	9	9	9	8	8	9
Reorganize Existing Agency	10	5	8	4	10	5
Create Public Corporation	5	4	5	0	5	4
Abolish Existing Agency	2	4	2	8	2	4
Grant Agency Independence	2	4	3	0	2	4
Elevate Agency to Higher Status	3	1	3	0	3	1
Combination	2	2	1	8	5	0
No Structural Reform in Statute	53	54	51	68	51	56

Table 4.2 (Continued)

	Presidency		Congress		Government	
	Democratic	Republican	Democratic	Republican/ Divided	Unified	Divided
Procedural Tactic						
Establish New System	20	23	19	36	20	24
Broaden System	10	17	13	20	10	18
Revise System	9	6	9	0	8	6
Deregulate/Narrow System	5	9	9	0	5	9
Reauthorize System	9	4	5	8	8	4
Abolish System	0	1	0	4	0	1
Combination	2	0	1	0	2	0
No Procedural Reform in Statute	46	41	45	32	48	39
Target						
General Organization of Government	46	35	41	32	48	34
Procurement/Acquisition	5	13	8	20	5	14
Ethics/Standards of Conduct	10	11	13	0	10	11
Administrative Process	3	9	7	4	3	9
Pay Systems	7	4	6	0	7	4
Audit/Investigation	2	7	3	16	2	8
Rulemaking Procedures	7	2	5	0	7	3
General Personnel/Classification	9	1	4	4	8	1
Budget/Financial Management	2	7	5	4	2	8
Combination	5	4	3	12	5	4

Strategic Planning/Analysis	2	2	3	0	2	3
Debt Collection	2	2	1	8	2	3
Tort Claims	2	1	2	0	2	1
Scale						
Nature of Idea						
New Approach	49	56	53	56	51	55
Modification of Old	51	43	47	44	49	45
Scope of Impact						
Large	49	33	41	32	46	35
Small	51	67	59	68	54	65
Overall Scale of Reform						
New/Large	32	23	29	16	33	23
New/Small	19	33	24	40	20	33
Old/Large	19	11	14	16	15	14
Old/Small	31	33	33	28	33	31
Implementation						
Experimental Approach in Statute?	3	4	3	4	3	4
Time Horizon in Statute						
Temporary/Sunset	14	11	10	20	13	12
Permanent	86	89	90	80	87	89
Scope						
Single Agency	34	38	40	20	34	38
Several Agencies	19	11	15	12	20	10
Governmentwide	48	51	46	68	46	53

Table 4.2 (Continued)

	Presidency		Congress		Government	
	Democratic	Republican	Democratic	Republican/Divided	Unified	Divided
Oversight Approach						
Centralized	59	44	50	52	57	44
Decentralized	41	56	50	48	41	56
Impact						
Shift in Shared Powers						
Toward President	54	43	47	48	56	41
Toward Congress	24	31	32	8	23	31
Not Clear/No Shift Discernible	22	27	21	44	21	28
Impact on Cost of Government						
Increase	36	18	28	12	36	18
Decrease	5	11	7	16	5	11
Not Clear/No Impact Discernible	59	71	65	72	59	71
Impact on Role of Government						
Expand	44	20	31	24	46	18
Contract	9	12	10	16	8	13
Not Clear/No Impact Discernible	48	68	60	60	46	70
Impact on Shape of Government						
Thicken Hierarchy	64	54	61	44	66	53
Thin Hierarchy	10	20	14	24	10	20
Not Clear/No Impact Discernible	25	26	25	32	25	28

Impact on Administrative Speed						
Accelerate	32	39	35	40	31	40
Slow Down	20	31	26	28	2	31
Not Clear/No Impact Discernible	48	30	39	32	49	29
Impact on Interest Group Access						
Enhance	22	13	17	16	25	11
Reduce	17	29	22	32	15	31
Not Clear/No Impact Discernible	61	57	60	52	61	58
Impact on Public Access						
Enhance	20	17	22	0	20	18
Reduce	5	9	6	12	5	9
Not Clear/No Impact Discernible	75	74	72	88	75	74
Impact on Government Morale						
Improve	29	23	26	24	28	24
Reduce	2	2	1	8	2	3
Not Clear/No Impact Discernible	70	74	73	68	71	74
Impact on Bureaucratic Balance						
Strengthen Line Units	58	39	53	20	59	38
Strengthen Staff Units	36	50	40	64	34	51
Not Clear/No Impact Discernible	7	11	8	16	7	11

N = 141

to make a difference in efforts to make government work, whether in each institution or across government as a whole. The influence of party, however, is not always as strong at both ends of Pennsylvania Avenue.

Influence of the President's Party

Table 4.2 provides a long list of mostly weak to moderate impacts in predicting the rise and fall of the tides, depending upon which party occupies the White House. Of those impacts, three bear quick review. First, a Democratic Congress is more likely to be active when a Republican president is in office. Second, whether in control of Congress or the presidency, Democrats show a clear preference for scientific management. They may not be the party of tax and spend, as Republicans charge, but they have historically been the party of blend and coordinate. Third, Democrats show a clear preference for management reforms that expand the role of government.

Otherwise, the findings are less than dramatic. Having a Republican in the White House creates greater momentum toward a philosophy of compliance accountability, while having a Democrat increases the tendency toward capacity. The party of the president makes little significant difference to change philosophy, scale of reform, and implementation, except for a clear preference among Democrats for centralization. Having a Democrat in the Oval Office reveals a range of moderate preferences regarding impacts, not the least of which is an expanded role for government in strengthening line units. As I have argued, Democratic presidents tend to favor thickening of the delivery units of government, Republicans of the staff/advisory units.[11]

Notwithstanding these occasional differences, the question for the moment is why a president's party does not have a much greater impact in table 4.2. After all, the choice of a Democrat or Republican for president should have some significant bearing on how the chief executive actually behaves in this most central of offices, or at least that is what the principles of administration would have departments and agencies believe. Alas, the supposed true masters of government studied here appear lightly influenced at best by their party heritage.

Consider three possible explanations for the underwhelming significance of presidential party in shaping the tides of reform. First, it may be that party influence in the White House has been eclipsed by much greater activism elsewhere. As I shall shortly suggest, congressional party clearly matters much more to the rise and fall of the tides, in large measure because the volume of congressional interest in making government work has increased dramatically over time. In a sense, the presidential parties may have stood still as a source of leadership on management reform while the rest of the solar system has varied. Thus Reagan's influence is unique to Reagan, Clinton's influence to Clinton.

Second, it may be that the durability of any president's influence has been sharply weakened by the decay of institutional memory in the White House and Office of Management and Budget (OMB). The once-powerful Division of Administrative Management slowly disappeared over the years as OMB went through one internal reorganization after another. In 1970, the management side of OMB had roughly 224 full-time employees. By 1980, the number had dropped to 70, by 1990 to 46; by 1994 the management side had been reorganized to barely a dozen. At the same time, Congress strengthened its sources of management advice, building the General Accounting Office (GAO) into a significant presence in the debate about making government work. Although the relative number of staff at OMB and GAO is far from a perfect measure of relative influence, a strong case can be made that GAO has replaced OMB as the federal government's institutional memory on reform, with predictable results for a heavier focus on financial management as the fulcrum for improvement.

Perhaps to confirm the rising influence of financial management reform in the 1980s, the little management capacity that remained at OMB was steadily "subordinated," as Ronald Moe puts it, to support a host of new statutes championed by GAO, starting with the Federal Managers' Financial Integrity Act in 1983 and culminating with the Chief Financial Officers Act seven years later. According to Moe, the White House and OMB seemed to believe "that if they conducted enough financial management improvement projects, this would equal a management philosophy."[12]

Third, it may be that no institution or party has complete influence over all four tides of reform. Unlike the earth's moon, which dominates the rise and fall of the great ocean tides, it may be that different parties in different institutions have highly targeted influence over just one or two tides—that is, that the tides of reform are influenced by more than one moon and one sun. The notion that the tides might be driven by rather different constellations of forces might explain why the hurricanes of reform seem to be coming with greater frequency and force lately. To stretch the tides analogy to its virtual breaking point, imagine the impact on the ocean tides of a second or third moon. The waves would come and go with much less predictability; the gravitational pulls would change much more rapidly.

Influence of Congressional Party

The notion that congressional party makes a difference in making government work was certainly a central theme in the Republicans' 1994 Contract with

America. Although the ten bills on the contract did not contain any manage-ment reform per se, the preamble argued that a Republican majority would be the "end of government that is too big, too intrusive, and too easy with the pub-lic's money," familiar rhetoric from the war on waste and watchful eye.[13]

Lacking a broad attack on government structure itself, new House Speaker Newt Gingrich (R-Ga.) believed that reinventing government was little more than "a cosmetic facelift of the old order."[14] Yet even as he argued that the 1994 election was not about *how* government works but about *what* it does, Gingrich was clearly sympathetic with some of the liberation themes raised in the National Performance Review, including efforts to push total quality man-agement and its customer concepts deeper into government.[15]

It is doubtful that adding the 104th Congress into Appendix A would alter the findings in table 4.2. In its first year, the new Republican Congress pro-duced a significant inventory of war on waste in the budget process, some of which was signed into law by Clinton, some of which prompted the vetoes that created two government shutdowns in late 1995. As already noted, Republi-cans also produced a pair of particularly significant watchful eye reforms, at least one of which (lobbying reform) would easily make the list in Appendix A. Republicans had not shown any interest whatsoever in scientific management reforms; nor, for that matter, had the president, and liberation appeared to be on hold during the 1996 campaign.

The influence of congressional party is evident throughout table 4.2. On legislative history, for example, a Republican/divided Congress is much more frequently the source of ideas than a Democratic Congress, with legislative passage much more likely to be unanimous. During the six years of a divided Congress in 1981–1987, fourteen of the nineteen initiatives in Appendix A passed unanimously. No doubt this finding reflects the general popularity of war on waste during the period. However, it may also reflect the inability to get much else past a reluctant Senate. As noted in Chapter 3, there was no lack of fodder should the Senate have decided to move forward on department build-ing, nor any absence of opportunity for liberation.

Congressional party shows a dramatic impact in predicting the rise of war on waste philosophy. What is not shown in table 4.2 is the even greater impact of divided control *within* Congress on the tides of reform. Whereas Demo-cratic Congresses over the years drew just 10 percent of their initiatives from war on waste, the divided Congresses of 1981–1987 drew 68 percent. And whereas the two Republican Congresses that came into office in 1947 and 1953 drew 100 percent of their initiatives from scientific management and none from watchful eye, the three divided Congresses that entered office beginning in 1981 drew just 16 percent from scientific management and 16 percent from watchful eye.

This remarkable commitment to war on waste is in sharp contrast to the Democratic Congresses that both preceded and followed the 97th–99th. War on waste accounted for just 15 percent of the initiatives in the three Democratic Congresses that preceded the 97th Congress, which convened in 1981, and just 13 percent in the three Democratic Congresses that followed the 99th, which passed into history in January 1987. Scientific management (36 percent) and watchful eye (33 percent) dominated the first three Democratic Congresses, and watchful eye (40 percent) and liberation management (30 percent) dominated the last three.

Clearly, there was something about the first six years of the Reagan administration that allowed the war on waste to reach its peak. It could not have been just a Republican presidency, for the two Democratic Congresses that shared power with Republican George Bush drew just 36 percent of their reforms from war on waste. Nor could it have been just Ronald Reagan himself, for the Democratic Congress that served with him in 1987–1989 drew 50 percent from war on waste, a respectable showing for the tide but nowhere near the 74 percent established in the previous three Congresses. Rather, it had to be a combination of divided Congresses and Ronald Reagan that added up to the remarkable strength of war on waste in 1981–1986.

Again, there is no doubt that such findings reflect the remarkable popularity of war on waste during the Reagan years. Reagan never tired of calling the troops to battle, and Congress never tired of producing more supplies for the fight. Between 1980 and 1986, for example, the number of employees in already-established offices of inspector general (OIGs) increased 23 percent, even as federal civilian employment held virtually steady. In a zero-sum personnel game resulting from an employment freeze imposed by executive order on Reagan's first day in office, the OIGs were clearly the winners. Total civilian employment at the Department of Commerce fell 29 percent between 1980 and 1986, while the OIG actually grew by 20 percent. Even in agencies where the OIGs lost staff, they lost less than the rest of the agency. Total employment at HUD fell 30 percent, while the OIG fell by just 2 percent.[16]

Part of the growth was fueled by the spread of the IG concept to other agencies. The Agency for International Development got an IG in 1981, the Department of Defense in 1982, the Railroad Retirement Board in 1983, the U.S. Information and Disarmament Agency in 1986. Much of the expansion originated in the House, where Representative Jack Brooks (D-Tex.) and his

Government Operations Committee remained dedicated advocates of the IG concept.

Part was due to a separate OIG budget process at OMB. Starting in 1981 and continuing through the end of the Reagan administration in 1989, all OIG budget requests were subject to a "special director's review." The review allowed OMB to assure a specific dollar increase for the war on waste (funding for the already existing OIGs increased from $248 million in 1981 to $500 million seven years later), and also permitted earmarking of personnel slots.

Finally, part was due to an effective defense by the IGs themselves and their House allies. The IGs proved skillful defenders of their own turf and took full advantage of the backlash against the 1981 firings to establish what some called a "trade union" to lobby OMB on behalf of expansion. The IGs also proved effective in drawing upon the natural House support for the war on waste. It was the House, for example, that held Reagan to account for the IG firings, the House that provided 60 percent of the IG committee and subcommittee appearances, and the House that authored the major ten-year review in 1986 that created the basis for the final push to Justice and Treasury and the federal small agencies in the 1988 Inspector General Act amendments.

Given this history, it seems reasonable to suggest that the high level of war on waste activity in the divided Congresses of the early 1980s may have had more to do with Senate willingness to pass House bills than any deep commitment to war on waste per se. Although the Congress and the presidency are surely able to agree on major policies during periods of divided government, a point well made by David Mayhew in his pioneering *Divided We Govern,* it may be that the two chambers of Congress are mostly able to agree on war on waste.[17]

As such, the Senate may have acted as a legislative tidal gate during the Reagan years, allowing virtually every last liberation management initiative to drift back out to sea (none was approved during the three divided Congresses), keeping but a handful of reforms from scientific management and watchful eye (16 percent of the total each), while holding a remarkable reservoir from war on waste (68 percent). As I shall shortly suggest, the notion is well supported by the long House history of war on waste activism.

There are other differences between Democratic and Republican/divided Congresses in table 4.2. The two parties clearly disagree on general view of government, for example, with congressional Democrats the party much more likely to be trusting. As noted in Chapter 3, of course, that trust has declined in the post-Watergate era. Democrats were willing to give liberation management a hearing in Clinton's first two years, but their parallel commitment to watchful eye betrays continuing confusion over just how much to trust government, particularly when it comes to freedom of information and ethics. The congressional Republicans harbor no such mixed feelings. Their trusting days are to be found in the early years of this analysis, not the most recent.

The two parties also disagree on the change strategy of reform. Republicans have far less interest in structure than Democrats and tend to focus their interests on very different targets. Not surprisingly, they favor procurement/acquisition and audit/investigation to a much greater extent than congressional Democrats, while completely eschewing interest in producing initiatives dealing with ethics/standards of conduct.

It is ironic that congressional Democrats mastered the watchful eye tide under Nixon but plied it under Democrat and Republican presidents alike. It never mattered who was in the White House. The Republican Senate took a decidedly different approach in the early 1980s, defending the Republican White House against watchful eye expansions and rarely launching the kinds of highly visible hearings and investigations that so often lead to further management reform. Ten years later, with a Democrat in the White House, the new Republican Senate majority showed no such reticence in pushing forward on the Whitewater case. If precedents hold, however, one would expect no such intensity should a Republican inherit the White House.

Table 4.2 also shows that congressional Republicans show slight preferences toward new/small initiatives, temporary time horizons, and governmentwide reforms, all of which reflect the sizable number of reforms generated in 1981–1986. Congressional Democrats were heading in the same direction. As for impacts, Republicans show preferences for presidential power, somewhat less interest in increasing the cost and role of government, and a remarkable reluctance to strengthen the line units of government. As with Republican presidents, Republican Congresses show greater concern for tightening the delivery side of government, which political scientists such as Terry Moe would argue makes perfect sense, given the prevailing incentives facing parties and interest groups that are normally out of power. Such groups "work against effective performance," Moe writes, favoring stronger oversight. "Opposing groups are dedicated to crippling the bureaucracy and gaining control over its decisions, and they will pressure for fragmented authority, labyrinthine procedures, mechanisms of political intervention, and other structures that subvert the bureaucracy's performance and open it up to attack."[18]

The question, of course, is whether congressional Republicans would behave differently should a Republican gain the White House. Moe doubts that they would, for a group in power "favors structural designs it would never favor on technical grounds alone: designs that place detailed formal restrictions on bureaucratic discretion, impose complex procedures for agency decision making, minimize opportunities for oversight, and otherwise insulate the agency from politics."[19] There is at least some evidence here to suggest that Moe is right.

Divided We Still Govern

As I have noted, Appendix A clearly confirms Mayhew's notion that government can produce plenty of important policy during periods of divided government. The list of major statutes emerging from the 80th, 84th–85th, 91st–94th, 97th–99th, and 101st–102d Congresses show the effect. From the National Security Act of 1947, which created the modern defense establishment, to passage of a one-sentence first version of the Freedom of Information Act, from the Omnibus Budget and Reconciliation Act of 1981 to the Goldwater-Nichols Department of Defense Reorganization Act of 1985, divided government does produce.

As table 4.2 shows, however, divided government appears to produce a rather different *kind* of statute. With regard to legislative history, for example, divided government produces a much higher number of congressional origins and a related higher number of unanimous and near-unanimous votes. This higher level of unanimity is, in part, the product of a lesser number of recorded votes. (All voice votes were considered unanimous.)

The reform philosophy of divided government draws less upon scientific management and much more on both war on waste and watchful eye. Given the figures on general view of government, the preference for watchfulness likely reflects the natural incentives in Congress to stoke the fires of potential scandal for future elections. A similar impulse explains the moderate preference in divided government for compliance accountability.

Regarding change strategy, unified and divided government track rather closely on focus (a slight preference for procedures), and structural and procedural tactic. Where the two forms differ is on target, where divided government expresses a preference for procurement/acquisition and a decided distaste for fixing the general organization of government. This latter finding may reflect the simple unwillingness to give a sitting administration of the other party the opportunity to establish and staff new departments and agencies.

Unified and divided government again track closely on scale and implementation, showing their greatest differences on the scope of impact and overall scale of reform. As would be expected, divided government produces more new/small reform. Where innovation is possible, it is likely to be small. Table 4.2 also shows a slight preference for decentralization in initiatives produced by divided government.

Finally the two forms of government show sharp differences on impacts only with regard to the role of government and the impact on staff units. The former is clearly an effect of the Great Society—that is, the major expansion of government in the period covered by this book occurred under unified party control, while the most significant contraction occurred in 1981 under divided control.

Ultimately, Mayhew's broad conclusions about divided government's ability to act emerge relatively undisturbed in this analysis. His reasoning is simple: "The government floats in public opinion; it goes up and down on great long waves of it that often have little to do with parties. There is the obvious structural component—separation of powers—that brings on deadlock and chronic conflict, but also nudges officials toward deliberation, compromise, and super-majority outcomes."[20] In short, divided government will not deny the tides of reform. If the public is ready, or so Mayhew suggests, then divided government will produce reform.

THE PULL OF CONGRESS VERSUS THE PRESIDENCY

The four tides of reform have different institutional champions. As noted in Chapter 1, scientific management has historically been favored by presidents, and for good reason. The basic principles on which scientific management is based would naturally attract support from the supposed "one true master" of government. Unity of command, centralization, departments grouped by program, narrow spans of control, and staff assistance would only make the president more powerful, or at least so it would seem to a president fresh from the campaign. In fact, as I have written, scientific management and its inevitable thickening of government may do anything but strengthen the president's leadership: "Leadership is not measured by the number of people the president brings into office or the number of helpers at the top and middle of government. It is not achieved by further tightening of the command-and-control model that evolved under Eisenhower and his successors. Instead, a president's leadership is most likely to be judged by his clarity of mission, his articulation of cause, and the ultimate value produced by what government does. As such, it is likely to be stronger with fewer helpers, and clearer with fewer steps in the chain of command."[21]

Nevertheless, even as the Clinton administration tried to streamline the middle and lower levels of government, it steadfastly refused to consider any flattening at the seniormost layers of government. The NPR apparently considered and rejected a small reduction in political appointees—"the White House personnel office went ballistic," one participant told me—and eventually moved its recommendation for better training of new political appointees from the main body of the final report to the appendix.[22]

At the same time, presidents have become increasingly attracted to liberation management, particularly when it gives them greater authority vis-à-vis Congress. The NPR was anything but reluctant, for example, in advocating sharp cuts in congressional micromanagement, calling for a reduction in the line items, earmarks, and assorted personnel floors that Congress has historically used to limit administrative discretion, as well as a cut in the number of congressionally mandated reports. The NPR report promised: "We will ask Congress to pass legislation granting OMB the flexibility to consolidate and simplify statutory reports and establishing a sunset provision in any reporting requirements adopted by Congress in the future."[23] By autumn 1996, such legislation had not passed.

Congress is not without its favorite tides, of course. As I have argued, war on waste and watchful eye have long been popular on Capitol Hill. Driven in part by the growing professionalization of staff following the Legislative Reorganization Act of 1946 and in part by a thirst for information following the Budget and Accounting Procedures Act of 1950, Congress has shown a nearly unquenchable dedication to opening government to the sunshine, whether through new institutions such as the OIGs or through the public and media.

That the presidency and Congress—and, indeed, the House and the Senate—have different tastes in management reform is confirmed by tables 4.3 and 4.4. Where the idea originates clearly matters.

The Sun and Moon of Reform

Just as the sun and moon do not exert equal pulls on the tides of the ocean (although the sun is much larger in mass, the moon's proximity makes its pull much stronger), Congress and the presidency are not equally powerful in pulling the tides of reform. Start at table 4.3, which summarizes the differences between the presidency and Congress. The impact of origin shows early at the top of the table and continues all the way down. Presidential initiatives are far more likely, for example, to involve blue-ribbon commissions than congressional ones and are likely to involve somewhat greater controversy, much closer votes, and a higher number of on-the-record tallies.

The bipartisan nature of the two committees of origin provides a clue why Congress goes so easy on its own reform bills. It is fair, if a bit harsh, to note that the Senate Governmental Affairs and House Government Operations Committees have to achieve a certain level of bipartisanship to succeed, if only

Table 4.3 Origin of Ideas (percentages)

	Presidency	Congress
Time		
Era		
Pre-1974	66	22
Post-1974	34	78
Decade		
Glory Days	27	13
Great Society	25	3
Reassessment	34	33
New Proceduralism	14	52
Legislative History		
President's Party		
Democratic	63	25
Republican	38	75
Congressional Party		
Democratic	91	75
Republican	5	4
Divided Between Chambers	5	21
Party Control of Government		
Unified	64	26
Divided	36	74
Blue-Ribbon Commission Involved?	19	9
Interest Groups Involved?	31	27
Legislative Debate		
Routine	48	62
Controversial	52	38
Legislative Passage		
Unanimous	34	61
Near-Unanimous	33	25
Strong Majority (60 or more)	25	9
Close (less than 60)	8	5
Recorded Vote Taken?	69	53
Philosophy		
Tide		
Scientific Management	67	25
War on Waste	13	23
Watchful Eye	3	40
Liberation Management	17	12

Table 4.3 (Continued)

	Presidency	Congress
Purity of Statute		
No Other Tides Found in Statute	69	73
One Other Tide Found	25	21
Two Other Tides Found	6	7
Primary Accountability Mechanism		
Compliance	19	57
Capacity	72	25
Performance	9	18
General View of Government		
Trusting	70	30
Distrusting	30	70
Change Strategy		
Focus		
Structure of Government	63	23
Procedures of Government	33	69
Both	5	5
Create a Study Commission	0	3
Structural Tactic		
Create New Agency	17	16
Merge Existing Agencies	17	1
Reorganize Existing Agency	14	1
Create Public Corporation	8	1
Abolish Existing Agency	5	1
Grant Agency Independence	0	5
Elevate Agency to Higher Status	3	1
Combination	3	1
No Structural Reform in Statute	33	71
Procedural Tactic		
Establish New System	11	31
Broaden System	2	25
Revise System	8	8
Deregulate/Narrow System	6	7
Reauthorize System	8	4
Abolish System	2	0
Combination	2	0
No Procedural Reform in Statute	61	24
Target		
General Organization of Government	67	17
Procurement/Acquisition	5	14
Ethics/Standards of Conduct	5	16

Table 4.3 (Continued)

	Presidency	Congress
Administrative Process	0	12
Pay Systems	5	5
Audit/Investigation	0	9
Rulemaking Procedures	5	4
General Personnel/Classification	5	4
Budget/Financial Management	5	5
Combination	3	5
Strategic Planning/Analysis	0	4
Debt Collection	2	3
Tort Claims	0	3

Scale

Nature of Idea

New Approach	58	49
Modification of Old	42	51

Scope of Impact

Large	48	33
Small	52	68

Overall Scale of Reform

New/Large	38	18
New/Small	22	31
Old/Large	13	16
Old/Small	28	35

Implementation

Experimental Approach in Statute?	2	5

Time Horizon in Statute

Temporary/Sunset	14	14
Permanent	86	86

Scope

Single Agency	47	27
Several Agencies	21	8
Governmentwide	32	65

Oversight Approach

Centralized	63	40
Decentralized	38	60

Impact

Shift in Shared Powers

Toward President	73	26
Toward Congress	14	39
Not Clear/No Shift Discernible	13	35

Table 4.3 (Continued)

	Presidency	Congress
Impact on Cost of Government		
Increase	44	10
Decrease	13	5
Not Clear/No Impact Discernible	44	84
Impact on Role of Government		
Expand	53	10
Contract	17	5
Not Clear/No Impact Discernible	30	84
Impact on Shape of Government		
Thicken Hierarchy	59	57
Thin Hierarchy	20	12
Not Clear/No Impact Discernible	20	30
Impact on Administrative Speed		
Accelerate	47	27
Slow Down	8	42
Not Clear/No Impact Discernible	45	31
Impact on Interest Group Access		
Enhance	20	14
Reduce	16	31
Not Clear/No Impact Discernible	64	55
Impact on Public Access		
Enhance	9	26
Reduce	6	8
Not Clear/No Impact Discernible	84	66
Impact on Government Morale		
Improve	17	33
Reduce	2	3
Not Clear/No Impact Discernible	81	65
Impact on Bureaucratic Balance		
Strengthen Line Units	69	29
Strengthen Staff Units	22	62
Not Clear/No Impact Discernible	9	9

$N = 141$

because the issues on which both work are so inherently boring to most members that any hint of division is often enough to scuttle forward motion.

Differences in origin also show strongly under philosophy of reform. As suggested above, Congress clearly favors watchful eye above all else, with war on waste a distant second, while the presidency favors scientific management, with no other tide even close. This result obviously reflects the timing patterns discussed in Chapter 3. As presidents have been eclipsed by Congress as a source of management ideas, scientific management has faded steadily from shore. It is possible that the fading of scientific management is precisely what caused the decline of the presidency as a source of reform, but Clinton's success in pushing liberation management suggests the potential for presidential leadership of a different tide.

Much of table 4.3 repeats these preferences for one tide or the other. Accountability mechanism and general view fall in expected directions, with the presidency much more willing to apply capacity accountability and trust and Congress drawn more to compliance and distrust. Interestingly, however, Congress has shown a more recent willingness to experiment with performance accountability, the most notable expression being the Government Performance and Results Act, which emerged from a long Senate incubation in 1993.

Change strategy shows similarly expected results. Of particular note is the much higher congressional tendency to broaden established systems. As Kingdon argues, Congress has a tendency to mine a given vein of reform until it plays out. This is clearly the case with repeated congressional expansions and fine-tunings of previously successful statutes. Thus did the 1962 effort to consolidate bribery, graft, and conflict of interest statutes lead to the Ethics in Government Act of 1978, which, in turn, produced the independent counsel reauthorizations, independence for the Office of Government Ethics, and further expansion of the Ethics Act in 1989. Thus did the Freedom of Information Act of 1966 spawn a half dozen amendments over the years covered by this book. And thus did the 1976 establishment of an OIG at HEW spawn a host of expansions.

Congress tends to prefer, or accept, smaller innovations than the presidency and clearly favors governmentwide, decentralized implementation. It is useful to note that Congress has been the source of four of the five experiments recorded in Appendix A, the lone exception being the 1978 Civil Service Reform Act that emerged mostly from the presidency. The total number of experiments is admittedly small, but Congress nonetheless seems more tolerant of piloting than the White House. At the same time, however, the White House seems somewhat tolerant of sunsets and other time horizons. Ultimately, of course, neither branch is particularly interested in either experimentation or sunsets.

Finally, the two branches show a range of significant differences on the impacts of reform. Not surprisingly, the presidency favors shifts of power toward the White House, while Congress shows much greater enthusiasm for shifts toward Capitol Hill. This congressional bias toward strengthening its own role in management is actually higher in the pre-1974 period, when congressional initiatives shifted power toward Congress more than half of the time. This curious inversion is largely due to the congressional preference for a war on waste. Many of the statutes passed during the early 1980s gave the commander in chief greater authority to ferret out fraud, waste, and abuse. Member self-interest in claiming a role in that war apparently outweighed institutional interests in shifting power toward the Hill.

That Congress must share the blame for the thickening of government is confirmed in table 4.3, as is its impact on slowing administrative speed, increasing public access to government, and strengthening staff units of government. These impacts are largely a function of Congress's fascination with watchful eye. Although presidents can be held accountable more for increasing the cost and role of government, Congress has itself to blame in part for the bureaucratic red tape about which it so frequently complains.

Congress Against Itself

Turn next to table 4.4, which summarizes the fifty-eight congressional initiatives that originated in either the House or the Senate. (The other fourteen congressional initiatives are set aside as joint efforts.) As the figures suggest, Congress is often divided against itself.[24]

The Senate, for example, had its most active years during the last decade, while the House has been working at government reform since Watergate. It may be that the Senate was simply more reluctant to second-guess the presidency as a source of ideas, in part because the Senate has historically been an incubator of presidential candidates. If a substantial minority of senators envision themselves as future chief executives, perhaps the chamber is more sympathetic toward unified command, staff assistance, and so on. And because the Senate is constitutionally responsible for the confirmation of presidential appointees, perhaps there is also greater empathy toward those who must navigate the bureaucratic seas.

The Senate is by far the more accommodating chamber for its own proposals. Its debates tend to be routine, not controversial, and its margins of passage unanimous or near-unanimous. Both chambers show an equal disdain for blue-ribbon commissions as a source of ideas, and both show a similar tolerance for interest group involvement.

The two chambers begin to diverge more sharply on philosophy of reform. The Senate emerges as much more committed to watchful eye, the House to war on waste. As we have seen with regard to the divided Congresses under

Table 4.4 Chamber of Origin

	House	Senate
Time		
Era		
Pre-1974	21	21
Post-1974	79	79
Decade		
Glory Days	13	9
Great Society	0	3
Reassessment	41	27
New Proceduralism	46	62
Legislative History		
President's Party		
Democratic	25	21
Republican	75	79
Congressional Party		
Democratic	83	74
Republican	0	0
Divided Between Chambers	18	26
Party Control of Government		
Unified	21	18
Divided	79	82
Blue-Ribbon Commission Involved?	2	1
Interest Groups Involved?	25	32
Legislative Debate		
Routine	46	71
Controversial	54	29
Legislative Passage		
Unanimous	48	68
Near-Unanimous	30	24
Strong Majority (60 or more)	13	6
Close (less than 60)	9	3
Recorded Vote Taken?	63	59
Philosophy		
Tide		
Scientific Management	26	23
War on Waste	30	23
Watchful Eye	26	49
Liberation Management	17	6

Table 4.4 (Continued)

	House	Senate
Purity of Statute		
No Other Tides Found in Statute	74	80
One Other Tide Found	22	14
Two Other Tides Found	4	6
Primary Accountability Mechanism		
Compliance	50	65
Capacity	29	21
Performance	21	15
General View of Government		
Trusting	42	18
Distrusting	58	82
Change Strategy		
Focus		
Structure of Government	33	18
Procedures of Government	63	77
Both	4	6
Create a Study Commission	0	0
Structural Tactic		
Create New Agency	21	11
Merge Existing Agencies	0	3
Reorganize Existing Agency	0	3
Create Public Corporation	4	0
Abolish Existing Agency	4	0
Grant Agency Independence	4	6
Elevate Agency to Higher Status	4	0
Combination	0	0
No Structural Reform in Statute	63	77
Procedural Tactic		
Establish New System	21	43
Broaden System	21	31
Revise System	17	3
Deregulate/Narrow System	8	3
Reauthorize System	0	3
Abolish System	0	0
Combination	0	0
No Procedural Reform in Statute	33	17
Target		
General Organization of Government	29	11
Procurement/Acquisition	13	17
Ethics/Standards of Conduct	8	20

Table 4.4 (Continued)

	House	Senate
Administrative Process	13	14
Pay Systems	8	3
Audit/Investigation	17	3
Rulemaking Procedures	0	9
General Personnel/Classification	8	3
Budget/Financial Management	0	9
Combination	4	0
Strategic Planning/Analysis	0	6
Debt Collection	0	6
Tort Claims	0	0
Scale		
Nature of Idea		
New Approach	44	54
Modification of Old	57	46
Scope of Impact		
Large	39	34
Small	61	66
Overall Scale of Reform		
New/Large	22	20
New/Small	22	34
Old/Large	17	17
Old/Small	39	29
Implementation		
Experimental Approach in Statute?	0	11
Time Horizon in Statute		
Temporary/Sunset	8	12
Permanent	92	88
Scope		
Single Agency	50	12
Several Agencies	8	8
Governmentwide	42	79
Oversight Approach		
Centralized	48	31
Decentralized	52	69
Impact		
Shift in Shared Powers		
Toward President	35	20
Toward Congress	39	46
Not Clear/No Shift Discernible	26	34

Table 4.4 (Continued)

	House	Senate
Impact on Cost of Government		
Increase	8	12
Decrease	13	3
Not Clear/No Impact Discernible	79	85
Impact on Role of Government		
Expand	13	6
Contract	8	6
Not Clear/No Impact Discernible	79	88
Impact on Shape of Government		
Thicken Hierarchy	50	62
Thin Hierarchy	13	12
Not Clear/No Impact Discernible	38	27
Impact on Administrative Speed		
Accelerate	17	18
Slow Down	50	41
Not Clear/No Impact Discernible	33	41
Impact on Interest Group Access		
Enhance	9	20
Reduce	22	37
Not Clear/No Impact Discernible	70	43
Impact on Public Access		
Enhance	17	38
Reduce	8	3
Not Clear/No Impact Discernible	75	59
Impact on Government Morale		
Improve	26	26
Reduce	0	3
Not Clear/No Impact Discernible	74	71
Impact on Bureaucratic Balance		
Strengthen Line Units	38	15
Strengthen Staff Units	46	79
Not Clear/No Impact Discernible	17	6

$N = 58$

Reagan, the Senate's support for watchful eye may be conditioned on party control of the two branches. Senate Republicans may have been reluctant to lead watchful eye investigations of a Republican president in the early 1980s but have been anything but reluctant to do so under a Democratic president in the mid-1990s.

Interestingly, the House is also a greater source of liberation management, suggesting that it also shares some sympathy toward those in government. Part of the finding is explained by the historic House involvement in procurement reform. Given its leadership in the war on waste, it may be that the House has the political freedom to loosen the controls from time to time. Moreover, it is the House, not the Senate, that produces the more trusting statutes. Recalling the maxim of former House Speaker Thomas P. "Tip" O'Neill that "all politics is local," the House can wage war on waste and abolish agencies at the same time it authors a Foreign Service employee bill of rights, argues for comparable worth, protects hiring preferences for veterans, pushes for pay increases for U.S. postal workers, and launches a campaign to elevate the Veterans Administration to Cabinet status. Thus, it is the Senate, not the House, that is the author of more compliance accountability, and the Senate, not the House, that shows the much more distrusting hand.

With regard to change strategy, both chambers show a general dislike of government structure, with the House displaying the greater willingness to use structure as a means to making government work. Confirming the House preference for war on waste, the figures include the first two IG acts and the base closure commission (an idea first proposed by Representative Dick Armey [R-Tex.], who would emerge as majority leader in the 104th Congress). The base closure commission suggests that the House can, indeed, put the war on waste above local politics.

Surprisingly, the Senate leads the House in the percentage of initiatives related to procurement/acquisition. That finding reflects the special interest of Senate Republicans in procurement reform in the early to mid-1980s. It was an interest that emerged from a series of high-profile Senate Governmental Affairs Committee investigations of defense procurement fraud that began under the Republican majority and continued when the Democrats returned to power in the 100th Congress.

This is not to argue that the House ignored the defense scandals of the period. But no one committee can investigate everything. The House Government Operations Committee handled most of the IG legislation in the early 1980s, including a high percentage of the audit/investigation bills, and it also took on the HUD scandal in 1987. As a result, the Senate produced a significant number of procurement reforms, among them the Major Fraud Act of 1988, which made procurement fraud against the federal government a clear criminal offense.

The Senate shows a greater preference for new approaches, most notably in ethics and freedom of information, yielding a higher percentage of new/small innovations. At the same time, the Senate is more open to experimental approaches in statute—all four experiments that originated in Congress came from the Senate—and shows a slightly greater inclination than the House toward sunsets (recall that the failed 1977 Sunset Act originated in the Senate Governmental Affairs Committee). Notwithstanding its support for such limits, the Senate is by far the most active in promoting governmentwide reforms and in using decentralized implementation.

There are more similarities between the two chambers than sharp differences with regard to impacts. Of particular note is the willingness to let the presidency take the lead in proposing expansions in the cost and role of government, along with the shared desire to slow down the administrative process. The Senate shows a clear preference for greater public access, reflecting its broad commitment to watchful eye, while the House is more inclined to strengthen line delivery units, suggesting its predominant concern for assuring that government goods get delivered on time back home.

Origin, Party, and Time

It is difficult if not impossible to rank the competing explanations for the ebb and flow of the tides. What is clear is that time, individual presidents, party, and origin of idea are all important influences. What is not clear is whether time, presidents, party, or origin is the most important factor, and how the factors vary in influence across each separate tide.

Although there are advanced statistical techniques for assessing the precise influence of each factor on the four tides, the number of initiatives involved here is so small and the kinds of measures used to sort the 141 initiatives so weak that such techniques would produce speculative results at best. In addition, the number of categories involved in the measures discussed in the past two chapters makes a single table impossibly unwieldy. Ten presidents, four decades, two eras, two congressional parties, two presidential parties, two forms of party government, two origins of ideas, and two chambers would yield far too many cells with zero initiatives.

Thus the best one can do is attempt a brief comparison of what appear to be the three most important predictors of the tides: time, party, and origin of idea. Table 4.5 shows the results. The problem with reading the table is evident: the small number of initiatives in some cells limits meaningful comparisons. The two Republican Congresses in the pre-1974 period originated exactly three initiatives between them, which means that the figures for Congress as *Origin of Idea* under the subheadings *Republican Congresses* and *Pre-1974* must be taken with a rather sizable concern for generalizability to the present.

In spite of these caveats, table 4.5 generates two broad conclusions for pre-

Table 4.5 Changes in Sources of Ideas (percentages)

	President				Congress			
	Democratic		Republican		Democratic		Republican/Divided	
	Pre-1974	Post-1974	Pre-1974	Post-1974	Pre-1974	Post-1974	Pre-1974°	Post-1974
Tide								
Scientific Management	78	39	80	56	43	18	100	13
War on Waste	11	23	0	22	0	16	0	69
Watchful Eye	4	8	0	0	43	50	0	19
Liberation Management	7	31	20	22	14	16	0	0
Accountability Mechanism								
Compliance	19	23	13	22	50	59	0	69
Capacity	74	77	75	56	36	21	100	13
Performance	7	0	13	22	14	21	0	19
Focus								
Structure of Government	67	46	80	44	21	30	33	6
Procedures of Government	33	39	20	44	79	64	0	88
Both	0	15	0	11	0	7	0	6
Study Commission	4	0	0	0	0	0	67	0
Oversight								
Centralized	70	39	67	67	36	41	67	38
Decentralized	30	62	33	33	64	59	33	63

N = 141
°N = 3

dicting the tides. First, Democratic presidents have moved somewhat faster from scientific management toward liberation management than Republicans. Note the 39-point drop in scientific management over the period and the 24-point rise in liberation. Although Republican presidents also changed over the period, the movement is not quite as sharp: a 24-point drop in scientific management, a 22-point rise in war on waste. The rise in Democratic support for liberation management appears to reflect the party's effort to find a way to keep the debate focused on how government works, not what government does.

Democratic presidents show far more stability in accountability mechanism, holding steady on all three approaches. Here it is the Republican presidents who change over time, with a sharp drop in capacity-based accountability and a parallel rise in performance. To be fair, at least two Democratic presidents, Johnson and Clinton, made performance a centerpiece of executive reform. LBJ's Programming, Planning, Budgeting System was the subject of a governmentwide order in August 1965, while Clinton's customer service approach became the focus of an executive order late in his first year. So noted, neither can be credited with drafting any of the performance-oriented initiatives in Appendix A. Clinton's 1993 reinventing package was much more about capacity accountability—stripping Agriculture of needless layers, streamlining the acquisitions process—than about creating incentives toward performance.

Second, Democratic Congresses show far less change than Democratic presidents. Although there is a 25-point drop in the share of scientific management initiatives, Democratic Congresses show remarkable stability in their commitment to watchful eye. Watergate is best viewed as an accelerator, not an originator, of the watchful eye rise. If Congress was interested in the sunshine long before the dark hours of executive privilege in the late 1960s and early 1970s, it was Watergate that clearly upped the volume of watchful eye initiatives. As Congress became a much more active participant in making government work, it appears inevitable that watchful eye would emerge as its preferred tide.

The relative stability of Democratic Congresses is confirmed by the steadiness of preferences for compliance, procedures, and decentralized oversight. There is little support here for the notion that the 1940s and 1950s were somehow the "good old days," when a compliant Congress minded its own business. Congress most certainly was less active during the pre-1974 period, but it was hardly minding its own business. It was learning the legislative techniques and honing the statutory tools that would make it the dominant force in making government work in the 1970s and 1980s.

Nevertheless, the pre-1974 years clearly favored a more trusting view of government. When they had to, presidents, not Congress, authored the war on waste initiatives, singling out agencies and programs for trimming. This is not to suggest that Congress was completely silent about waging the war on waste. Congress expressed its concerns about the size of government in amendments to the 1949 Classification Act and passed a Post Office appropriations bill amendment sponsored by Jamie Whitten (D-Miss.) in 1952 that required departments and agencies to review all positions created or placed in a higher pay level and to abolish all positions found to be unnecessary.

For the most part, however, Congress was content to add amendments here and there to make its points about smaller government or to focus those concerns through the two Hoover Commissions. It was reasonably content to let Agriculture Secretary Orville Freeman establish an IG by department order in the early 1960s, and it deferred, albeit with tough criticism, to Assistant Secretary Joseph Wright when he abolished the office by department order ten years later. It was not until the mid-1970s that Congress began producing major statutes of its own. No longer willing to defer to the president or blue-ribbon commissions, Congress opened its own legislative assembly line. It is not clear that Congress will ever go back, particularly given the persistent levels of public distrust, or that the presidency is equipped to stake a claim to its once singular leadership of government reform.

None of this means that reforms originating in Congress are somehow inferior to those emanating from the presidency. Such a claim would be difficult to sustain, if only because presidents often claim congressional initiatives as their own when they first enter office. There is no inherent reason why either Congress or the presidency should be better or worse at making government work. Indeed, Congress's greater tolerance for pilot programs might make it more effective in making government work over the long haul.

What may make Congress a more difficult orginator of reform, however, is the fact that it is home to 535 individual entrepreneurs, each one of whom is free to surf his or her pet wave. It is no surprise that the tides of reform appear to be accelerating as Congress takes a more active role as an originator of ideas. With more sources of reform, and arguably much less control over the legislative agenda, Congress is rife with opportunities for both accretion and contradiction in the ebb and flow of reform.

Some who page through this chapter and the evidence of congressional assertiveness will long for a return to the strong presidency of the 1940s and 1950s, hoping against hope that making government work will somehow be restored as a purely executive responsibility. Others, however, will rightly note that the presidency was never the great engine of reform that so many armchair historians imagine it was.

In fact, the presidency was always sharing power with the Congress, just as the House was always competing with the Senate. Ever was it thus in America's constitutional system. As such, table 4.5 confirms Charles O. Jones's description of the role of the presidency in making policy of whatever kind: "The plain fact is that the United States does not have a presidential system. It has a *separated* system. It is odd that it is so commonly thought of otherwise since school-children learn about the separation of powers and checks and balances. . . . Simply put, the role of the president in this separated system of governing varies substantially, depending on his resources, advantages, and strategic position."[25]

This separated system most certainly shows itself in table 4.5. Presidents are leaders in government reform for only a brief moment in historical time, and even then with very different preferences. Their role changes as Congress grows more assertive, ebbs with the rise of war on waste in the 1980s, then rises again with the emergence of liberation management in the 1990s. As Jones argues, it is unreasonable to assume that presidents will be solely responsible for any policy area, whether making war or making government work. As table 4.5 suggests, just about the only thing ultimately predictable about the rise and fall of the tides is the rise and fall itself. Those who are ready to declare liberation management the one true answer will soon be contradicted by advocates of a return to science or a restoration of watchfulness.

What remains for this book are questions of how to make the best of the natural ebb and flow. Although an individual president or Congress can change the climate of reform, there is no evidence that any tide ever completely subsides. Therefore, the issue is how to harness the tides to assure the best possible result. Just as seaside communities protect themselves from the tidal surge, so, too, might government protect itself from the momentary hurricanes of reform. Before turning to such issues in more detail in Chapter 6, however, it is first useful to ask a bit more about what makes a given tide controversial, what makes a given idea innovative, and how one might measure the consequences of reform.

5

The Consequences of Reform

Making government work is such an easy promise for candidates to make in part because there is virtually no way to know whether the promise is ever kept. Candidates may promise that they will finally make government (1) more businesslike, (2) less wasteful, (3) more watchful, or (4) more efficient and less expensive, but there is precious little evidence that any of the 141 initiatives in Appendix A accomplished those lofty goals.

The fact that the IGs continue to set records in their statistical inventories of dollars saved and funds put to better use, for example, is not necessarily evidence that the war on waste is being won. The yearly records might even be evidence that the "visible odium" of deterrence is neither as visible nor as odious as the IGs imagine. As I have written, the reason is not that the "IGs have done their job poorly, but that they may be doing the wrong job entirely—putting too much emphasis on compliance and not enough on performance and capacity building."[1] After fifteen years of a steadily escalating war on waste, the light at the end of the tunnel is still nowhere to be seen.

Nor is there any evidence that the public has noticed an improvement. The number of Americans who say they have a great deal of confidence in the executive branch held steady at 12 percent in late 1994, a single percentage point lower than its 1975 mark, while 93 said that the federal government wastes their money, a dramatic increase over the previous two decades.

It is not clear, however, why making government work would affect public confidence. The two are poorly linked at best. Political scientists have long argued that confidence in government rises and falls more with economic performance, the president's personal approval, and individual social trust than with real progress made on procurement reform, administrative procedures, even paperwork reduction.[2] Thus, even the most successful management reforms might not affect confidence.

MEASURING CONSEQUENCES

The question, therefore, is how to measure the broad consequences of reform. At a very minimum, for example, each of the 141 initiatives had an impact on the legislative process. After all, it is no small accomplishment just to make the statute books. There were roughly four hundred thousand bills introduced in Congress over the fifty-year period covered by this book, of which fewer than twenty thousand actually become public law.[3] Given such odds, getting through both chambers and across the president's desk is no small sign of impact.

Nevertheless, mere passage is hardly a sign of lasting consequence. The question here is not whether an initiative passed but whether it made any difference in making government work—obviously, a much more difficult question to answer. It is very rare, for example, to find an acknowledged failure on the list. The closest one might come to complete failure are the pay-setting measures passed over the years, most of which failed to reduce the conflict surrounding executive, legislative, and judicial salaries. Only by resorting to pay based on local cost of employment indexes did the federal government finally figure out a way to boost employee salaries without requiring a battle on congressional pay.

Much more common on the list are partial successes. Almost all of the initiatives were successfully implemented with at least marginal results. Because of the Administrative Procedure Act, all federal rules must go through a notice-and-comment stage; because of the Ethics in Government Act, all presidential appointees must correct conflicts of interest; because of the Presidential Transitions Effectiveness Act, all incoming and outgoing presidents receive federal dollars to come and go; and because of a host of department- and agency-creating statutes, NASA, FAA, the Departments of Education,

Energy, HUD, Transportation, and Veterans Affairs all still exist, though threatened from time to time.

It is when the initiatives are measured against the promises they made that almost all suffer. Take merit pay as but one of dozens of examples. Created under the 1978 Civil Service Reform Act, merit pay was designed to give federal employees an incentive for higher performance. "Rewarding excellence and discouraging lackluster performance is very difficult under the present system," the Senate Governmental Affairs Committee explained in 1978. "Performance appraisals now are virtually meaningless, with almost every employee receiving a 'satisfactory' rating. Pay increases are awarded almost automatically."[4]

The new Merit Pay System, which took half of every manager's general pay increase to establish a pool for rewarding top-performing employees and, in doing so, clearly punished poor performers, lasted exactly three years after being implemented in 1981. It was replaced by a new Performance Management and Recognition System in 1984, which gave every manager, top-performing or not, a nearly automatic general pay increase, and established a new hierarchy of merit increases, awards, and bonuses for rewarding top-performing employees, thereby removing any sanctions for poor performers. It continues into the present but is generally viewed as a failure, in part because money for pay increases of any kind has been scarce, in part because of continuing impressions that poor performance rarely gets punished. In addition, scholars appear to agree that pay for performance has never been fully tested as a tool for motivating employees.

"Why does a seemingly good idea such as [pay for performance] so frequently fail to achieve expectations?" asks the public administration scholar James Perry. "One answer may be that it is *not* a good idea, depending on the motivational theory to which you subscribe." After reviewing the competing theories, Perry argues that pay for performance systems "must continue to be viewed as experimental."[5]

Even if government could design a statistically valid experiment on pay, or on any other management reform for that matter, the challenge would be in finding a common metric for measuring the results. There is no general agreement on how to measure public effectiveness.

Some reformers, most notably Al Gore, put their faith in customer satisfaction as the final arbiter of success. But as we have seen, customer satisfaction may be poorly linked to actual agency performance, and public expectations may be so low that mediocre performance is satisfactory. Other reformers, such as the public management scholar Mark Moore, argue that government must be measured by the public value it creates.[6] But the "eye-of-the-beholder" quality of public value makes it exceedingly weak as a measure against which to test specific reforms. Still others suggest that the answer is to be found in the performance plans and outcome indicators of the Government Performance and Results Act (GPRA). As the Senate Governmental Affairs Committee explained, "This reform has the potential to make a significant change in the way that managers, policymakers, and the American people think about what services the government should provide, and how well it does at providing them. The legislation will provide the information necessary to strengthen program management, to make objective evaluations of program performance, and to set realistic, measurable goals for future performance."[7]

As I shall argue in Chapter 6, the GPRA may yet provide the needed baselines for harnessing, if not stopping, the hurricanes of reform that blow through Washington with what seems to be increasing frequency and, dare one suggest, damage. With GPRA implementation still years away, however, the best this book can do to measure consequences is to ask how the 141 initiatives may have reshaped the debate about making government work.

Beyond the measures of cost, role, shape, speed, bureaucratic balance, and so on presented throughout this book, this chapter deepens the search for consequences through three additional questions: First, to what extent do certain kinds of reform yield legislative controversy? Second, what kinds of reform constitute the kinds of breakthroughs that might change the prevailing image of reform? And, third, what kinds of reform appear to make the greatest difference in shifting the institutional balance between Congress and the presidency?

Before tackling each question in order, it is important to emphasize that this book does not attempt to measure the ultimate success or failure of any given reform. No one knows whether government is actually better off after these past fifty years of reform than it would have been absent the effort or even whether the individual tides have been successful. Is it fairer than it was because of all the watchful eye or less wasteful because of the war on waste? Is it more coordinated because of the scientific management or better managed because of the liberation? The federal government has more than enough measures of inputs (budget, employment, clients) and activity (cases opened, audits conducted, dollars spent, troops deployed), but very few measures of outcome (poverty reduced, jobs created, waste prevented) that would tell an objective observer what worked and what did not. The lack of such measures is particularly acute in making the link between management reform and policy outcomes. One cannot know, for example, whether the coordination that comes from scientific management, the deterrence from war on waste, the visibility from watchful eye, or the risk taking from liberation management actually produce any gains in desired outcomes, such as reducing poverty or creating better jobs. Nor can we know whether the reforms even produce the promised gains in management. Does war on waste actually reduce waste or merely catch it after the fact? Does liberation management produce innovation or merely reduce paperwork?

CREATING CONTROVERSY

Government management reform was far from the most controversial item on the legislative agenda during the fifty years covered by this book. There were no all-night debates, only a few presidential vetoes (most significantly on such watchful eye reforms as the Administrative Procedure Act and reauthorization of the independent counsel), a handful of filibusters (most notably on civil rights and the Federal Elections Campaign Act of 1974), and the very rare great debate (most centered on efforts to shift the balance of executive-legislative power, such as the 1974 Budget and Impoundment Control Act).

This is not to argue that government management reform is always routine. Even the most noncontroversial reform can create controversy simply by its popularity. The bill to elevate the Veterans Administration to cabinet status in 1988, for example, passed by an overwhelming margin in the House and earned Reagan's enthusiastic endorsement. In the Senate, however, VA elevation became a legislative hammer for driving home much broader veterans reform, including judicial review of veterans benefits decisions. Under the then-existing system, veterans could appeal benefit rejections within the VA system. They had lost the right to sue their government for redress back in 1933, when Congress passed the Economy Act, which simultaneously cut veterans benefits and closed access to the courts. When VA elevation was linked to the Veterans Judicial Review Act of 1988, the former became instantly controversial.[8]

Other entries in Appendix A were equally controversial, if not more so. The Administrative Procedure Act took most of a decade to pass, surviving a presidential veto along the way. The Tort Claims Act of 1946 took even longer, covering twenty years and a pocket veto in 1928. Increasing civil service pay was invariably intense, prompting repeated efforts to devise some foolproof way to protect members of Congress from the political consequences of raising their own salaries. And liberating federal employees from the Hatch Act restrictions took two decades and two vetoes, the first by Ford in 1976, the next by Bush in 1990, with a threatened veto from Reagan enough to scuttle reform in 1988. Although there are no veto overrides in Appendix A, the history of making government work has more than enough excitement to ask what makes a reform controversial. The answers are summarized in table 5.1.

Table 5.1 confirms an assortment of previous findings, while offering a clear pattern of advice for reformers who wish to avoid controversy. Before turning to that advice, it is useful to note that controversy has been in decline of late, in large measure because of the rising popularity of war on waste, not because making government work has become any easier.

Of particular note here is the remarkable number of noncontroversial items emerging from the divided Congresses of 1981–1987. Is this because divided Congresses get along better than unified ones? Is this some grand new insight on the nature of intraparty conflict? Not at all. By now, it should be clear that the low level of controversy in divided Congresses is an agenda-setting effect—that is, divided Congresses appear to screen out the more difficult issues before final passage. What emerges by way of management reform is likely to reflect the least common denominator between the two chambers. And at least in recent years, the easiest kind of reform to push through Congress has been war on waste. Divided Congresses may not be able to agree on budgets, invasions, even old-growth forests, but they most certainly can coalesce around fighting the good fight.

This general conclusion is confirmed in the legislative history surrounding controversial reforms. Note again the impact of origin of idea on controversy. Congress does go easy on itself. Note also the role of blue-ribbon commissions in soothing the potential for friction.

As I shall soon suggest, commissions may not be particularly useful in generating spectacular new ideas, but they are helpful in wrapping old/large ideas in a more palatable package. The 1983 Social Security rescue is a prime example. There was nothing particularly new in the final package, just a rather familiar mixture of tax increases, benefit cuts, and assorted thinly disguised revenue raisers, like taxation of benefits (an option that could be labeled a benefit cut or a tax increase, depending on the audience). But what made the National Commission on Social Security Reform important was the political cover that allowed negotiators to finally reach agreement on an obvious package of reform.[9]

In contrast, just as a commission signals a likely drop in legislative tension, interest group involvement signals a likely rise. It may be that interest groups get involved in government management reform only when the stakes are great. That was certainly the case in the Department of Education Act, a Carter priority that pitted the National Education Association against the American Federation of Teachers in a struggle for control of the education

Table 5.1 Sources of Legislative Controversy (percentages)

	Routine	Controversial
Time		
Era		
Pre-1974	58	42
Post-1974	55	45
Decade		
Glory Days	56	44
Great Society	56	44
Reassessment	51	49
New Proceduralism	61	39
Legislative History		
President's Party		
Democratic	53	48
Republican	59	41
Congressional Party		
Democratic	54	46
Republican	67	33
Divided Between Chambers	63	37
Party Control of Government		
Unified	54	45
Divided	58	43
Origin of Idea		
President	48	52
Congress	62	38
Blue-Ribbon Commission Involved?	58	42
Interest Groups Involved?	24	76
Legislative Passage		
Unanimous	83	17
Near-Unanimous	43	58
Strong Majority (60 or more)	22	79
Close (less than 60)	0	100
Recorded Vote Taken?	38	62
Philosophy		
Tide		
Scientific Management	55	45
War on Waste	62	39
Watchful Eye	58	42
Liberation Management	50	50

Table 5.1 (Continued)

	Routine	Controversial
Purity of Statute		
No Other Tides Found in Statute	57	43
One Other Tide Found	53	47
Two Other Tides Found	56	44
Primary Accountability Mechanism		
Compliance	64	36
Capacity	48	52
Performance	60	40
General View of Government		
Trusting	59	41
Distrusting	54	46
Change Strategy		
Focus		
Structure of Government	41	59
Procedures of Government	69	31
Both	29	71
Create a Study Commission	100	0
Structural Tactic		
Create New Agency	35	65
Merge Existing Agencies	50	50
Reorganize Existing Agency	50	50
Create Public Corporation	22	67
Abolish Existing Agency	0	100
Grant Agency Independence	75	25
Elevate Agency to Higher Status	33	67
Combination	33	67
No Structural Reform in Statute	70	30
Procedural Tactic		
Establish New System	64	35
Broaden System	70	30
Revise System	50	50
Deregulate/Narrow System	70	30
Reauthorize System	75	25
Abolish System	0	100
Combination	100	0
No Procedural Reform in Statute	43	57
Target		
General Organization of Government	43	57
Procurement/Acquisition	93	7
Ethics/Standards of Conduct	47	53

Table 5.1 (Continued)

	Routine	Controversial
Administrative Process	67	33
Pay Systems	43	57
Audit/Investigation	71	29
Rulemaking Procedures	67	33
General Personnel/Classification	50	50
Budget/Financial Management	29	71
Combination	83	17
Strategic Planning/Analysis	100	0
Debt Collection	100	0
Tort Claims	50	50
Scale		
Nature of Idea		
New Approach	55	45
Modification of Old	58	42
Scope of Impact		
Large	38	63
Small	68	32
Overall Scale of Reform		
New/Large	40	61
New/Small	71	29
Old/Large	35	65
Old/Small	67	33
Implementation		
Experimental Approach in Statute?	80	20
Time Horizon in Statute		
Temporary/Sunset	50	50
Permanent	57	43
Scope		
Single Agency	45	55
Several Agencies	50	50
Governmentwide	66	34
Oversight Approach		
Centralized	52	48
Decentralized	60	40
Impact		
Shift in Shared Powers		
Toward President	52	48
Toward Congress	54	46
Not Clear/No Shift Discernible	66	34

Table 5.1 (Continued)

	Routine	Controversial
Impact on Cost of Government		
Increase	36	64
Decrease	33	67
Not Clear/No Impact Discernible	67	33
Impact on Role of Government		
Expand	45	55
Contract	27	73
Not Clear/No Impact Discernible	67	33
Impact on Shape of Government		
Thicken Hierarchy	49	51
Thin Hierarchy	50	50
Not Clear/No Impact Discernible	76	24
Impact on Administrative Speed		
Accelerate	51	49
Slow Down	62	38
Not Clear/No Impact Discernible	57	43
Impact on Interest Group Access		
Enhance	50	50
Reduce	50	50
Not Clear/No Impact Discernible	60	40
Impact on Public Access		
Enhance	62	39
Reduce	50	50
Not Clear/No Impact Discernible	55	45
Impact on Government Morale		
Improve	56	44
Reduce	0	100
Not Clear/No Impact Discernible	58	42
Impact on Bureaucratic Balance		
Strengthen Line Units	52	49
Strengthen Staff Units	66	34
Not Clear/No Impact Discernible	31	69

N = 141

bureaucracy. That was also the case in the creation of most of the government corporations listed in Appendix A. Comsat, the Postal Service, Amtrak, Conrail, Legal Services, and National Service all involved controversy of one kind or another, in part because government corporations were often used as a way of rescuing doomed government programs (Amtrak, Legal Services) or packaging controversial issues to begin with (Comsat, National Service). And virtually anything involving nearly one million federal employees (the Postal Service) is bound to generate more than a passing interest-group involvement.

Table 5.1 also shows already familiar patterns regarding the four tides of reform. War on waste is the least controversial of the four tides, while liberation management is the most. Although none of the other measures of philosophy shows much of an impact on controversy, it is interesting to note the increasing controversy attendant with the number of tides represented in a statute. This phenomenon appears to be more a consequence of controversy than a cause, however. It may be that particularly controversial reforms are loaded with extra freight to make them more salable to a reluctant Congress. Certainly that has been the case in the use of war on waste as a secondary reform in support of both scientific and liberation management.

Attempts to change the structure of government clearly produce far greater controversy than efforts to alter procedures. Part of the explanation may reside in sheer visibility. It is relatively easy to move a procedural reform through the Congress and past the president with very little notice. After all, but for signature reforms like the Freedom of Information Act or Ethics in Government, procedure is a relatively simple legislative issue. Single authorizing committees are usually involved, with little need to engage appropriations or budget. Although this analysis does not record the exact number of amendments involved in each initiative, the legislative record suggests that there was much less amending activity on procedural reforms than on structural. Congress may be generally willing to defer on procedure to the originating committees, most notably the two government operations committees, while elevating structural bills to a much more prominent position.

This general notion is confirmed in part by the mix of controversy under each tactic. The most controversial structural initiative involves either the creation of a new agency (fifteen out of twenty-three were controversial) or its abolishment (four out of four). The least controversial structural reform is granting independence (one out of four), perhaps because such action is often a sign of broad congressional agreement on an agency's overall value or importance. In contrast, the least controversial procedural initiative involves the broadening of an existing system (fourteen out of twenty were routine) and the most controversial a revision (just four out of ten). Congress may care about building new agencies but not necessarily about the systems that bind those creations. "If you build it," Congress might rewrite the *Field of Dreams* message, "who cares how the infield gets mowed?"

This pattern continues with the reform target. Among the categories with five or more entries, procurement/acquisition reform is by far the least controversial. It seems reasonable to conclude that Congress will not only pass just about any reasonable procurement reform—provided, of course, that it advances the war on waste—but that it will give such reforms the easiest treatment possible. Two thirds of all procurement/acquisition reforms pass without a recorded vote, compared to just one fifth of general organization initiatives, and just one sixth of pay-setting reforms. And of the five procurement/acquisition reforms that came to a recorded vote, all but one passed unanimously. Although there is only so much Congress and the president can do to change procurement law, it is easily the most popular reform to pass.

Small reforms are much less controversial than large. As might be expected, the larger the reform (hence the greater the cost and impact on government), the more controversial the process. It is important to note, however, that Congress is not at all hostile to innovation. Quite the contrary. The least controversial items in Appendix A are new/small reforms such as the 1990 Negotiated Rulemaking Act. Although Congress also treats old/small reforms with kid gloves, it reserves its most gentle process for small-scale innovations that might well form the basis for the kinds of experiments that would allow the federal government to truly learn what works and what does not.

The difficulty with demanding a greater congressional commitment to experimentation in management reform is twofold. The first challenge is the relative popularity of governmentwide initiatives, which are roughly half again as easy to pass as single-agency efforts. The second is the slight preference for permanent time horizons. As a general rule, Congress finds small/new ideas less controversial, but as a specific rule, it is small/new/permanent ideas that get the most favored treatment. Roughly three quarters of all small/new/permanent ideas pass through Congress on a routine basis, compared to 50 percent of small/new/temporary, 44 percent of large/new/permanent, and exactly 0 percent of large/new/temporary.

The question, therefore, is why members of Congress prefer governmentwide reform to single-shot applications. One answer is the simple nature of the legislative process. Much small/new reform simply cannot attract enough interest to achieve legislative velocity. Often it is only by overpromising and overapplying that management reform can reach the legislative calendar at all. In all but the rarest of cases, management reform is neither a career breaker nor a career maker. If a bill cannot be advertised as a be-all and end-all in making government work, can it pass at all?

With regard to impacts, table 5.1 shows mostly expected results. For starters, the absence of impact is often the least controversial option available. "Not discernible" leads on routine legislative passage for shift in shared powers, impact on the cost, role, and shape of government and is a close second on administrative speed and public access. It appears that the more management reform takes a stand on these key issues, the more likely it is to be controversial. The fact that procurement reform is the least likely target of reform to show such impacts is one reason for its popularity. Although Congress is far from thinking about management reform as solely a problem of passing a new small-purchase threshold, procurement has become the safest bet for showing that Congress and the president truly care about making government work.

This is not to argue that management reform must be completely bland to avoid controversy. Enhancing public access, for example, generates significant support, in part because it is a product of watchful eye, in part because opening government to greater participation is almost as American as apple pie, the flag, and promises to make government work. That access comes at a cost, of course, in its tendency to strengthen staff units. The public may get more access but less efficiency, a trade-off Congress has long deemed more than acceptable.

Finally, table 5.1 suggests that controversy is more often associated with reducing government morale, a reassuring finding for those worried about the future of the public service. It is important to remember, however, that only three initiatives out of the 141 could be clearly defined as reducing morale. The first was the 1946 Tort Claims Act, which exposed federal employees to civil liability, the second was the 1981 Omnibus Budget Reconciliation Act, which involved some of the most hostile rhetoric toward government and its employees in the period covered by this book, and the third was the Gramm-Rudman-Hollings budget reform, which theoretically exposed government to automatic cuts in the event Congress and the president failed to meet annual budget reduction targets. Even though many other statutes listed in Appendix A involved harsh rhetoric, and well over half involved a generally distrusting view of government and its employees, it is difficult to draw sharp conclusions about the ultimate impacts on morale.

Indeed, the fact that a distrusting view of government provokes only slightly greater controversy than a trusting view may be the most damning finding on morale. Presidents and members of Congress have long been rewarded, not punished, for attacking the government they seek to reform. "The Carter administration repeatedly castigated the federal civil service in presidential comments, press releases, and one entire [Personnel Management Project] report," writes Chester Newland of the selling of the 1978 Civil Service Reform Act (CSRA), "giving the impression that the bureaucracy was filled with career loafers and incompetents who could not be fired. The negative image of civil service that resulted was one of the most powerful and enduring products of the politics of CSRA—but it helped to get the reform adopted."[10] Thus, even a reform that is classified as strengthening government morale, which the 1978 CSRA most surely did, was sold with rhetoric that ultimately undermined the very service it sought to repair.

Ultimately, this analysis of controversy yields a rather substantial inventory of advice for would-be reformers, advice that is summarized in table 5.2. As the list suggests, the easiest way to get management reform passed is to wage

Table 5.2 Avoiding Legislative Controversy

Legislative History
> *Create a blue-ribbon commission*
> *Avoid interest group involvement*
> *Give Congress the credit*

Philosophy
> *Launch a war on waste*
> *Avoid scientific and liberation management*
> *Try to stay pure*

Change Strategy
> *Focus on the procedures of government*
> *When in doubt, create a commission*
> *Avoid creating new agencies and public corporations*
> *Give an agency independence, but not elevation*
> *Establish a new procedural system*
> *Broaden, revise, deregulate, or reauthorize an existing procedural system*
> *Target procurement/acquisition or administrative process*

Scale
> *Stick to the small stuff, whether new or old*

Implementation
> *Try an experiment*
> *But make the experiment permanent and adopt the reform governmentwide*
> *Be decentralized in oversight*

Impacts
> *Stick to reforms in how government works, not what it does*
> *Neither increase nor decrease cost*
> *Neither expand nor contract the role of government*
> *Stay thin*
> *Enhance public access*
> *Strengthen staff units, not line*

---

war on waste, giving credit to Congress along the way and steering clear of the three other tides; to focus on procedures over structure, how government works, not what it does; to go governmentwide with a long time horizon; and to be innovative, but not too innovative.

The fact that such reforms are the most likely to emerge from the legislative process unscathed may help explain why it is so difficult to know whether government is working any better today than it did fifty years ago. The reforms most likely to survive the legislative process are those with the least potential for teaching future Congresses about what reform might work when and where. The tendency to go governmentwide, for example, creates a layering of reform over time that is virtually impossible to untangle in a search for actual consequences.

CHANGING THE CONVENTIONAL WISDOM

One of the most important consequences of reform is the evolution of conventional wisdom about what constitutes good government. That wisdom changes with the ebb and flow of the tides. The principles of administration, for example, held that good government existed in a unified hierarchy with tight spans of control, staff assistance, specialization, and clear rules for behavior.

It was that wisdom, for example, that generated enormous momentum behind the thickening of the federal hierarchy. Sparked by the Brownlow Committee's argument that the president needs help, and driven forward by the first Hoover Commission, the layering and widening of the federal government has survived virtually every reinventing effort of the past fifty years. As I have written, "One president adds a layer of help, only to be followed by another who layers over. Since layers almost never disappear, the constant struggle to gain control of the executive branch produces an onslaught of leaders but no guarantee of leadership."[11]

This *bureaucratic paradigm*, as Michael Barzelay and Babak Armajani call it, was clearly ascendant from the late 1800s to the 1950s. Over the years, most Americans came to believe "that administrative decisions should be made in a businesslike manner, that the executive branch should be organized hierarchically, that most agency heads should be appointed by the chief executive, that most positions should be staffed by qualified people, that materials should be purchased from responsible vendors based on objective criteria, and that systems of fiscal control and accountability should be reliable."[12] That was once the conventional wisdom about making government work.

The *postbureaucratic* paradigm, as Barzelay and Armajani describe it, contradicts scientific management at every turn, as if one must completely obliterate any allegiance to the bureaucratic paradigm in order to get on with the reinventing. Consider the following sample of comparisons drawn from Barzelay and Armajani's *Breaking Through Bureaucracy:*

- A bureaucratic agency is focused on its own needs and perspectives. A customer-driven agency is focused on customer needs and perspectives.
- A bureaucratic agency is focused on the roles and responsibilities of its parts. A customer-driven agency is focused on enabling the whole organization to function as a team.
- A bureaucratic agency sticks to routine. A customer-driven agency modifies its operations in response to changing demands for its services.
- A bureaucratic agency fights for turf. A customer-driven agency competes for business.
- A bureaucratic agency separates the work of thinking from that of doing. A customer-driven agency empowers front-line employees to make judgments about how to improve customer services.[13]

There are two basic problems as the postbureaucratic paradigm fights to become the conventional wisdom. First, as I have already argued here, the postbureaucratic (or liberation management) paradigm is not the only tide competing against the bureaucratic (or scientific management) paradigm. War on waste and watchful eye still impose enormous constraints on government and its employees. Woe to the federal agency or employee who ignores the Privacy or Freedom of Information Act or the IG who fails to monitor and enforce the Major Fraud Act.

Second, at least some of the failures that prompt calls for liberation involve problems of mission and funding, not freedom from rules. Give a bureaucratic agency a clear mission and the capacity to achieve it, and it can work very well indeed, as NASA proved in putting a man on the moon. Give a postbureaucratic agency a fuzzy mission and no resources to reach it, and it can fail very nicely. Bureaucratic agencies do not always follow routines just because they are bureaucratic, just as postbureaucratic agencies are not allowed to merely ignore statutes just because customers say so.

Ultimately, the greatest challenge to the postbureaucratic paradigm is not in scientific management at all but in a *neobureaucratic* paradigm represented by war on waste and watchful eye. Driven by its distrust of government and its employees, this paradigm sees itself more perhaps as a counterbalance to scientific management than as an alternative. Unlike the postbureaucratic paradigm, which holds hope that government and its employees will act in the public interest if just given the customer standards and the occasional market pressure to do so, the neobureaucratic paradigm holds no illusions about ever trusting government to do other than the self-interested thing. And unlike the postbureaucratic paradigm, which celebrates innovation and risk taking, the neobureaucratic paradigm sees innovation as dangerous and risk taking as the first step toward a breach of the public trust. Thus, to the samples from Barzelay and Armajani's list, neobureaucratic reformers might add the following kinds of caveats:

- A bureaucratic agency sticks to routine. A customer-driven agency modifies its operations in response to changing demands for its services, *provided that any modifications are subject to appropriate notice and comment and all affected parties have equal access to information.*
- A bureaucratic agency fights for turf. A customer-driven agency competes for business, *provided that all competition is fair, bidders have equal access to information, and losing parties have the opportunity to protest all bids within a certain number of days.*
- A bureaucratic agency separates the work of thinking from that of doing. A customer-driven agency empowers front-line employees to make judgments about how to improve customer services, *provided that the integration does not create a conflict of interest, violate prohibitions against self-dealing, or otherwise create vulnerabilities to fraud, waste, and abuse.*

Lacking answers on whether and when to trust government and its employees, the neobureaucratic reformers are not soon going to retire. And their ropes on the self-interest of government cannot be ignored. As Joel Aberbach argues, "What we call red tape serves a variety of real purposes in government, including ensuring that groups can get access to the administration and guaranteeing fair procedures in decision making. Groups and citizens would miss the procedures and requirements that are at the core of red tape, should they lose them, and demand them back. Empowering an agency's employees by decentralizing decision making is likely to fall victim to the first significant scandal that occurs (as it inevitably will in any organization), with Congress reacting by putting restrictions in place to prevent future scandals."[14] Thus would the liberation tide go out and two others, war on waste and watchful eye, come in.

Much as the postbureaucratic reformers might flinch, their "new era" rhetoric would be remarkably familiar to Andrew Jackson and his spoilsmen of the 1830s. Jackson wanted freedom from the staid bureaucratic routines of the early Federalists and saw his mission as "empowering" citizens. The language might be different, updated to keep pace with an information society, but the impulse that led one Tennessean to proclaim a new era of government in

1830 is hardly different from the instincts that led another to call for reinventing anew more than 150 years later.

In a sense, therefore, declaring any idea as innovative is risky business. Because innovation challenges the prevailing wisdom, its definition is dependent on just what the prevailing wisdom is. It can be large or small, but innovation must above all be different. In the case of making government work, the prevailing wisdom over the past fifty years has been mostly scientific management. Because of its dominance in the early years covered by this study, any effort to measure the newness of ideas is going to define scientific management as mostly old.

Yet just as surely as the tides come and go, scientific management will someday soon be easily defined as new. Just as Jackson's image of good government eventually prompted the rise of the merit system, so, too, will reinventing government someday soon provoke another reinventing. The danger is to confuse a short-term rush of support for a long-term acceptance of reform. Having failed to answer the essential question of whether and when to trust government and its employees, and, therefore, having rejected the notion of carefully designed tests, each new reform movement carries the seeds of its own eventual demise.

For the time being, however, this book can only look backward in time to track the ebb and flow of ideas in good currency over the past fifty years. According to table 5.3, scientific management is definitely "out" and liberation management "in." The table also confirms that innovation, large and small, involves a different set of histories, strategies, tactics, and impacts from simply building on past success.

Starting with time, the post-1974 era shows the greatest share of new ideas, large or small. The final quarter of the twentieth century has been anything but staid, with new/small ideas of particular prominence in the final decade of the period covered by this book. The choice of "reassessment" to label the 1970s appears particularly apt, for the decade involved a mix of old and new. In a sense, the 1970s offered the last gasp for the kinds of old/small ideas that were so often carried through reorganization plans. When the president's reorganization authority lapsed in the 1980s, to be renewed but once in 1984 and then only for the briefest moment, government lost a particularly valuable device for making the kinds of small-scale adjustments to existing practice that are neither big enough to attract congressional interest nor small enough to be executed through departmental order.

This is not to argue that large-scale reorganizations are easy, of course. As the organizational theorists James March and Johan Olsen conclude, "Neither presidents nor congresses succeed often in major reorganization projects. What is proposed is regularly defeated or abandoned. Presidents, in particu-

Table 5.3 Evolution of Ideas (percentages)

	New/ Large	New/ Small	Old/ Large	Old/ Small
Time				
Era				
Pre-1974	47	37	45	40
Post-1974	53	63	55	60
Decade				
Glory Days	21	11	25	22
Great Society	18	11	10	11
Reassessment	37	37	30	29
New Proceduralism	.24	42	35	38
Legislative History				
President's Party				
Democratic	50	29	55	40
Republican	50	71	45	60
Congressional Party				
Democratic	90	74	80	84
Republican	3	3	10	4
Divided Between Chambers	8	24	10	11
Party Control of Government				
Unified	53	32	45	44
Divided	47	68	55	56
Origin of Idea				
President	63	37	40	40
Congress	37	63	60	60
Blue-Ribbon Commission Involved?	11	11	20	16
Interest Groups Involved?	40	29	35	18
Legislative Debate				
Routine	40	71	35	67
Controversial	61	29	65	33
Legislative Passage				
Unanimous	29	58	55	56
Near-Unanimous	40	21	25	27
Strong Majority (60 or more)	26	18	0	13
Close (less than 60)	5	3	20	4
Recorded Vote Taken?	71	50	70	56
Philosophy				
Tide				
Scientific Management	42	37	50	49
War on Waste	16	24	15	18
Watchful Eye	21	16	30	29
Liberation Management	21	24	5	4

Table 5.3 (Continued)

	New/ Large	New/ Small	Old/ Large	Old/ Small
Purity of Statute				
No Other Tides Found in Statute	68	79	70	67
One Other Tide Found	24	18	25	24
Two Other Tides Found	8	3	5	9
Primary Accountability Mechanism				
Compliance	32	40	45	44
Capacity	58	42	50	38
Performance	11	18	5	18
General View of Government				
Trusting	42	61	35	49
Distrusting	58	40	65	51
Change Strategy				
Focus				
Structure of Government	47	45	45	31
Procedures of Government	34	55	50	66
Both	18	0	0	0
Create a Study Commission	0	0	5	2
Structural Tactic				
Create New Agency	32	21	10	0
Merge Existing Agencies	13	13	10	0
Reorganize Existing Agency	5	0	10	13
Create Public Corporation	5	5	5	2
Abolish Existing Agency	8	3	0	0
Grant Agency Independence	0	0	5	7
Elevate Agency to Higher Status	3	0	5	2
Combination	0	3	0	4
No Structural Reform in Statute	34	55	55	69
Procedural Tactic				
Establish New System	40	40	0	2
Broaden System	0	3	30	29
Revise System	0	0	10	18
Deregulate/Narrow System	8	13	0	4
Reauthorize System	0	0	10	13
Abolish System	0	0	0	0
Combination	3	0	0	0
No Procedural Reform in Statute	47	45	50	33
Target				
General Organization of Government	53	34	45	31
Procurement/Acquisition	38	21	5	9
Ethics/Standards of Conduct	8	8	15	13

Table 5.3 (Continued)

	New/ Large	New/ Small	Old/ Large	Old/ Small
Administrative Process	8	3	10	7
Pay Systems	0	3	0	13
Audit/Investigation	0	5	15	4
Rulemaking Procedures	5	8	0	2
General Personnel/Classification	3	3	5	4
Budget/Financial Management	13	0	0	4
Combination	3	3	5	7
Strategic Planning/Analysis	3	3	0	2
Debt Collection	0	5	0	2
Tort Claims	3	3	0	0
Implementation				
Experimental Approach in Statute?	8	5	0	0
Time Horizon in Statute				
Temporary/Sunset	11	11	15	20
Permanent	90	90	85	80
Scope				
Single Agency	45	42	30	27
Several Agencies	13	11	20	16
Governmentwide	42	47	50	58
Oversight Approach				
Centralized	50	37	55	60
Decentralized	50	63	45	40
Impact				
Shift in Shared Powers				
Toward President	53	45	50	44
Toward Congress	32	18	45	24
Not Clear/No Shift Discernible	16	37	5	31
Impact on Cost of Government				
Increase	45	29	20	9
Decrease	16	5	5	7
Not Clear/No Impact Discernible	40	66	75	84
Impact on Role of Government				
Expand	34	32	30	24
Contract	24	11	0	4
Not Clear/No Impact Discernible	42	58	70	71
Impact on Shape of Government				
Thicken Hierarchy	71	53	80	42
Thin Hierarchy	21	18	5	13
Not Clear/No Impact Discernible	8	29	15	44

Table 5.3 (Continued)

	New/ Large	New/ Small	Old/ Large	Old/ Small
Impact on Administrative Speed				
Accelerate	40	45	35	27
Slow Down	26	18	35	29
Not Clear/No Impact Discernible	31	37	30	44
Impact on Interest Group Access				
Enhance	26	16	20	9
Reduce	26	18	40	20
Not Clear/No Impact Discernible	47	66	40	71
Impact on Public Access				
Enhance	29	16	25	9
Reduce	11	3	10	7
Not Clear/No Impact Discernible	61	82	65	84
Impact on Government Morale				
Improve	16	26	35	29
Reduce	8	0	0	0
Not Clear/No Impact Discernible	76	74	65	71
Impact on Bureaucratic Balance				
Strengthen Line Units	47	47	40	49
Strengthen Staff Units	37	40	60	47
Not Clear/No Impact Discernible	16	13	0	4

N = 141

lar, go through a cycle of enthusiasm and disappointment. Most commonly (Franklin Roosevelt and Richard Nixon are particular counterexamples), they start reorganization studies at the beginning of their terms, but by the time the studies are completed, they seem to have concluded that reorganization either will not solve their administrative problems or will not be worth the political costs."[15]

Such large-scale reorganizations are not the stuff of which reorganization plans were made, however. To the contrary. The vast majority of the fifty-three reorganization plans (which are recorded as thirteen entries in Appendix A) covered relatively small adjustments of the prevailing order—transferring the Bureau of Economic Security from the Federal Security Agency (which would become part of the new Department of HEW) to Labor in 1949, reorganizing the Internal Revenue Service in 1952, transferring regulatory responsibilities from the Federal Maritime Board to the Commerce Department's Maritime Administration in 1961 or the Community Relations Service from Commerce to Justice in 1966, and merging the Peace Corps and VISTA under the umbrella of ACTION in 1971. (Hence, eleven of the thirteen reorganization plans fall into the small/old category.)

Although there are exceptions to the small-scale nature of most reorganization plans—most notably creation of the Department of HEW in Reorganization Plan No. 1 of 1953 and the Environmental Protection Agency under Reorganization Plan No. 3 in 1970—the president's reorganization authority has served more often as a tool for fine-tuning than an instrument for major reform. And when it did perform this latter role, it almost invariably provoked strong congressional resistance, as in Truman's two efforts to create HEW in the late 1940s. Although future administrations called for restoration of reorganization authority, as Clinton's did in the fine print of *Creating a Government That Works Better and Costs Less,* Congress is not likely to budge. It is Congress, not the executive branch itself, that is now the source of most fine-tuning.

Small-scale innovation is much more likely to involve Republican presidents and divided government, while large-scale innovation is more likely to be linked to Democratic presidents and Democratic Congresses. Given their frequent marriages with large Democratic congressional majorities, Republican presidents may have had little choice but to favor the small over the large. "There was no point in presenting a full set of comprehensive programs," a Ford legislative liaison staffer told me in explaining the White House preference for small-scale domestic policy ideas. "Congress would not have acted. Even if we had moved a series of heavy measures, we wouldn't have won. After the 1974 midterms, we only had 144 Republicans in the House. How could we hope for any major success?"[16]

Such political calculations aside, Republicans may also have a natural preference for small-scale reforms. A Nixon aide explained the administration's attraction to new/small domestic proposals: "We had several critical items, but our preference was to start with a smaller intervention and see how it worked. Our orientation was to present the first draft as a limited program and build on it later."[17]

Republican presidents are not alone in thinking that small is beautiful, at least as far as management reform goes. The Republican Senate that served with Ronald Reagan also preferred small-scale initiatives over large. Of the nine initiatives that originated in the Republican Senate during 1981–1986, six were new/small initiatives: the Prompt Payment Act, the Debt Collection Act, Competition in Contracting, a new federal retirement system, the Program Fraud and Civil Remedies Act, and the Federal Debt Recovery Act.

As the titles suggest, innovation in the Republican Senate meant innovation in the war on waste. Two of the six gave the federal government new tools for collecting bad debts, two provided new procedures for spurring lower costs, and one created incentives for prompt payments and new penalties for late payments to contractors. Even the new retirement system involved significant budget savings, in the form of higher employee payments into a system modeled on the rising tide of 401(k) plans in the private sector. It is not immediately clear why the Republican Senate preferred smallness in the war on waste. It was certainly not fear of the House. Indeed, House Democrats probably would have accepted larger-scale initiatives on competition in contracting, debt collection, and prompt pay. Members were particularly attracted to anything that would give the OIGs more tools in the search for fraud, waste, and abuse.

Rather, it may be that the Senate Governmental Affairs Committee simply preferred to go small. Although it was not committed to an experimental ethic per se, the committee did show a growing fascination during the 1980s with using small-scale initiatives as a wedge in a long-term battle against waste and inefficiency. It produced the first of its four experimental statutes in 1986 (the Debt Recovery Act) and laid the legislative groundwork for both the Chief Financial Officers Act and the Government Performance and Results Act, both of which contained clear commitments to pilots as a first step toward full-scale implementation.

The committee's interest in experimentation survived the transition back to a Democratic majority following the 1986 elections. The committee promptly expanded the Prompt Payment Act, and it criminalized procurement fraud later the same year, building on its earlier small-scale work with two slightly larger reforms. It also produced the two other experiments: the Regulatory Negotiation Act, which encouraged agencies to try the new technique for producing rules, and the Government Performance and Results Act, which established a series of pilots leading to governmentwide performance plans and outcomes measurement. There is simply no evidence elsewhere in Congress—or the White House, for that matter—of a similar commitment to trial and error.

Divided government also appears to be healthy for generating small-scale initiatives. Recall, for example, that roughly half of all initiatives produced in divided Congresses involve new/small ideas. So noted, divided party control of government also produces old/small ideas. Almost 40 percent of the initiatives produced in divided government fall into this less innovative category, another 25 percent fall into new/small, 20 percent into new/large, and just 16 percent into old/large. Unified government may produce a higher *percentage* of new/large initiatives, but not a larger *absolute* number. Of the twenty-nine new/large reforms recorded in Appendix A, seventeen came from divided government.

The question is where the instinct for innovation arises. Elsewhere in table 5.3, the answer appears to be Congress. It is the presidency that more frequently supports the expansion of old systems and structures, and the Congress that more often pushes against the prevailing wisdom. And, as noted in Chapter 4, it is the Senate, not the House, that most often incubates the new/small ideas. This may be the Senate's job, of course. Freed from the constant campaigning that representatives must do, buffeted by national issues in their elections, often imagining a future of their own in the White House, perhaps the Senate is simply the more natural source of innovation.[18]

Three factors intersect to make new/small ideas the most routine of legislative issues. The first is that the new/small category contains a very high number of war on waste ideas. Nine of the twenty-six entries involve this most popular of the tides. The second is that a very high percentage of new/small ideas comes from Congress, which, as noted earlier, goes much easier on its own initiatives. The third is that new/small ideas are inherently attractive to Congress. They allow a margin of credit-claiming for something new, but relatively low risk of great controversy.

The tides show different preferences regarding the scope of ideas. Because it is the dominant tide during the early period studied here, scientific management locates heavily in the old categories. Recall that exactly half of all scientific management initiatives are old/small ideas, with another 19 percent in the old/large category.

So noted, scientific management still shows the largest percent of new/small ideas, accounting for fourteen of the thirty-eight items in the category. Scientific management clearly had its day in redefining the prevailing wisdom. Alas for its advocates, that day is now long past. Two thirds of its new/large reforms and 71 percent of its new/small ones came before 1974. It also had its day in defending its old success. Sixty percent of its old/large reforms and 64 percent of its old/small ones came before Watergate.

Not surprisingly, the timing patterns for the three other tides are mostly the opposite. One hundred percent of war on waste's new/large, new/small, and old/large reforms came after 1974, and only 38 percent of the old/small came before. For watchful eye, 37 percent of its new/large and 33 percent of its new/small and old/large reforms came before 1974, while 100 percent of its old/small ideas came after.

Given its current fashionability, it may be a bit of a surprise that a substantial minority of innovation in liberation management occurred before 1974: 37 percent of its new/large, 22 percent of its new/small, its one old/large (conversion of the Post Office Department into a government corporation), and 50 percent of its old/small reforms came before Watergate. Again, it is useful to remind liberation advocates that theirs is hardly a new venture in making government work. The postbureaucratic paradigm has been at work in the initiatives covered by this book since the 1950s.

The purity of statute is roughly equal across the four categories of ideas, with new/small initiatives freer perhaps to move forward on a single tide. Accountability mechanism is also roughly equal, the one exception being new/small initiatives, which show a split personality of sorts. Performance accountability highest under new/small, as is compliance. The former reflects the rather large influence of liberation management on the category, while the latter involves war on waste. Whereas scientific management shows its greatest strength in the old/small category and watchful eye in a mix of new/large and old/small, war on waste and liberation management have contested each other on new/small reforms.

The sharpest differences in table 5.3 involve general view of government, with new/small initiatives being the most likely to carry a more trusting view. The view confirms the role of distrust as the driver for major reforms, with old/large initiatives carrying the highest level, following by new/large. Although almost half the initiatives in Appendix A carry a trusting message to government and its employees, that message is clearly drowned out by the size of the initiatives that convey distrust.

Moreover, the strength of the message has changed over time. Whereas 86 percent of the new/small initiatives were trusting before 1974, just 46 percent were trusting after; whereas two thirds of the new/large initiatives were trusting before 1974, just 20 percent were trusting after. Perhaps this is why the postbureaucratic paradigm puts so much emphasis on customers as the driver of reform. Getting the customers to think positively of government is no small step toward addressing the rather staggering impact of distrust on making government work.

With regard to change strategy, the four categories show a mix of preferences toward structure and procedures. Old/small ideas concentrate most heavily on procedures, while new/large leans more toward structure. Indeed, the new/large category is the only one of the four that shows any percentage under the "both structure and procedure" category. The two best examples of this combination came in 1978. The Civil Service Reform Act simultaneously codified both a new personnel system and a split administrative structure composed of the Office of Personnel Management and the Merit Systems Protection Board, while the Ethics in Government Act established new financial disclosure and conflict of interest rules to be administered by the Office of Government Ethics.

The figures for implementation show a collection of expected results. It is hardly a surprise, for example, that experimentation would fall into the new category, large or small, or that single agencies would show up more frequently under the new category as well. Whereas old ideas concentrate on a broad mix of targets, innovation rarely focuses on several agencies at a time, choosing either a targeted approach (mostly liberation management) or a governmentwide implementation (mostly war on waste).

Whether single agency or governmentwide, however, new/small ideas in particular prefer decentralized implementation. In fact, decentralization is what makes many new/small ideas new. Looking back to Jackson yet again, of course, decentralization is anything but a new idea. It shows up as such here, again, as an artifact of the dominance of scientific management over the early decades covered in this analysis.

Most of the findings regarding impacts show similarly expected patterns, if any patterns at all. Old ideas of either size tend to strengthen the president, even as old/large ideas show the greatest shift toward Congress, most notably through revisions of great watchful eye reforms like the Freedom of Information Act amendments of 1974. New/large ideas have the greatest impact on the cost of government, while old ideas of either size expand the role of government and tend to strengthen line units over staff. The overall lack of differences within these cells is interesting because it confirms the inherent confusion about how best to make government work. Lacking an answer about when and where to trust government and its employees, reformers drift from one approach to another, marking the field more with confusion than clarity.

SHIFTING SHARED POWERS

A recurring theme in making the government work is just who will lead the effort. Congress has clearly been ascendant in reform during the post-Watergate period, becoming the most frequent originator of reform ideas. The question for the next few pages is to what extent reform has also shifted power to one institution or the other.

Making judgments about how a given reform might shift power toward one institution or the other is no small task. For every obvious decision, such as the Budget and Impoundment Control Act (toward Congress) or most agency creations (toward the president), there is one nearly impossible to assess, such as the Prompt Payment Act. Thus 34 of the 141 initiatives are left out of table 5.4, which summarizes patterns in the shift of shared power over administrative discretion. Of the 106 initiatives left, 69 shift power toward the president, 37 toward Congress.

The table shows the growing role of Congress as a voice in influencing, overseeing, and/or actually managing the operations of government. The president is still active, of course, and, as Reagan proved, can still shape the climate of reform in a way Congress cannot. Nevertheless, the president is no longer the one true master. It is a conclusion that becomes particularly clear when we look at the four decades separately. The president was much closer to being the one true master in the 1950s than the 1980s.

This finding is hardly novel to this analysis. A number of scholars, from Joel Aberbach to Donald Kettl, have noted the rising congressional interest in administration.[19] Focusing on congressional micromanagement in defense policy as his indicator, Kettl points out that twenty-nine committees and fifty-five subcommittees are directly or indirectly interested in the issue, giving Congress ample venues for developing policy ideas. Noting that Congress is criticized for overseeing government both too much and too little, Kettl concludes that "both sides are right. Congress often does not control administrative activities very effectively, and sometimes when it tries to exert control, it only makes things worse by dealing with micro-level details instead of macro-level policy."[20] In short, regardless of the result, Congress has the needed tools for reform, tools that I shall argue in the next chapter are in a state of disrepair at 1600 Pennsylvania Avenue.

As the legislative history cells in table 5.4 suggest, Congress once showed a greater generosity toward the presidency. Roughly four in ten reforms that originated in Congress actually shifted power down the Avenue, most coming in the pre-1974 period. In establishing the two Hoover Commissions, for example, Congress clearly accepted the general notion that the president should be in charge of administrative reform.

Even after Watergate, Congress was still quite capable of loaning the keys to administrative reform to the presidency. Congress gave the president sweeping authority to reduce the flow of paperwork under the Paperwork Reduction Act of 1980, for example, authority that Reagan used to build a regulatory clearance process under Executive Order 12498. Using the Paperwork Act to require agency compliance, the order created a cradle-to-grave agenda-setting process clearly designed to slow, if not kill, regulatory activism in the executive branch. Given a chance to reduce the president's authority when the act came up for reauthorization during the 1980s, liberal members of Congress fought to change the statute but were able only to delay the inevitable.

Congress still shows a surprising readiness to defer to the commander in chief with regard to war on waste. Although table 5.4 does not quite reveal a "two presidencies" phenomenon—a label that Aaron Wildavsky once used to describe what he saw as the president's greater freedom to act in foreign policy—it does suggest a willingness to strengthen presidential authority as long

Table 5.4 Shifts in Institutional Balance (percentages)

	Toward the Presidency	Toward Congress
Time		
Era		
Pre-1974	74	26
Post-1974	53	47
Decade		
Glory Days	87	12
Great Society	69	31
Reassessment	56	44
New Proceduralism	50	50
Legislative History		
President's Party		
Democratic	70	30
Republican	58	42
Congressional Party		
Democratic	60	40
Republican	100	0
Divided Between Chambers	75	25
Party Control of Government		
Unified	71	29
Divided	57	43
Origin of Idea		
President	84	16
Congress	40	60
Blue-Ribbon Commission Involved?	83	17
Interest Groups Involved?	62	39
Legislative Debate		
Routine	63	38
Controversial	52	54
Legislative Passage		
Unanimous	61	39
Near-Unanimous	57	43
Strong Majority (60 or more)	79	21
Close (less than 60)	67	33
Recorded Vote Taken?	61	39
Philosophy		
Tide		
Scientific Management	91	9
War on Waste	72	27
Watchful Eye	0	100
Liberation Management	53	47

Table 5.4 (Continued)

	Toward the Presidency	Toward Congress
Purity of Statute		
No Other Tides Found in Statute	59	41
One Other Tide Found	67	33
Two Other Tides Found	100	0
Primary Accountability Mechanism		
Compliance	24	77
Capacity	81	19
Performance	86	14
General View of Government		
Trusting	87	13
Distrusting	37	63
Change Strategy		
Focus		
Structure of Government	72	28
Procedures of Government	52	48
Both	50	50
Create a Study Commission	100	0
Structural Tactic		
Create New Agency	64	36
Merge Existing Agencies	92	8
Reorganize Existing Agency	100	0
Create Public Corporation	20	80
Abolish Existing Agency	100	0
Grant Agency Independence	0	100
Elevate Agency to Higher Status	67	33
Combination	100	0
No Structural Reform in Statute	58	42
Procedural Tactic		
Establish New System	29	71
Broaden System	36	64
Revise System	83	17
Deregulate/Narrow System	86	14
Reauthorize System	57	43
Abolish System	100	0
Combination	100	0
No Procedural Reform in Statute	73	27
Target		
General Organization of Government	77	23
Procurement/Acquisition	100	0
Ethics/Standards of Conduct	0	100

Table 5.4 (Continued)

	Toward the Presidency	Toward Congress
Administrative Process	0	100
Pay Systems	80	20
Audit/Investigation	0	100
Rulemaking Procedures	75	25
General Personnel/Classification	100	0
Budget/Financial Management	75	25
Combination	80	20
Strategic Planning/Analysis	0	100
Debt Collection	0	0
Tort Claims	0	0
Scale		
Nature of Idea		
New Approach	66	35
Modification of Old	61	39
Scope of Impact		
Large	59	41
Small	67	33
Overall Scale of Reform		
New/Large	63	38
New/Small	71	29
Old/Large	53	47
Old/Small	65	36
Implementation		
Experimental Approach in Statute?	67	33
Time Horizon in Statute		
Temporary/Sunset	69	31
Permanent	62	38
Scope		
Single Agency	69	30
Several Agencies	80	20
Governmentwide	48	53
Oversight Approach		
Centralized	75	25
Decentralized	48	52
Impact		
Impact on Cost of Government		
Increase	85	15
Decrease	57	43
Not Clear/No Impact Discernible	53	48

Table 5.4 (Continued)

	Toward the Presidency	Toward Congress
Impact on Role of Government		
Expand	88	13
Contract	91	9
Not Clear/No Impact Discernible	40	60
Impact on Shape of Government		
Thicken Hierarchy	55	45
Thin Hierarchy	80	20
Not Clear/No Impact Discernible	88	13
Impact on Administrative Speed		
Accelerate	81	19
Slow Down	18	82
Not Clear/No Impact Discernible	78	22
Impact on Interest Group Access		
Enhance	61	39
Reduce	38	62
Not Clear/No Impact Discernible	76	24
Impact on Public Access		
Enhance	16	84
Reduce	29	71
Not Clear/No Impact Discernible	78	22
Impact on Government Morale		
Improve	52	48
Reduce	100	0
Not Clear/No Impact Discernible	67	33
Impact on Bureaucratic Balance		
Strengthen Line Units	81	19
Strengthen Staff Units	41	59
Not Clear/No Impact Discernible	44	56

$N = 106$

as the goal is ferreting out fraud, waste, and abuse.[21] Thus did many of the war on waste reforms of the early 1980s redound to the president's favor.

Congress may go much easier on its own ideas, but not necessarily on ideas that shift power to Congress. This finding reflects the controversy surrounding watchful eye, which never shifts power toward the presidency. Although Congress has clearly been the leader on watchful eye, there is little congressional unanimity as one pages back through the great debates over Freedom of

Information, the Privacy Act, Government in the Sunshine, and Ethics in Government. Members of Congress were and still are sharply divided over how much authority to take from the president, and they clearly recognize the trade-offs between opening government to the sunshine and assuring protection for individual citizens.

The trade-off was clear, for example, in passage of the 1978 IG Act, when the Senate refused to accept a House amendment that would have waived Privacy Act protections in the hunt for fraud. The House wanted the exemption to accelerate the use of computer-matching programs, while the Senate viewed the provision as much too threatening to individual rights. As the Senate Governmental Affairs Committee explained its objection: "The House language would grant to the Inspector and Auditor General [the Senate's preferred title for the IGs] a power that no other official of the executive branch has—the authority to require the transfer of personal information from any agency to the Inspector and Auditor General without regard for the protections of the Privacy Act. . . . Even if the committee believed that the Privacy Act hampered the carrying out of matching programs, the House language would still be troublesome. Matching programs constitute a very small part of the Inspector and Auditor General's work, but the exemption sought for those few cases would be a substantial loophole."[22]

The Senate prevailed in its defense of the Privacy Act, confirming its long-standing commitment to watchful eye, but lost on the title, confirming the House's emphasis on war on waste. The Senate had championed the Auditor and Inspector General title in an effort to lighten the war on waste rhetoric from the House. The title had been recommended by the General Accounting Office as a way to make sure auditing did not get lost in the new OIGs: "The name of the organizations established by the bill will set the tone for how they operate."[23]

Philosophical shifts toward one institution or the other clearly involve different tides, accountability mechanisms, and general views of government. Shifts toward the presidency are much more likely to involve scientific management and war on waste, while shifts toward Congress occur more frequently under liberation management. As already noted, watchful eye is unequivocally a shift toward Congress.

The two institutions prosper under very different accountability mechanisms. Compliance is the central tool in shifts toward Congress. Compliance allows Congress to conduct the kind of relatively inexpensive fire-alarm oversight that often results in greater visibility back in home districts, using the IGs, media, and individual citizens to pull the alarms. Compliance also establishes baselines against which Congress can hold the executive branch accountable. These baselines may be little more than simple checklists of expected behavior, but they are baselines nonetheless. As I have suggested elsewhere, compliance accountability produces findings that involve higher volume, visibility, ease of measurement, and credit-claiming yield for Congress, and it can be strengthened at lower cost and in less time with much greater legislative consensus and jurisdictional neatness than either performance or capacity accountability: "A high degree of political consensus surrounds the simple goal of most compliance recommendations: to punish the cheaters and abusers. Republicans and Democrats rarely disagree; liberals and conservatives have plenty of common ground. But when the issue is one of paying employees for successful performance or recruiting the best and brightest to government, those agreements quickly break down. Why pay for something government workers should produce automatically? Why hire the most capable when the less capable (and less expensive) will do?"[24]

The link between compliance and Congress reflects a distrusting view of government. Only by writing clear rules and creating credible enforcement can government and its employees be expected to do the right thing. Unlike performance accountability, which puts its faith in incentives, or capacity, which puts its faith in technologies (people, structures, training), compliance argues that the incentives are weak predictors of behavior. Congress has supported performance accountability over the years, most notably in the pay-for-performance provisions of the CSRA, but its preference for watchful eye tips the balance in table 5.4 toward compliance.

Change strategy also shows clear patterns in institutional balance. With regard to structure, the presidency benefits in the institutional tug-of-war by creating new agencies and merging or reorganizing old, while Congress is strengthened only in creating public corporations and granting agency independence. Congress benefits by creating new procedures and expanding old, while the presidency is strengthened only by revising, deregulating, reauthorizing, and abolishing old. The reason reauthorizations show strengthening of the presidency is simple: Congress tends to put shorter time lines on statutes that strengthen the presidency.

These differences hold on the target of reform, too. The presidency is strengthened when reform involves the general organization of government, procurement/acquisition reform (where six of the fifteen initiatives fall into the "not clear" category), pay systems, rulemaking, budget/financial management, and combinations of the above. It is important to note that not all initiatives in Appendix A are created equal. The presidency may have benefited from most of the budget and accounting reforms during the period covered by this book, but Congress won the one reform that mattered most, the 1974 Budget and Impoundment Control Act.

Congress is strengthened when reform involves ethics, administrative process, audit/investigation, and strategic planning (where two of just three initiatives fall to Congress). The three most important statutes in the audit/investigation category are all IG acts, which explains why every agency called to testify on the 1978 IG Act argued against passage. As Else Porter, then assistant secretary for administration at the Department of Commerce, argues, the opposition involved the dual reporting relationship to Congress and the president: "It boggles the mind! Had the legislation merely created the IGs in GAO's image and left them as the agency's relatively independent auditing and investigating arm, reporting to the head of the agency, I think the model might work. But in forcing dual allegiance (and, therefore, dual dependency) of the IG to both the Executive and Congress, the legislation creates an enormous problem of trust for the IGs to overcome. Put another way, it plants the seeds of distrust."[25]

Congress is favored more by large-scale reform and combinations thereof. It also benefits in governmentwide reforms, an artifact of the role of watchful eye in shifting power toward Congress, and is favored by decentralization. To the extent the unity of command is weakened, Congress benefits. Conversely, the presidency is strengthened by small-scale reforms, an artifact of changing congressional attitudes toward executive authority. Bluntly put, Congress has grown increasingly reluctant to grant authority to the presidency except in small-scale reforms, a point well made in the reluctance to reauthorize the Reorganization Act in recent years.

The final set of shifts in institutional balance involve questions of the cost, role, speed, and shape of government. Interestingly, the presidency tends to benefit in initiatives that either increase/expand/thicken or decrease/contract/thin the cost, role, and shape of government. It may be that doing *either* is so difficult that the presidency can only be helped, while doing *neither* invariably helps Congress.

The presidency is also helped by initiatives that accelerate the administrative process, while Congress benefits from slowing down. The finding is a natural fit with the congressional preference for watchful eye. The more Congress can see what is going on in the executive branch, the more it is strengthened. Therein may lie the seeds of ultimate defeat for the NPR recommendations on reducing congressional micromanagement (mandated reports, budget earmarks, and so forth). Congress will almost always put its need to see ahead of a manager's need to act.

The most curious finding on the list involves public access, where Congress benefits in both increasing and decreasing access. The benefit from increasing is clearly linked to watchful eye. Recall that more than half of watchful eye initiatives enhance access, while none reduce it. The benefit from decreasing access involves a blend of initiatives that created public corporations, established a highly insulated multilayered pay-setting process, and the military base–closing commission. By simultaneously reducing the public's access and the president's authority, the five statutes strengthened Congress.

Thus far, this chapter has addressed what are mostly intended consequences of reform through what are ultimately blunt measures of controversy, images of what constitutes good government, and shifts of institutional power toward either end of Pennsylvania Avenue. Flawed as the measures are, the results suggest that the four tides have very different impacts, often clashing along the way.

There are other ways to assess the impact of reform, of course, most notably through case studies of specific statutes. There is general agreement, for example, that the Administrative Procedure Act has worked rather well in standardizing the rulemaking process while opening what are very important decisions to greater public scrutiny. At the same time, however, the Regulatory Negotiation Act clearly recognized that the APA process may bind agencies too tightly, resulting in long delays and needless conflict.

There is also general agreement that the Ethics in Government Act has worked well in deterring at least some of the conflicts of interest that face presidential appointees. In spite of the headlines about good appointees caught in seemingly minor mistakes, the statute has no doubt screened out many unsuitable individuals who might have otherwise served. Its success notwithstanding, there is no doubt the Ethics in Government Act has also exacted a toll on the speed of the appointments process. As the political scientist G. Calvin Mackenzie argues, "The modern presidential appointments process barely resembles its constitutional design or intent. In fact, it differs dramatically from the way presidents made appointments as recently as the late 1940s. There are more jobs to fill than ever before, and many of them have complex and technical duties. The appointment process is much more formal and structured. It takes longer, often many months longer, to fill an appointive position than it did just a few decades ago. And the process is more visible and consistently contentious than ever."[26]

In a sense, ethics reform is both a cause and a consequence of the changes. It clearly added a time-consuming burden to the appointive process, a burden illustrated in Mackenzie's figures on the length of time needed to make the key appointments at the start of a presidential term. Yet it was also a product of the increasing congressional and media scrutiny of the executive branch, and of growing public concerns about the role of money in politics.

Unfortunately, even the most detailed case studies of reform may end up yielding more heat than light. My effort to measure the impact of the IG Acts resulted in a rather frustrating inventory of tepid indicators of success. Whether one looks at the professionalism of the OIGs, staffing ratios, amount of savings claimed, quality of outputs, or visibility of results, the bottom line is always the same—rather, there *is* no bottom line for measuring how well a reform makes government work. It is a problem to be addressed in more detail in the next chapter. Suffice it to note here that government has virtually no established baselines against which to measure its success.

Beyond hunch, the occasional measure of activity (audits performed, files processed, forms received), and customer satisfaction surveys, reformers have little basis for claiming either success or failure. The lack of hard baselines may be one reason why customer service standards are so popular these days in the reinventing movement. Flawed as they can be, and contrary to the founders' intent as they most certainly are, such surveys at least allow some tracking of performance. On the old notion that one can't beat something with nothing, those who argue against customer satisfaction are obligated to push forward with alternative measures.

6

Against the Tides

The Danish Conqueror, on his royal chair,
Mustering a face of haughty sovereignty,
To Aid a covert purpose, cried—"O ye
Approaching Waters of the deep, that share
With this green isle my fortunes, come not where
Your Master's throne is set."—Deaf was the Sea;
Her waves rolled on, respecting his decree
Less than they heed a breath of wanton air.
—William Wordsworth, "A Fact and on Imagination or,
Canute and Alfred, on the Seashore," 1816

The tides of reform can no more be ordered to a halt than can the tides of the ocean. Those who long for an end to reinventing government are little more than modern-day King Canutes, doomed to failure as the waves of reform roll on. Just as the high tide swallowed King Canute's throne, so, too, will their calls fall on deaf congressional and presidential ears.

Yet if the tides of reform cannot be stopped, perhaps their impact can somehow be lessened, even deflected. Just as coastal cities can protect themselves against high tides and hurricanes by careful engineering, tidal gates, and ocean jetties, perhaps the federal government can be insulated against the hurricanes of reform by better analysis and greater experimentation. Even though analysis and experimentation smack of scientific management, they may be well worth the long-term investment.

To accept the inevitability of the tides is not to deny the value of building on higher ground. And to acknowledge the futility of beach restorations, which so often wash away with the next great storm, is not to refute the returns from occasionally battening down the hatches. Moreover, even as reformers wonder how to protect government against the inevitable tidal surges, they might challenge themselves to think about ways to change the climate of reform and the force of gravity. Continuing to sit at the dock of the bay just watching the tides of reform roll in is worse than a waste of time if those tides wash over the dock and drown the tide watcher.

THE PROBLEM WITH THE TIDES

Naturalists might argue that efforts to slow or redirect the tides of the ocean are futile at best, harmful at worst. Far better to let the tides work their will even if that work sometimes produces damage and frustration. Building jetties and altering climates is not only aesthetically offensive to the environment, or so the naturalist might argue, but expensive and mostly unsuccessful.

Analogous risks hold for changing the tides of reform, not the least of which is raising the cost of trying new ideas and making needed investments in capacity. Tidal gates close off all the water entering a bay, not just the water tide watchers like the least. Nevertheless, there are at least four patterns in the tides discussed in this book that make an effort at reforming how Congress and the president make government work.

Accretion

The first reason to abandon bureaucratic naturalism is that the tides of reform create *cumulative,* not isolated, effects. Ironically, whereas the impact of the ocean tides is often erosion, the tides of management reform appear always to produce accretion, whether in the form of paperwork, rules, or administrative thickening—that is, more layers of management and more managers at each layer.

Between 1960 and 1992, for example, the number of assistant secretaries devoted to advisory functions—budget, evaluation, acquisitions, personnel, and so forth—grew from thirty-five to eighty-eight, as each tide worked its will on the thickening of government. Scientific and liberation management combined to produce a rise in the number of assistant secretaries for evaluation, planning, and policy analysis from three in 1960 to fourteen in 1992, while the war on waste boosted the number of budget, controller, and chief financial officer titles from five to seventeen, and accounted for the rise in the number of IG slots from three to fourteen. And although all departments had general counsels in 1960, watchful eye most certainly affected the number of staff, which grew fivefold over the period.[1]

Whatever the tide involved, each one of these new staff assistant secretariats acquired its own support staff, agenda, and constituency. In an expression of organizational isomorphism—which is simply a formal way of restating Senator Daniel Patrick Moynihan's Iron Law of Emulation—each one of these units became more like the other. And, in doing so, each one became extremely difficult to abolish. Hence, the National Performance Review recommended "reorienting" the inspectors general but certainly not abolishing them.

Even the effort to thin government can require a certain amount of thickening. Clinton may have ordered a 50 percent reduction in "internal management regulations" under Executive Order 12861, but he needed regulations in order to enforce it. He also needed regulations to create streamlining plans, require annual reports to customers, enforce paperwork reduction, and honor commitments to small, small disadvantaged, and small women-owned businesses. As for the target of the 50 percent cut, "internal management regulations" were defined only as "an agency directive or regulation that pertains to its organization, management, or personnel management," meaning that regulations of the kind found in statutes like the Administrative Procedure Act were off limits.

It may never be known just how much regulation Clinton actually cut. Certainly, procurement and personnel regulation fell sharply under the order. Whether the drop offset the new requirements for streamlining and customer service standards is not clear. It is interesting to note, however, that Executive Order 12861, cutting regulations, was quickly followed by Executive Order 12863, requiring departments and agencies to create streamlining plans. As excerpts from the latter order itself suggest, creating streamlining plans was hardly a paperless exercise:

1. Each executive department's and agency's plans should address, among other things, the means by which it will reduce the ratio of managers and supervisors to other personnel, with a goal of reducing the percentage who are supervisors or managers in halving the current ratio within 5 years.

2. The streamlining plans should be characterized by (a) delegation of authority, (b) decentralization, (c) empowerment of employees to make decisions, and (d) mechanisms to hold managers and employees accountable for their performance.
3. Each plan shall address ways to reduce overcontrol and micromanagement that now generate "red tape" and hamper efficiency in the Federal Government. Each streamlining plan should also propose specific measures to simplify the internal organization and administrative processes of the department or agency.
4. The streamlining plans should further seek to realize cost savings, improve the quality of Government services, and raise the morale and productivity of the department or agency.[2]

One can almost feel the drafter struggling to break free of the traditional command-and-control language of most executive orders. But an order is an order, in this case meaning that it must generate micromanagement in order to reduce it, and create extra paperwork for the federal employees about to be liberated.

Comprehensiveness

The second problem with naturalism is that the tides are increasingly concerned with *comprehensive,* governmentwide effects. As noted in Chapter 3, the number of new/large initiatives may have declined over time, but the number of governmentwide reforms has grown steadily. Congress and the president may be increasingly trading size against scope. "The problem with most strategic reforms," write the organizational scholars George Downs and Patrick Larkey of comprehensive policy initiatives, "is that they involve so many details with important consequences for 'Who gets what, when, and how' that they can never be implemented without losing their basic character to the point that they are unrecognizable as well as ineffectual. Most of the time they do not get implemented at all but simply persist in the background as hollow monuments to great expectations and great naïveté."[3]

The advantage of small-scale, targeted reforms is not in lower cost, however. Indeed, such reforms may be just as expensive to design and launch as governmentwide reform, if not more so. Nevertheless, targeted initiatives have lower political costs, are most certainly less expensive to evaluate and terminate, and can be more easily allowed to fail. Alas, because their resulting credit-claiming yield for members of Congress is corresponding lower than comprehensive reform, small-scale reforms may be much more expensive to pass. "If it is widely believed that billions are casually tossed away through bureaucratic waste," Downs and Larkey argue, "it is hard to capture much political attention and inspire political support by advocating modest programs that save a few hundred thousand or even a million dollars."[4] Hence the tendency is always to go comprehensive.

Consider the call for decentralization. There is no question that decentralization is an idea in good currency. Witness the Clinton administration's de facto dismantlings of the Office of Personnel Management (OPM) and the last remnants of OMB's Division of Administrative Management. Some agencies have clearly earned the right to freedom, while others would best be monitored closely.

The risks of too much freedom are evident in the thickening of government. Federal managers have never done particularly well when given their freedom to classify positions. Indeed, position management has been one of the few areas in government that has been highly decentralized for the better part of the last half century. And the result has been a steady grade inflation at the hands of sometimes less-than-courageous managers.

Congress held hearings on the problem as early as 1949 and demanded annual reviews of position classification under the Whitten Amendment in 1952. Lacking strong enforcement from the Civil Service Commission, the precursor to OPM, the inflation continued; the average grade rose from roughly 5.5 on a 16-point scale in 1956 to 6.6 in 1961 and 7.8 by 1970.[5] Although the changing mix of federal jobs clearly produced some of the increase, so, too, did abuse of agency discretion, a fact noted by GAO in a particularly critical 1975 assessment of the role of managers in grade creep: "People are people," GAO argued on behalf of tighter central oversight. "Some may remain unaware of the legal requirements. Some will consciously flout the law, balancing the risk of discovery against the grade gains. Some will rationalize their actions on the grounds that higher grades will enhance mission accomplishments. Others will fragment duties to stay within the law but not within the spirit of the law."[6] That some agencies continue to abuse their position management authorities is indisputable. What has changed is OPM's ability to mount even a tepid oversight effort in the face of overwhelming pressure for decentralization.

It is no small irony, of course, that liberation management demands decentralization as an all-or-nothing option. Agencies have no choice but to accept the new authorities, even if they would prefer to remain under the comfortable tutelage of strong central agencies. The one-size-fits-all problem is hardly restricted to liberation management, however. All four tides have characteristically operated with a governmentwide zeal. Even scientific management and liberation management, which have the highest percentages of single- and several-agency implementations, are best seen as a comprehensive philosophy implemented selectively. If the Hoover Commissions and the NPR had any doubt about the ultimate value of governmentwide implementation, it is not evident in their rhetoric. The Hoover Commission's agency-by-agency reorganizations and the NPR's reinvention laboratories were but a proving ground for what was already assumed to be an inevitable expansion.

The fact is that not all agencies are created equally competent. It may be that tight hierarchies and specialization are particularly appropriate for certain kinds of high-volume processing agencies, such as the Social Security Administration or the Internal Revenue Service, but inappropriate for knowledge-producing agencies like the National Institutes of Health or NASA's Jet Propulsion Laboratory. It may also be that employee teams and empowerment are much more suitable for such highly professionalized workforces as air traffic controllers or customs inspectors but a poor fit for agencies with long histories of internal division or high vulnerability to fraud, waste, and abuse. The point here is simply to suggest the potential benefits of asking just where and when a given reform might fit best. Giving air traffic controllers the freedom to innovate is much easier to support after the plane has landed than before it takes off.

Contradictions

The third problem with bureaucratic naturalism is that the tides of reform often create *contradictory,* not compatible, effects. This is a recurring theme throughout this book. The four tides have different goals, inputs, products, participants, and champions, as well as very different defining moments, statutes, and patron saints.

War on waste emerges as the most compatible of the four streams. Even when it is clearly incompatible with another tide, as with liberation management, it is often attached as a selling point for passage. Thus, the NPR clearly advertised itself not as just a way to make government work better but also as a way to cut costs. War on waste is also surprisingly compatible with watchful eye, despite the fact that the two almost never appear together in the same statute. Both tides are driven by a distrustful general view of government and its employees, both thrive on openness and access to information, and both use compliance as a central tool of accountability. Where the two differ is in implementation, with war on waste focused on centralized oversight and watchful eye on decentralized.

Liberation management emerges as the least compatible of the four tides. Its champions pride themselves on having divorced themselves entirely from the machine bureaucracies of the 1930s. And, notwithstanding the occasional expressions of scientific management in the creation of chief operating officers and centralized oversight of streamlining plans, the tide has generally sustained a clear break with the past. Whereas scientific management, war on waste, and watchful eye all flow from a general acceptance of bureaucracy as an inevitable, if no longer quite so enviable instrument, liberation management is self-consciously disdainful of such compromises with structural machinery. It tends to view itself more as a social movement for rescuing government than as a mere engine of tinkering with the structure of the past.

Liberation management is a tide still very much in the making. It is not yet sure whether it is primarily about empowering the front line, liberating agencies to be more businesslike, creating market forces, or releasing managers from the Lilliputian ropes of internal management regulation. Much as its champions might declare it all of the above, privatization advocates on the right and union organizers on the left may soon force liberation management to choose between pure market forces and employee empowerment (and its focus on job security).

As if to prove its evolutionary character, there was even a time when liberation management could be described as a branch of scientific management, its current nemesis. At least in the 1960s and early 1970s, government corporations were viewed as just another form of structure, albeit a form that offered greater freedom to operate in a businesslike fashion—with profit-and-loss statements, for example, and greater personnel and procurement flexibility. There was no question, for example, that Congress and the president hoped that the U.S. Postal Service and Amtrak would operate in a businesslike fashion, with unified chains of command, narrow spans of control, staff assistance (if not for the president of the United States, then at least for the president of the corporation), and, ultimately, declining federal subsidies. Indeed, it was the businesslike nature of their work that gave Congress and the president confidence to grant the needed release from traditional personnel, procurement, and financial management routines.

As noted earlier, creating a government corporation today is much more a device for disguising an otherwise traditional bureaucracy than a way to achieve businesslike operations. Hence the National Service Corporation has absolutely no need to operate as a corporation, indeed has no source of revenue other than congressional appropriations, but was designated a corporation in large measure to make it look like something other than what it is.

Compatibility is, of course, partially driven by the institutional sponsor of reform. As Congress has become increasingly involved in making government work, the tides have become more clearly divided against each other. This may be a natural consequence of bicameralism. The differing electoral and policy goals of each chamber—and of the presidency, for that matter—create clear incentives to draw ever-sharper distinctions in each institution's view of how best to improve government, a point well made in the House-Senate debate on whether to give the IGs special authority to suspend the Privacy Act. To the extent that each institution has its own preferred tide, and to the extent that these tides are used to fulfill electoral and policy goals, the four tides will steadily drift apart, eventually making every relation between the tides incompatible.

Acceleration

The final problem with bureaucratic naturalism is that the tides of reform appear to be accelerating. The interval between the last reform and the next appears to be shrinking. More than a third of the 141 initiatives in Appendix A rolled in during the fourteen years from 1981 through 1994, compared with less than a fifth for the sixteen years from 1945 through 1960.

Part of the apparent acceleration comes from a more active Congress, part from the presence of three more active tides upon which to draw reform, and part from the fact that public distrust increases the political credit to be gained by claiming victories in making government work. Part may also involve the simple entropy of reform—that is, the more government is reformed, the more it needs reforming. If so, one can expect government to be increasingly littered with reform.

CHANGING THE TIDES

Given the potential cost to government of cumulative, comprehensive, conflicting, and accelerating tides, it seems reasonable to ask what might be done to improve the odds that the tides of reform might eventually come to complement each other. Much as one can admire the ebb and flow of the tides, perhaps there are ways to assure that the occasional hurricanes of reform do less damage, even as each tide contributes in its own way to making government work.

Consider three broad approaches that might serve as a starting point for debate: (1) building barriers to haphazard reform by strengthening institutional memory in Congress and the presidency, (2) working to restore public trust by addressing the broader causes of the current climate, and (3) changing the underlying pulls of reform by creating an ethic of experimentation in management reform. Table 6.1 summarizes the specific recommendations that follow.

Table 6.1 Recommendations Against the Tides

Building Tidal Barriers

In Congress

Create a Joint Congressional Committee on Federal Management

Require automatic and unrestricted sequential referral of all management reform bills to the House and Senate Government Reform/Governmental Affairs Committees

In the White House

Create a Special Assistant for Federal Management in the Office of General Counsel, Office of Policy Development, or a broadened Office of Presidential Personnel

Create an Office of Federal Management within the Executive Office of the President

In the Departments and Agencies

Create career-reserved statutory Undersecretaries and Underadministrators for Management appointed under five- to seven-year performance-based contracts

Governmentwide

Establish a "Clean-Out Commission" with a base-closure mechanism to present Congress and the president with a list of statutes for sunset

Altering the Climate for Reform

Make the renewal of civic life a central goal of the public administration/public management profession

Make the citizen a central concern of public administration/public management curricula

Altering the Gravitational Pulls of Reform

Create credible performance baselines against which to measure the impact of specific reforms

Promote an ethic of experimentation by using the Government Performance and Results Act waiver process to create credible tests of the four tides of reform

Allow for the creation of "charter agencies" modeled on charter schools as settings for government management experimentation

---

Building Tidal Barriers

One of the most important barriers to the hurricanes of reform is a deep institutional memory of what has come before. Although it hardly makes sense to ask reformers to read the *Federalist Papers* or Woodrow Wilson's 1887 paper on the study of administration, there is some value in deepening the institutional expertise available to reformers. Contrary to the urging of scientific management, this expertise cannot be available just to the president. Given its increased role in making government work, Congress must have its own sources of expertise, too.

Building Congressional Memory In theory, Congress has enormous access to institutional memory about making government work. The Congressional Research Service (CRS) of the Library of Congress has several of the top public administration scholars in the country, and the General Accounting Office (GAO) has nearly five thousand employees dedicated to answering congressional inquiries. In reality, however, the House and Senate have too much information and not enough memory. The CRS and GAO both complain that their agendas are increasingly dominated by individual member requests, leaving less time for the kind of governmentwide studies that might shed light on what works and what does not by way of government reform.

In a similar vein, every committee in Congress has the freedom to engage in government management reform. Unlike the revenue and appropriations committees, which have exclusive jurisdiction over their respective issue areas, dozens of committees and subcommittees were involved in the 141 initiatives covered by this book, from Judiciary and Commerce to Government Reform (formerly Government Operations) and Labor. Whether the norm of specialization exists anywhere on Capitol Hill today, it is most assuredly absent in government reform.

The question on Capitol Hill is not how to stimulate a greater interest in reform but how to reduce the cacophony of legislation. Consider two small steps. First, Congress could create a Joint Committee on Federal Management to parallel its already active Joint Committee on Taxation, which acts as a kind of "holding company" for a professional staff that works with the two tax-writing committees of Congress, and the Joint Economic Committee, which conducts ongoing studies and hearings on domestic and international economic issues.

Although Congress does conduct governmentwide management studies from time to time—most recently and notably the deep investigation conducted by Representative Stephen Horn's (R-Calif.) Government Reform and Oversight Subcommittee on Government Management, Information, and Technology—the costs of such efforts are prohibitive and exhaustive for an individual committee with other legislative duties. With a staff supplied by senior CRS and GAO specialists, a Joint Committee on Federal Management could conduct the kind of integrative research and hearings that might help its two client committees, Governmental Affairs in the Senate and Government Reform and Oversight in the House, discipline Congress as a whole.

Second, Congress could give these two committees much greater power to review government management legislation as it moves through other committees. The easiest path to such oversight is to grant the two committees automatic sequential referral on any legislation that would alter management practices anywhere in the federal government. Congress could also provide point-of-order authority for chairs of the two committees to challenge floor amendments in a similar fashion. Although the Senate Governmental Affairs Committee has such sequential authority on confirmation of inspectors general, which are ordinarily reviewed by the authorizing committee responsible for the given department or agency, the referral has an automatic discharge timer, meaning that the Committee rarely has enough time to conduct full review. Thus, any such referral and point-of-order authority would need to be unrestricted.

Building Presidential Memory The presidency faces a very different challenge in building institutional memory. In contrast to Congress, which has too much information and not enough memory, the presidency has experienced a broad disinvestment in information, some of it driven forward by Congress. Gone in the budget cuts of 1994 was the Advisory Commission on Intergovernmental Relations, a durable source of information on federal-state-local relations; gone, too, was the Administrative Conference of the United States, a small jewel of an agency dedicated to studying and improving administrative procedures across the government.

Much of the damage, however, came from simple neglect by the Executive Office of the President (EOP). Start with the decline of OMB's Division of Administrative Management and its once proud Organizational Studies unit as one sign of the steady narrowing of presidential advice on reform. As I have noted, the division was once a central player in the scientific management movement, staffing the first Hoover Commission and generating much of the analysis undergirding Nixon's "good people caught in bad systems" speech in 1970.

Ironically, the decline appears to have accelerated with Nixon's effort to place management on an equal footing with budget in his 1970 reorganization of the Bureau of the Budget into OMB. The *M* of OMB was to provide a reform beacon within the executive branch. Indeed, under the original proposal, there would have been no *B* in the title. The Ash Council originally wanted to call the new entity the Office of Executive Management, which would have included budget, program evaluation, presidential personnel, and management improvement. Congressional worry about a lack of focus on the budget, and the budget deficits that might follow, led to the title change.[7] Congress had nothing to worry about, of course. Over time, the *B* began to crowd out the

M, partly because the budget became such an important vehicle for setting the president's policy agenda, partly because many of the management experts who had served as the backbone of the old Division on Administrative Management were "exiled" to the General Services Administration.[8]

The *M* in OMB also suffered from repeated reorganizations itself as one administration after another tried to find a way to use the management staff on time-sensitive issues.[9] The first effort to combine the two sides had actually occurred in 1953, when Eisenhower transferred much of the management staff to line positions in the budget divisions. The *M* side had mostly recovered by 1970 when Nixon's first OMB director, George Shultz, merged the two sides again. Over the next two decades, the *M* remained in flux, slowly dwindling in total staff even as it tried to build some new mission that might catch the eye of the president and the OMB director. During the 1980s, for example, the management side became preoccupied with financial management reform and the war on waste. It also provided much of the leadership for Reagan's "Reform '88" initiative, a mix of proposals largely designed to shave costs, collect bad debts, and strengthen internal management controls.

By 1992 there was barely enough left of the *M* to bother. Staff was down to a few dozen, most clustered around the deputy director for management created under the Chief Financial Officers Act. And the reorganizations continued, as the office was reshuffled more times than an old deck of cards: eight directors in twelve years, six different organization charts.[10] It was no surprise, therefore, when yet another president, Clinton, decided to once again embark on a merger of the *M* and *B* by transferring most of the remaining management staff to the line budget divisions one last time.[11] Although the reorganization did strengthen concerns for management within the line budget units, it came at a very high price in maintaining a governmentwide watch on the tides of reform. The reorganization was made possible in part by the continuing work of Gore's National Performance Review, which assembled a large staff, collected data, conducted hearings, encouraged reinventing experiments, and provided governmentwide leadership of the management agenda. Much as one can admire the NPR's work, it was designed to be temporary. Once its work is completed, its staff will disperse and its data will be archived, and OMB's lack of concentrated focus on management will be painfully evident again.

The question is what might be done to rebuild the lost sources of information and assemble it into broad institutional memory. The first place to build is the White House itself, where the Clinton administration set an important precedent in having the vice president put a visible focus not only on strengthening government but on creating a positive rationale for having a government at all.

Not all future administrations will be led by a vice president who cares so deeply about management, of course. But someone in the White House must take an interest in making government work if there is to be any incentive for senior political and career executives to care about the future of reform. And even if the vice president can be convinced to provide leadership, the president should appoint a senior aide with explicit responsibility for tracking federal management issues. Such a position could fit easily into several existing White House units, including the Counsel's Office, the Office of Policy Development, or a broadened Office of Presidential Personnel.

A second place to look for institutional memory is the EOP more broadly. Whoever leads the effort from inside the White House, building institutional memory at 1600 Pennsylvania Avenue must involve governmentwide policy guidance, which means having an institutional focus somewhere else in EOP. If not OMB, then where?

Some, once including this author, believe the answer is in rebuilding the old Division of Administrative Management, the notion being that the budget is a crucial lever for enforcing whatever management reforms a president might pursue. Far better to leave the M in OMB than to have it ignored entirely. Others, including senior members of the National Academy of Public Administration (NAPA), have argued for the creation of an entirely new Office of Federal Management, the argument being that budget will always crowd out management. Far better to have the M ignored on its own than completely submerged by budget. After waiting for three decades for OMB to begin the rebuilding, it appears that advocates of a separate office operating elsewhere in the EOP have the winning argument.

Building Departmental and Agency Memory The erosion of institutional memory involves more than congressional fragmentation and the slowly fading M in OMB, however. The executive departments and agencies have also lost institutional memory, particularly through the steady weakening of the assistant secretaryships for administration (ASAs). Part of the weakening involves the fragmentation of the once-unified offices. Recall the Hoover Commission recommendation that each department create a single assistant secretary to oversee the general counsel, chief financial officer, chief supply officer, chief management research officer, publications officer, and director of personnel. Led by a career civil servant to assure continuity over time, the ASA would act as a source of day-to-day operating advice and as a bulwark against management fads.

The ASA concept was not to last. It is not clear, for example, that any department ever created a chief management research officer, in part because the Hoover Commission never quite explained what the officer was to do. The Hoover Commission itself began breaking its own rules almost immediately in its detailed agency-by-agency reorganization plans. The Interior, Labor, and Treasury Departments were allowed to keep their separate general counsels, while the State Department was given a deputy undersecretary for administration with no apparent reporting authority over the general counsel, office of public affairs, or planning apparatus.

More importantly, the tides of reform began washing away separate pieces of the ASAs. Assistant secretaries for planning and evaluation expanded first, driven in part by the push for better policy analysis and measurement in the 1960s. The number of assistant secretaries for planning and/or evaluation and/or policy increased threefold between 1960 and 1972, with all fourteen departments covered by 1992.

Assistant secretaries for legislation, public affairs, and intergovernmental relations moved up next, driven in part by Nixon's fondness for the new federalism. The number of assistant secretaries covering these broad functions tripled between 1968 and 1976, with all departments covered by 1980. Assistant secretaries for budget grew next, rising almost inexorably with the federal deficit. The number of chief financial officers increased from just six departments to all fourteen with passage of the Chief Financial Officers Act in 1990.

The audit function also escaped, driven by the ever-expanding war on waste. The number of offices of inspector general (OIG) increased from three departments in 1976 to all fourteen by 1988. Along the way, secretaries gained more sources of management advice, but at the cost of increased fragmentation, a point well argued by the NPR in recommending the creation of chief operating officers (COO) to lead the reinvention charge. "Transforming federal management systems and spreading the culture of quality throughout the federal government is no small task," the NPR first report argued. "To accomplish it, at least one senior official with agencywide management authority from every agency will be needed to make it happen."[12] That is exactly what the Hoover Commission had declared, of course, in recommending the scientific establishment of the ASAs, a recommendation that was steadily weakened by time and the tides.

The problem with the COO concept is simple: the deputy secretary or administrator is best seen as the alter-ego of the secretary or administrator and must have a flexible portfolio to fight the inevitable management and policy fires that flare up over time. Moreover, deputy secretaries and administrators have little capacity to exert a significant presence on day-to-day management, let alone create much institutional memory. Their offices are small and their tenure relatively short. Whatever memory they gain is quickly dissipated with turnover.

Moreover, even though deputy secretaries have agencywide oversight, they cannot bring together what the tides of reform have torn asunder. Again, they simply do not have the capacity to integrate the far-flung activities of what has become a huge number of political subordinates. By 1992, there were 14 deputy secretaries in all of government to oversee 21 associate deputy secretaries, 32 undersecretaries, 52 deputy undersecretaries, 11 assistant and 11 associate deputy undersecretaries, and 212 assistant secretaries, a list that does not include the occasional chief of staff to the deputy secretary, principal deputy undersecretary, or principal associate deputy undersecretary.[13]

Nevertheless, although I have made the case elsewhere against needless thickening of hierarchy, the NPR's recommendation for high-level leadership is still well taken. Toward that end, Congress should create a statutory undersecretary or underadministrator for management in each federal entity to provide central management focus. The undersecretary or underadministrator should be put in charge of the traditional management functions, including evaluation, strategy planning, budget, personnel, equal opportunity, acquisitions, and intergovernmental relations, but, contrary to the Hoover ideal, not the general counsel or legislation. Those two functions are too politically sensitive to be moved so far from the secretary or administrator's direct report.

If these undersecretaries or underadministrators for management are to successfully rebuild and refresh the institutional memory, they and their assistant secretaries should be neither short-term political appointees nor long-term civil servants. Political appointees move out much too frequently to establish the needed continuity, while career civil servants tend to stay much too long to stay as fresh as possible. Rather, the undersecretaries and their direct reports might be most effective under five- to seven-year performance-based contracts.

These contracts would create a de facto, if not de jure, federal management service, allowing higher pay rates, easier movement in and out of government, and restoration of a certain prestige once associated with public service, thereby borrowing from scientific management. Such contracts would also clearly create incentives for performance, borrowing a bit from the market forces school of liberation management.

A Brief Note on Beach Restoration Perhaps the most vexing problem of the constant ebb and flow of the tides is the accumulation of conflicting reforms.

As we have seen, the federal statute books are littered with reforms that have long since outlived their usefulness. The Gore NPR attacked two specific areas, personnel and procurement, but left administrative procedure and war on waste mostly undisturbed. The political costs of being seen as weak on individual rights and fraud, waste, and abuse make it nearly impossible for any sitting administration or house of Congress to do the revisions.

It may be time, therefore, for a kind of blue-ribbon "clean-out commission" to sort through the various management titles of the *U.S. Code* in search of needed sunsets. Such a commission, to be appointed by Congress and the president, could be given the same authority to recommend an all-or-nothing sweep of outmoded, unnecessary statutes and federal regulations that helped the Base Closure and Realignment Commission do its jobs. The clean-out commission could also be charged with thinning the government of unnecessary layers of political and career management.

Altering the Climate of Reform

This is not the book to catalogue the assorted causes, consequences, and potential remedies for the public's deep distrust toward government and its leaders. Suffice it to suggest that the distrust is a blend of healthy skepticism and corrosive anger that will not yield easily to any single approach. Trust in government may have very little to do with the reality of what government does, however, a point well made by Charles Goodsell in his *Case for Bureaucracy*.[14]

One place to start rebuilding trust is with elections, arguably the most important event in democratic life. Scholars and practitioners who worry about trust in government would almost rather election campaigns not take place. Americans have come to believe that campaigns are about exactly the wrong issues. They say they are tired of the mudslinging and want candidates to talk about issues that matter. They say that campaign spending is too high, and they have learned to distrust just about everything candidates say. And they most certainly believe campaigns are too long.

At the same time, most Americans know that they are at least partly to blame. They may say they want more issue coverage, but they are addicted to negative advertising and news about the horse-race quality of the campaign. They know they do not follow campaigns as closely as they once did but cannot seem to find the time to pay more attention. They know they cannot have lower taxes and higher spending but still expect government to do it all. They know they should vote for candidates who tell it like it is but remain attracted to candidates who promise the world.

To date, public administration scholars and practitioners have mostly avoided questions of campaign conduct. It is increasingly obvious, however, that effective public administration is being undermined by the staggering levels of public anger toward politics. If the field of public administration cannot take a position on issues—campaign finance reform, for example—that so obviously undermine public confidence in government, who will?

In a similar vein, if the field cannot take an interest in citizens as central partners in making government work, even to the point of having citizens render government intervention less necessary by solving more of their own problems, who will? For too long, the field of public administration has left politics to others, enshrining the old politics-administration dichotomy as a bright line guiding their work. It is increasingly obvious, however, that public administration must renew its own intellectual capital in and contributions to the ongoing debate about how to renew civic life in the United States.

Altering the Gravitational Pulls of Reform

Tidal barriers like a Joint Committee on Federal Management or undersecretaries for management may improve the coordination of reform, thereby increasing the odds that hurricanes can be spotted early and tidal gates closed more quickly. But such barriers can do little to change the gravitational pulls of reform.

The only way to alter the gravity of reform is to introduce much greater knowledge about what succeeds and what does not in actually making government work. And the best route to that knowledge is through better measures of the performance of government, a greater commitment to experimentation in reform, and clean settings in which to conduct the needed tests. The measures provide the essential baselines against to measure reform, the commitment supplies the needed will to declare a given reform a failure, and the settings provide a place to generate valid data.

Building Baselines   To date, the answer to the first challenge—improving the quality of knowledge—has been a mixture of hunch and relatively weak measures of performance. Most oversight hearings on management reform are driven by opinion on how well X or Y statute has worked, or broad measures of activity. Inspector general effectiveness has mostly been measured, for example, by dollars saved and funds put to better use, not by whether government is somehow more or less vulnerable to fraud, waste, and abuse, and not on how well the OIGs have done in restoring public faith that government does not waste tax dollars. As a result, Congress and the president know a great deal about what the OIGs do in terms of audit cycles and investigative strategy but far less about how to target the war on waste to assure maximum deterrence.

Alas, getting government to make the commitment to performance-based accountability has been anything but easy. As the public management scholar Harry Hatry argues, the effort to develop the necessary baselines has been hampered by a lack of money, technical difficulties in actually collecting the needed information, a tendency to aggregate measures of performance into meaningless lumps, and a lack of training in recognizing the difference between good and bad performance information.[15] It is also not always clear that Congress and the president want to know if a program is failing, a point well illustrated by the need for a military base closure commission to do the dirty work on folding down obsolete installations that Congress and the president had long protected.

Congress began to remedy the problem with passage of the Government Performance and Results Act in 1993. Although the statute is best seen as an expression of liberation management, it holds significant promise for sorting through all four tides. It is important to note, however, that GPRA was not designed to produce performance measures as a way to test competing philosophies of reform. Rather, it was designed to use performance measures as a way to hold programs accountable for achieving results. "Whether the goal is defending the nation or immunizing children against disease," GAO had argued in a key 1985 report undergirding eventual passage, "government officials and the public need to know how well government is accomplishing its intended objectives. Assessing government accomplishments requires the measurement of employee and program performance. Though the size and complexity of the government make it difficult, developing effective performance measurement systems is clearly possible."[16]

That the measures were designed to track missions, goals, and objectives, while strengthening congressional oversight and presidential budgeting along the way, does not mean they cannot be used to test the impacts of management reform. Indeed, given the difficulties in writing the performance plans mandated under GPRA, measuring the impacts of management reform may be the best one can hope from the overall effort.[17] Thus, whatever the potential that a full-blown performance accountability system will emerge, the effort to create credible measures of impacts cannot come soon enough for the tides of reform.

The British Audit Commission has already demonstrated one model for progress, using its statutory mandate to develop a range of performance measures for local government. Although the measures often mix and match traditional activity measures, such as arrest rates and number of police per 100,000, the Audit Commission has also developed some innovative measures of public satisfaction and outcomes. In turn, local governments have begun to pay attention to the measures as one tool for evaluating success.[18]

Creating an Ethic of Experimentation Putting baselines into place is only half the challenge in strengthening the commitment to knowing. Equally important is developing an ethic of experimentation on management reform, a daunting task that makes developing good measures seem like child's play. Recall, for example, that only five of the 141 initiatives in Appendix A can remotely be characterized as including a commitment to experimentation. One of the five just happens to be GPRA, which mandated ten pilots en route to full implementation.

The GPRA is hardly a model case of experimentation, however. Indeed, it actually reflects one of the great challenges in forging a deeper commitment to trial and error. The original Senate proposal started off well enough. Ten pilots would be conducted, at least five "managerial accountability and flexibility" pilots to "see if the influence of incentives will . . . increase the chances for successfully implementing better accountability systems." After three years, OMB and GAO would report to Congress on the results, followed by joint resolutions in each chamber requiring governmentwide implementation. As the Senate Governmental Affairs Committee explained, "Focusing on doing it right in a handful of programs—often learning on a trial-and-error basis—maximizes the likelihood of ultimate, government-wide success."[19] As such, GPRA merely followed the precedent set in the Chief Financial Officers Act, which had required six pilots of agencywide financial statements on the way to a joint resolution en route to full governmentwide implementation.

The Governmental Affairs Committee was hardly worried about the ultimate outcome, however. "The Committee fully expects that Congress will want to go forward with program performance measurement," it explained, "but felt it was important that Congress first have the opportunity to review the experience of the pilot projects and to be satisfied with the results."[20] So noted, the Committee did acknowledge that there was some possibility that Congress would not approve the resolutions, noting that the president and OMB would still have authority to collect performance data under the Chief Financial Officers Act.

One year later, however, the review process was gone, the only obvious difference being a new Democratic president. Not only did a Democratic Congress feel perhaps more generous toward a Democratic president, the Clinton administration took umbrage at being asked to experiment when full-scale reform held such promise for liberating agencies. Testifying before the Senate Governmental Affairs Committee, OMB Director Leon Panetta did not ask for the outright abolishment of the trigger. Rather, he simply asked that the president be allowed to report to Congress on needed modifications in the GPRA plans, and, in turn, that the president's report be allowed to form the basis of the joint resolutions introduced in each chamber. Given a choice between a trigger pulled by the president or no trigger at all, Congress simply deleted the offending provision.

In the end, all ten pilots were approved, as was full governmentwide implementation, to occur not later than September 30, 1997. Because of the long lead times involved in full implementation, OMB issued instructions to all agencies on the preparation and submission of the required strategic plans in September 1995, barely a year into the pilots.[21]

As if to demonstrate its overall commitment to the cause of performance measurement, OMB authorized not ten but fifty-three pilots, covering twenty-one departments and agencies, 375,000 employees, and $48 billion in annual operating costs.[22] The pilots covered everything from the single-family housing program at the Farmers Home Administration to the airway facilities division of the Federal Aviation Administration, from the nuclear bomb plants in the Department of Energy to the snow survey at the National Oceanographic and Atmospheric Administration. Piloting became so popular with the agencies that OMB allowed a second round of nominations. By September 1994, seventy-one pilots had begun in twenty-seven departments and agencies, virtually assuring that any lessons learned from the pilots would follow, not precede, the 1997 governmentwide implementation.

The problems with keeping even a weak trigger on full implementation in the GPRA suggest the difficulties in building a greater commitment to experimentation. Experiments have at least four drawbacks when compared with governmentwide, pedal-to-the-metal reforms.[23] The first drawback, as the increased number of GPRA pilots suggests, is that Congress and the president are reluctant to go slow on reforms with potentially high credit-claiming yields. "For too long," Gore explained in announcing the fifty-three pilots, "the federal government has measured quantity, not quality: What it puts in instead of what it gets out. The American taxpayers want to be assured that their tax dollars are being put to the very best use possible. The pilot projects will lead the way toward measuring not just what the government spends, but what it accomplishes."[24] At the same time, an original GPRA author, Senator William Roth (R-Del.), argued, "For the first time, the American people will be told what levels of service and program results they can expect from their tax dollars, followed by reports on what was actually achieved. It may sound like common sense for government to do this—and it is—but it has not been done before by the federal government."[25] Experiments that promise political returns in the war on waste, for example, are not experiments for long.

The second drawback is that management experiments usually occur in contaminated settings. The GPRA was hardly the only experiment taking place in 1994. Reinventing government was under full steam, with agencies moving forward with work teams, employee empowerment, customer service standards, performance measurement, procurement streamlining, employee buyouts toward a 272,900 reduction in federal employment, and deregulation all at the same time. Even if government improves as a result of this broad-spectrum treatment, it will be nearly impossible to know which initiative caused the effect. Perhaps employee empowerment could not work without the discipline created by the job cutbacks; conversely, perhaps it would have worked much better without the anxiety.

The third drawback is that Congress and presidents may be entirely unsympathetic to the small effects that most management experiments are likely to demonstrate. This is not to suggest that policymakers are immune to such evidence. Indeed, passage of the Family Support Act of 1988 suggests that, at least for welfare reform, very small effects can propel very large legislative reform. Rather, it is simply not clear that small gains in productivity are enough to catch legislative attention. Unlike welfare reform, which has a high visibility and credit-claiming yield, management reform has historically been an issue of last resort on the legislative agenda. It is difficult to imagine Congress finding the will to move major management reform on the basis of a 2 or 3 percent gain in productivity—unless, of course, that gain can be linked to huge savings.

The fourth drawback is that Congress has been entirely unwilling to experiment with watchful eye reforms, particularly those involving ethics, information, and privacy. The history of watchful eye is one of governmentwide implementation, long-term time horizons, and a fundamental rejection of the kind of trial-and-error thinking found in the history of GPRA and other piloting statutes. Congress is not at all interested in learning where financial disclosure or sunshine might work best. To attend to those questions would be a tacit admission that presidents might be right in claiming broad privileges to keep the inner workings of government private. Although Congress has shown a somewhat greater willingness to experiment in war on waste, allowing federal agencies to use private firms to collect bad debts in a three-year pilot under the Federal Debt Collection Act, it seems reasonable to suggest that most government management experiments are likely to involve either scientific or liberation management. Congress seems willing to experiment when it comes time to trust government and its employees, but opts for permanency when it comes to distrust.

Given these obstacles, the question is what might be done to strengthen the commitment to experimentation. A first answer involves creating more advocates. Experimentation in government management reform has few if any advocates either inside or outside government. Beyond the Senate Governmental Affairs Committee, which appears committed to the cause, it is not clear just where one might expect greater support for trial and error. It is not likely to come, for example, from blue-ribbon commissions, advocacy-based think tanks, or national performance reviews, all of which tend to put government-wide implementation far above experimental evidence. Although the NPR called for a certain amount of trial and error in its recommendation for reinvention laboratories, for example, it was a call mostly in the context of moving ahead with unequivocal support for liberation management. The labs, while carrying an experimental label, were mostly about finding the best way to proceed governmentwide. Whether a laboratory could or would ever declare liberation management an impossible goal is in some doubt.

Those who work in reinvention laboratories are inevitably reluctant to declare the liberation goal impossible. Indeed, the final quotation highlighted in *Creating a Government That Works Better and Costs Less* is Daniel Burnham's call for boldness: "Make no little plans; they have no magic to stir men's blood, and probably themselves will not be realized. Make big plans; aim high in hope and work, remembering that a noble logical diagram, once recorded, will never die, but long after we are gone will be a living thing, asserting itself with ever-growing insistency."[26] Advocates of a specific tide will always find experimentation an awkward endeavor, particularly if it might call into question their favored tide of reform.

Setting aside commissions, performance reviews, and advocacy groups as better at promoting a specific tide of reform than at evaluating its effectiveness, consider three alternative sources of advocacy, the first two being inside government, the third outside. The first two involve already existing units: offices of evaluation and analysis across the departments and the offices of inspector general. The former has long had a faith in experimentation, albeit mostly in the context of policy, not management reform. Although weakened over the past decade by budget cuts, evaluation units should be encouraged to accept a greater role in understanding *how* government works alongside their already well-established expertise in *what* government does.

The offices of inspector general will strike most readers as a less likely fit for experimentation advocacy. After all, the IGs are a clear expression of the war on waste. However, as I have argued elsewhere, their dual reporting relation gives them a certain level of independence from both Congress and the presidency. They have the kind of protection to make the tough calls on experiments more easily, say, than reinvention laboratories. As the evaluation expert Eleanor Chelimsky argues, "Because of the carefully protected independence of audit offices, program evaluation can actually escape from politicization there. The fact is that, today, speaking truth to power is a pretty uncommon luxury in a government environment in which merely identifying a *problem* has become as hard as it used to be to agree on a solution."27 In a sense, the OIGs could provide a safe harbor for experimentation and clearly have the authority to do so under the 1978 IG Act and its amendments. Whether they will ever be willing to engage in such leading-edge work is unclear. But since they owe allegiance in part to the Senate Governmental Affairs Committee, perhaps the committee could give them the needed push.

The third source of advocacy for experimentation is outside government in the community of public administration and management scholars. The field has produced some very useful work on what works and what does not, including case studies of particular philosophies, such as Donald Kettl's work on contracting out; statistical analysis of specific reforms, such as James Perry's work on models of pay for performance; and a growing list of teaching cases on innovation that occasionally gets summarized into rich analyses like Martin Levin and Mary Bryna Sanger's study of public entrepreneurs.28 Such studies have the potential to make government work better. The field has also produced a growing inventory of what is happening in other nations and in state and local government, where liberation management has gone further perhaps than in the United States.

Notwithstanding the good work by these and other talented scholars, the field has not been able to make much progress in specifying the conditions under which one reform or management style might succeed or fail. Comparisons across different governments have been relatively weak in specifying the historical, cultural, and political conditions in each "laboratory."

One way to stimulate a greater attention to both specification of such conditions and promotion of greater experimentation might be to establish a public administration and management analogue to the Manpower Demonstration Research Corporation (MDRC), a nonprofit research firm created in the 1970s to promote and conduct experimental research on income security reform. It is safe to say that no other organization had a greater effect in bringing experimentation to bear on welfare reform over the years that followed.

A similar effort in the field of government reform might produce the same kind of impacts, particularly if public administration and management scholars can decide which of the numerous targets of reform (general organization, ethics, procurement, pay, classification, etc.) hold the greatest promise for experimentation, and what aspects of administration to control (type of agency, mission, and so on) in the experiments that follow.

Finding Clean Settings for Experiments Even with strong advocates, experimentation will remain difficult, if not impossible, without cleaner settings in which to conduct the needed learning. Such pure experimental settings are likely to be rare in government reform, if they exist at all. But there are at least two ways to improve the clarity of what might be seen.

The first is to take advantage of the already scheduled GPRA waiver process to assure maximum learning. As currently designed, the waivers would be granted upon agency requests. Under the statute, OMB must make its decision based on the costs and benefits from each waiver, not necessarily on the potential for evaluating the workability of a given approach. However, nothing in the statute would prohibit OMB from encouraging agencies to create internal experiments of their own by matching field offices or subunits in a rough approximation of a controlled experiment, or from asking the assistant secretaries for advice. Nor would the OIGs be barred from helping design such efforts. There is no reason not to grant waivers in a pattern consistent with discovering whether the given waiver makes any difference to overall performance.

The second way to create cleaner settings for reform experimentation is to build them from scratch. Several states have done just that, for example, by allowing charter schools to compete for K–12 education dollars. Although often linked to the public choice movement in education, charter schools deserve special attention in their own right as fresh settings for the kind of experimentation that might help clarify what works and what does not in government reform.

Thus, it seems reasonable to suggest that Congress consider permitting charter agencies to compete for federal business. Such charter agencies might be composed entirely of current government employees who band together to cleave off a share of a given department to mount on their own or might be created by private firms to compete directly for the chance to provide federal services. One might imagine, for example, a charter agency forming around a social security district office, a national forest, or an Agriculture field office. Such a charter agency would have to follow the same watchful eye and war on waste statutes that currently affect all government agencies, but it could be structured to test a series of operating principles that might create robust learning opportunities for the rest of government.

Rebuilding institutional barriers and strengthening the potential for experimentation will not stop the tides from flowing, of course. At best, they might deflect the tides a bit, and protect government somewhat from the hurricanes of reform. But those tides and hurricanes will keep coming, driven in large part by the lack of a final answer to the question about when and where to trust government and its employees.

Some policy analysts would argue that the lack of a final answer to this vexing question is reason enough to call for market forces as the only tide worth riding. That is what the founders did in building their system of separate powers and checks and balances. Much as they hoped for virtuous behavior from America's leaders, they designed the constitutional system with distrust in mind. If human beings were angels, as Madison argued, there would be no need for government. In a similar sense, if government agencies and their employees were angels, there would be no need for reform. They would always act in the public interest.

The problem with market forces as the sole instrument of reform is embedded in the founders' own ambivalence about using self-interest as the sole driver of effectiveness. They explicitly rejected the calls of Anti-Federalists like Brutus to characterize government and its employees as incapable of virtue, and they clearly hoped that America's leaders would occasionally rise above narrow parochialism to reach for the common good. They recognized that a government built on pure self-interest might risk the very tyranny it hoped to prevent.

The same argument might hold today for those who argue for market forces. By reducing expectations to the lowest common denominator of self-interest, one will virtually guarantee that altruism never appears. As the political scientist Jane Mansbridge argues, "It would be absurd to give up the extraordinarily useful insights into political behavior that rational choice as an enterprise has given us, or to give up the intellectual power that modeling with reduction to a single motive can provide. . . . But the claim that self-interest alone motivates political behavior must be either vacuous, if self-interest can encompass any motive, or false, if self-interest means behavior that consciously intends only self as the beneficiary."[29]

There will be places where self-interest is, indeed, the driving force for government and its employees, and places where altruism will ascend. The question in the tides of reform is where each motive is strongest, and how government reform itself cultivates one or the other. That is fundamentally a question of better research, more experimentation, and a sensitivity to the fact that government reform is not an "either/or" issue. There will be agencies and types of employees for whom market forces would be the great motivator, and others for whom market forces would sap all altruism. The challenge is to find out when and where. Otherwise, making government work is reduced to merely sitting at the dock of the bay, watching each contesting tide roll in to little ultimate improvement.

Appendix A:
Major Government Reform Statutes,
1945–1994

79TH CONGRESS

1945   1. *Federal Employees Pay Act* (PL 79-106)
           Adjusted basic federal pay rates for the first time in fifteen years
        2. *Government Corporation Control Act* (PL 79-248)
           Brought government corporations under greater executive branch
           control
        3. *Reorganization Act* (PL 79-263)
           Restored presidential authority to submit reorganization plans to
           Congress

1946   4. *Administrative Procedure Act* (PL 79-404)
           Formalized administrative procedures of government agencies and
           established uniform standards for judicial review
        5. *Atomic Energy Act* (PL 79-585)
           Established Atomic Energy Commission
        6. *Federal Tort Claims Act* (PL 79-601)
           Established federal liability for the loss of property, injury, or death due
           to actions taken or not taken by federal employees

80TH CONGRESS

1947   1. *Commission on Organization of the Executive Branch of the Government* (PL 80-162)
Established first Hoover Commission

2. *National Security Act* (PL 80-253)
Reorganized national defense structure, creating National Security Council, Central Intelligence Agency, and National Defense Establishment

81ST CONGRESS

1949   1. *Reorganization Act* (PL 81-109)
Restored presidential authority to submit reorganization plans to Congress

2. *Reorganization Plans*
2: Bureau of Employment Security and Veterans Placement Service Board
3: Postal Service
4: National Security Council and National Security Resources Board
5: Civil Service Commission
6: Maritime Commission
7: Public Roads Administration

3. *Federal Property and Administrative Services Act* (PL 81-152)
Established General Services Administration

4. *National Security Act Amendments* (PL 81-216)
Established Department of Defense, reorganized National Security Council and Joint Chiefs of Staff, and established new pay levels and budget and fiscal procedures

5. *Classification Act* (PL 81-429)
Established new pay schedule for government employees

1950   6. *Reorganization Plans*
2: Department of Justice
3: Department of Interior
5: Department of Commerce
6: Department of Labor
8: Federal Trade Commission
9: Federal Power Commission
10: Securities and Exchange Commission
13: Civil Aeronautics Board
14: Labor Standards Enforcement
15: Alaska and Virgin Islands Public Works

16: Certain Education and Health Functions

17: Public Works Advance Planning and Other Functions

18: Building and Space Management Functions

19: Employees' Compensation Functions

20: Statutes at Large and Other Matters

21: Federal Maritime Board; Maritime Administration

22: Federal National Mortgage Association

23: Loans for Factory-Build Homes

25: National Security Resources Board

26: Department of Treasury

7. *Budget and Accounting Procedures Act* (PL 81-784)
Clarified accounting responsibilities between Congress and executive branch

82D CONGRESS

1951   1. *Renegotiation Act* (PL 82-9)
Authorized federal government to renegotiate war mobilization contracts under certain conditions

1952   2. *Reorganization Plan*
Bureau of Internal Revenue Reorganization

83D CONGRESS

1953   1. *Reorganization Plan* (PL 83-13)
Established Department of Health, Education, and Welfare

2. *Reorganization Plans*

2: Department of Agriculture

3: Office of Defense Mobilization

4: Attorney General

5: Export-Import Bank

6: Department of Defense and Joint Chiefs of Staff

7: Foreign Operations Administration

8: United States Information Agency

9: Council of Economic Advisors

10: Civil Aeronautics Board

3. *Commission on Organization of the Executive Branch of the Government* (PL 83-108)
Established second Hoover Commission

4. *Reconstruction Finance Corporation Liquidation Act; Small Business Act* (PL 83-108)
Established Small Business Administration

84TH CONGRESS

1956   1. *Government Budget and Accounting Procedure* (PL 84-863)
        Amended executive branch budget and accounting practices

85TH CONGRESS

1957   1. *Civil Rights Act* (PL 85-315)
        Established Civil Rights Commission
1958   2. *National Aeronautics and Space Act* (PL 85-568)
        Established National Aeronautics and Space Administration
        3. *Department of Defense Reorganization Act* (PL 85-599)
        Strengthened Secretary of Defense's authority over the branches of the
        military service
        4. *Availability of Information from Federal Departments and Agencies*
        (PL 85-619)
        Prohibited use of 1789 housekeeping statute for withholding
        information
        5. *Federal Aviation Act* (PL 85-726)
        Established Federal Aviation Agency

87TH CONGRESS

1961   1. *Reorganization Act, amendment* (PL 87-18)
        Restored presidential authority to submit reorganization plans to
        Congress
        2. *Reorganization Plans*
          3: Civil Aeronautics Board
          4: Federal Trade Commission
          6: Home Loan Bank Board
          7: Federal Maritime Commission
        3. *Foreign Assistance Act* (PL 87-195)
        Established Agency for International Development and separated
        military and economic aid budgets
        4. *Peace Corps Act* (PL 97-293)
        Established Peace Corps
        5. *Arms Control and Disarmament Act* (PL 87-297)
        Established Arms Control and Disarmament Administration
1962   6. *Communications Satellite Act* (PL 87-624)
        Authorized private, for-profit commercial communications satellite
        corporation
        7. *Postal Service and Federal Employees Salary Act* (PL 87-793)
        Established new pay-setting system for government employees

8. *Bribery, Graft and Conflicts of Interest* (PL 87-849)
Consolidated and strengthened conflict-of-interest laws for federal
employees

88TH CONGRESS

1964   1. *Presidential Transition Act* (PL 88-277)
Provided federal funding for incoming and outgoing administrations
2. *Civil Rights Act* (PL 88-352)
Established Equal Employment Opportunity Commission
3. *Economic Opportunity Act* (PL 88-452)
Established Volunteers in Service to America (VISTA) and Office of
Economic Opportunity (OEO)

89TH CONGRESS

1965   1. *Department of Housing and Urban Development Act* (PL 89-174)
Established Department of Housing and Urban Development (HUD)
1966   2. *Reorganization Plans*
1: Community Relations Service
2: Water Pollution Control Administration
3: Public Health Service
3. *Freedom of Information Act* (PL 89-487)
Enhanced public access to executive branch information
4. *Federal Claims Correction Act* (PL 89-508)
Authorized collection and settlement of government claims against
citizens
5. *Department of Transportation Act* (PL 89-670)
Established Department of Transportation

90TH CONGRESS

1967   1. *Public Broadcasting Act* (PL 90-129)
Established Public Broadcasting Corporation
2. *Postal Revenue and Federal Salary Act* (PL 90-206)
Established new pay-setting process

91ST CONGRESS

1970   1. *Reorganization Plans*
1: Established Office of Management and Budget
2: Established Environmental Protection Agency

      3: Established National Oceanographic and Atmospheric
        Administration
2. *National Environmental Policy Act* (PL 91-190)
    Required federal agencies to prepare environmental impact statements
3. *Postal Reorganization Act* (PL 91-375)
    Established U.S. Postal Service as a government corporation
4. *Rail Passenger Service Act* (PL 91-518)
    Established Amtrak as a government corporation
5. *Federal Pay Comparability Act* (PL 91-656)
    Created new pay-setting process based on comparable private
    sector pay

92D CONGRESS

1971   1. *Reorganization Plan*
        Established ACTION by merging the Peace Corps, VISTA, and other
        volunteer programs
1972   2. *Federal Advisory Committee Act* (PL 92-463)
        Opened advisory committees to public review
       3. *Consumer Product Safety Act* (PL 92-573)
        Established Consumer Product Safety Commission

93D CONGRESS

1973   1. *Reorganization Plans*
         1: Transferred various executive responsibilities to line agencies
         2: Established Drug Enforcement Administration
       2. *Amtrak Improvement Act* (PL 93-146)
        Strengthened Amtrak's authority to manage the nation's passenger rail
        system
       3. *Comprehensive Employment and Training Act* (PL 93-203)
        Established block grants for job training
       4. *Regional Rail Reorganization Act* (PL 93-236)
        Established Conrail as a government corporation
1974   5. *Federal Energy Administration Act* (PL 93-275)
        Established a temporary agency to manage federal programs dealing
        with short-term fuel shortages
       6. *Congressional Budget and Impoundment Control Act* (PL 93-344)
        Established new federal budget process and limited presidential
        authority to impound and rescind appropriations
       7. *Legal Services Corporation Act* (PL 93-355)
        Established Legal Services Corporation as a government corporation

8. *Government property procurement and services, simplified procedures* (PL 93-356)
Simplified procurement procedures
9. *Housing and Community Development Act* (PL 93-383)
Established block grants for community development
10. *Office of Federal Procurement Policy Act* (PL 93-400)
Established Office of Federal Procurement Policy
11. *Employee Retirement Income Security Act* (PL 93-406)
Established Pension Benefit Guaranty Corporation
12. *Energy Reorganization Act* (PL 93-438)
Established Nuclear Regulatory Commission, Energy Research and Development Administration (ERDA), and Energy Resources Council
13. *Federal Election Campaign Act Amendment* (PL 93-443)
Established Federal Election Commission
14. *Freedom of Information Act Amendments* (PL 93-502)
Enhanced public access to government information
15. *Privacy Act* (PL 93-579)
Established the right of individuals to inspect, challenge, correct, or amend information contained in agency files
16. *Transportation Safety Act* (PL 93-633)
Established National Transportation Safety Board as an independent agency
17. *Headstart, Economic Opportunity, and Community Partnership Act* (PL 93-644)
Established Community Services Administration

94TH CONGRESS

1975   1. *Executive Salary Cost-of-Living Adjustment Act* (PL 94-82)
Established new pay-setting process
1976   2. *Government in the Sunshine Act* (PL 94-409)
Prohibited agencies from closing meetings to the public
3. *Shriner's Hospital for Crippled Children, conveyance* (PL 94-505)
Established an Office of Inspector General at the Department of Health, Education and Welfare

95TH CONGRESS

1977   1. *Reorganization Act* (PL 95-17)
Restored presidential authority to submit reorganization plans to Congress

2. *Federal Salary Act Amendments* (PL 95-19)
Created new pay-setting process (leading to the passage of PL 95-66, denying Congress its next annual cost-of-living pay increase)

3. *Department of Energy Organization Act* (PL 95-91)
Established Department of Energy

1978   4. *Reorganization Plans*
1: Equal Employment Opportunity Commission
2: Civil Service Commission
3: Established Federal Emergency Management Administration
4: Administration of Employee Retirement Income Security Act

5. *Inspector General Act* (PL 95-452)
Established Offices of Inspector General in twelve federal agencies

6. *Civil Service Reform Act* (PL 95-454)
Complete revision of the civil service system

7. *Airline Deregulation Act* (PL 95-504)
Required phased deregulation of passenger airline industry

8. *Ethics in Government Act* (PL 95-521)
Established financial disclosure and postemployment restrictions on senior federal employees

9. *Contract Disputes Act* (PL 95-563)
Established procedures for resolving contract disputes

10. *Presidential Records Act* (PL 95-591)
Established public ownership of presidential records

96TH CONGRESS

1979   1. *Department of Education Organization Act* (PL 96-88)
Established Department of Education

1980   2. *Energy Security Act* (PL 96-294)
Established Synthetic Fuels Corporation

3. *Regulatory Flexibility Act* (PL 96-354)
Required regulatory impact statements as part of rulemaking procedures

4. *Foreign Service Act* (PL 96-465)
Modernized the Foreign Service

5. *Equal Access to Justice Act* (PL 96-481)
Required federal payments in certain administrative adjudications and civil court actions

6. *Paperwork Reduction Act* (PL 96-511)
Established Office of Information and Regulatory Affairs

7. *Defense Officer Personnel Management Act* (PL 96-513)
Revised military promotion and retirement practices

97TH CONGRESS

1981   1. *Omnibus Budget Reconciliation Act* (PL 97-35)
         Cut and/or eliminated a broad assortment of federal programs

1982   2. *Prompt Payment Act* (PL 97-177)
         Required agencies to pay federal contractors within thirty days of billing

         3. *Federal Managers' Financial Integrity Act* (PL 97-255)
         Required annual agency reports on internal accounting and administrative weaknesses

         4. *Debt Collection Act* (PL 97-365)
         Enhanced the ability of agencies to collect unpaid debts

         5. *Independent Counsel Reauthorization* (PL 97-409)
         Revised and reauthorized special prosecutor (renamed independent counsel) provisions of 1978 Ethics in Government Act

98TH CONGRESS

1983   1. *Office of Federal Procurement Policy Act Amendments* (PL 98-191)
         Reauthorized and strengthened the Office of Federal Procurement Policy

1984   2. *Competition in Contracting Act; Small Business and Federal Procurement Enhancement Act* (PL 98-369, PL 98-577)
         Required competition in federal contracts

         3. *Comprehensive Crime Control Act* (PL 98-473)
         Criminalized computer fraud against the federal government

         4. *Reorganization Act Amendments* (PL 98-614)
         Restored presidential authority to submit reorganization plan to Congress (authority lapsed before it could be used)

99TH CONGRESS

1985   1. *Defense Procurement Improvement Act* (PL 99-145)
         Revised procurement system

         2. *Balanced Budget and Emergency Deficit Control Act* (PL 99-177) (Gramm/Rudman/Hollings)
         Established new budget process designed to achieve balanced budget

1986   3. *Synthetic Fuels Corporation Act* (PL 99-272)
         Abolished the Synthetic Fuels Corporation

         4. *Federal Employees' Retirement System Act* (PL 99-335)
         Established new federal retirement system

         5. *Goldwater-Nichols Department of Defense Reorganization Act* (PL 99-433)
         Strengthened authority of Defense Department leadership

6. *Computer Fraud and Abuse Act* (PL 99-474)
   Expanded laws prohibiting federal computer fraud
7. *Electronic Communications Privacy Act* (PL 99-508)
   Established guidelines for federal government interception of electronic communications
8. *Program Fraud Civil Remedies Act* (PL 99-509)
   Established procedures to penalize persons who recklessly or knowingly misrepresent facts to federal agencies
9. *False Claims Amendments Act* (PL 99-562)
   Enhanced federal capacity to identify and sanction fraud against the federal government
10. *Federal Debt Recovery Act* (PL 99-578)
    Allowed the federal government to use law firms to collect debts

100TH CONGRESS

1987   1. *Independent Counsel Reauthorization* (PL 100-191)
           Revised and reauthorized independent counsel provisions
        2. *Computer Security Act* (PL 100-235)
           Strengthened security over government computers
1988   3. *Presidential Transition Effectiveness Act* (PL 100-398)
           Increased federal transition support and established reporting requirements governing private transition funds
        4. *Prompt Payment Act Amendments* (PL 100-496)
           Strengthened the Prompt Payment Act
        5. *Computer Matching and Privacy Protection Act* (PL 100-503)
           Imposed new safeguards on federal use of computer records
        6. *Inspector General Act Amendments* (PL 100-504)
           Established Offices of Inspector General at Justice, Treasury, Office of Personnel Management, Federal Emergency Management Administration, and Nuclear Regulatory Commission
        7. *Base Closure and Realignment Act* (PL 100-526)
           Established a commission to recommend all-or-nothing lists of military bases for closure
        8. *Department of Veterans Affairs Act* (PL 100-527)
           Elevated the Veterans Administration to cabinet status
        9. *Office of Government Ethics Reauthorization* (PL 100-598)
           Elevated Office of Government Ethics to independent agency status
        10. *Office of Federal Procurement Policy Act Amendments* (PL 100-679)
            Strengthened the authority of the Office of Federal Procurement Policy
        11. *Federal Employees Liability Reform and Tort Compensation Act* (PL 100-694)

Established protection for federal employees from liability for work-related actions
12. *Major Fraud Act* (PL 100-700)
Further criminalized procurement fraud against the federal government

101st CONGRESS

1989   1. *Whistleblower Protection Act* (PL 101-12)
Enhanced job protection for whistleblowers
2. *Financial Institutions Reform, Recovery and Enforcement Act* (PL 101-73)
Established Resolution Trust Corporation
3. *Ethics Reform Act* (PL 101-194)
Prohibited lobbying of former departments, established uniform financial disclosure laws, and raised pay for executive, judicial, and legislative officials
4. *Department of Housing and Urban Development Reform Act* (PL 101-235)
Strengthened internal controls at HUD; limited secretarial discretion in certain program areas

1990   5. *Administrative Dispute Resolution Act* (PL 101-552)
Authorized and encouraged administrative dispute resolution procedures by federal agencies
6. *Chief Financial Officers Act* (PL 101-576)
Established Deputy Director of Management and Office of Federal Financial Management at the Office of Management and Budget; established chief financial officers at fourteen executive departments and nine federal agencies
7. *Federal Employees Pay Comparability Act* (PL 101-601)
Established new pay-setting process based on local employment cost index
8. *Negotiated Rulemaking Act* (PL 101-648)
Authorized agencies to pursue negotiated rulemaking

102d CONGRESS

1992   1. *Federal Facility Compliance Act* (PL 102-386)
Prohibited federal agencies from claiming sovereign immunity in violating federal solid and hazardous waste laws
2. *Cost Savings Disclosures Awards Act* (PL 102-487)
Authorized employee awards for disclosing information on fraud, waste, and abuse in government

3. *Federal Housing Enterprises Financial Safety and Soundness Act* (PL 102-550)
Strengthened federal oversight of Federal National Mortgage Association (Fannie Mae) and Federal Home Loan Mortgage Corporation (Freddie Mac)

103D CONGRESS

1993   1. *Government Performance and Results Act* (PL 103-62)
Required federal agencies to develop and apply performance standards
2. *National and Community Service Trust Act* (PL 103-82)
Established Corporation for National Service as a government corporation
3. *Hatch Act Reform Amendments* (PL 103-94)
Clarified on-the-job and off-the-job restrictions on federal employee political activity

1994   4. *Federal Workplace Restructuring Act* (PL 103-226)
Authorized employee buyouts of up to $25,000
5. *Independent Counsel Reauthorization* (PL 103-270)
Expanded and reauthorized the independent counsel law for five years
6. *Social Security Independence and Improvement Act* (PL 103-296)
Elevated Social Security Administration to independent status
7. *Reinventing Government Package*
1: *Federal Crop Insurance Reform and Department of Agriculture Reorganization Act* (PL 103-354)
Authorized closure of more than 1,000 field offices
2: *Federal Acquisition Streamlining Act* (PL 103-355)
Simplified federal purchasing procedures
3: *Government Management Reform Act* (PL 103-356)
Revised federal administrative services

Appendix B:

An Overview of the Reform Statutes

Category	# of statutes	%
Time		
Era		
Pre-Watergate	59	42
Post-Waterate	82	58
President		
Truman	17	12
Eisenhower	10	7
Kennedy	8	6
Johnson	10	7
Nixon	17	12
Ford	13	9
Carter	17	12
Reagan	31	22
Bush	11	8
Clinton	7	5

(Continued)

Category	# of statutes	%
Decade		
Glory Days (1945–1960)	27	19
Great Society (1961–1968)	18	13
Reassessment (1969–1980)	47	33
New Proceduralism (1981–1994)	49	35
Legislative History		
President's Party		
Democratic	59	42
Republican	82	58
Congressional Party		
Democratic	116	82
Republican	6	4
Divided Between Chambers	19	14
Party Control of Government		
Unified	61	43
Divided	80	57
Origin of the Reform Statute		
President	64	45
Congress	77	55
Chamber of Origin in Congress		
House	23	31
Senate	35	47
Simultaneous/Not Clear	17	23
Blue-Ribbon Commission Involved?	19	14
Interest Groups Involved?	41	29
Legislative Debate		
Routine	80	57
Controversial	61	43
Legislative Passage		
Unanimous	69	49
Near-Unanimous	40	28
Strong Majority (60 or more)	23	16
Close (less than 60)	9	6
Recorded Vote Taken?	85	60
Philosophy		
Tide		
Scientific Management	62	44
War on Waste	26	18
Watchful Eye	33	23

(Continued)

Category	# of statutes	%
Liberation Management	20	14
Purity of Statute		
No Other Tides Found in Statute	100	71
One Other Tide Found	32	23
Two Other Tides Found	9	6
Primary Accountability Mechanism		
Compliance	56	40
Capacity	65	46
Performance	20	14
General View of Government		
Trusting	68	48
Distrusting	73	52
Change Strategy		
Focus		
Structure of Government	59	41
Procedures of Government	74	53
Both	7	5
Establish a Study Commission	2	1
Structural Tactic		
Establish New Agency	23	17
Merge Existing Agencies	12	9
Reorganize Existing Agency	10	7
Establish Public Corporation	6	4
Abolish Existing Agency	4	3
Grant Agency Independence	4	3
Elevate Agency to Higher Status	3	2
Combination	3	2
No Structural Reform in Statute	76	54
Procedural Tactic		
Establish New System	31	22
Broaden System	20	14
Revise System	10	7
Deregulate/Narrow System	10	7
Reauthorize System	8	6
Abolish System	1	1
Combination	1	1
No Procedural Reform in Statute	60	43
Target		
General Organization of Government	56	40
Procurement/Acquisition	14	10

(Continued)

Category	# of statutes	%
Ethics/Standards of Conduct	15	11
Administrative Process	9	6
Pay Systems	7	5
Audit/Investigation	7	5
Rulemaking Procedures	6	4
General Personnel/Classification	6	4
Budget/Financial Management	6	4
Combination	6	4
Strategic Planning/Analysis	3	2
Debt Collection	3	2
Tort Claims	2	1
Scale		
Nature of Idea		
New Approach	66	47
Modification of Old	75	53
Scope of Impact		
Large	56	40
Small	85	60
Overall Scale of Reform		
New/Large	38	27
New/Small	38	27
Old/Large	20	14
Old/Small	45	32
Implementation		
Experimental Approach in Statute?	5	4
Time Horizon in Statute		
Temporary/Sunset	20	14
Permanent	121	86
Scope		
Single Agency	51	36
Several Agencies	20	14
Governmentwide	70	50
Oversight Approach		
Centralized	71	50
Decentralized	70	50
Impact		
Shift in Shared Powers		
Toward President	67	48

(Continued)

Category	# of statutes	%
Toward Congress	39	28
Not Clear/No Shift Discernible	35	25
Impact on Cost of Government		
Increase	36	26
Decrease	12	9
Not Clear/No Impact Discernible	93	66
Impact on Role of Government		
Expand	42	30
Contract	15	11
Not Clear/No Impact Discernible	84	60
Impact on Shape of Government		
Thicken Hierarchy	82	58
Thin Hierarchy	22	16
Not Clear/No Impact Discernible	37	26
Impact on Administrative Speed		
Accelerate	51	36
Slow Down	37	26
Not Clear/No Impact Discernible	53	38
Impact on Interest Group Access		
Enhance	24	17
Reduce	34	24
Not Clear/No Impact Discernible	83	59
Impact on Public Access		
Enhance	26	18
Reduce	10	7
Not Clear/No Impact Discernible	105	75
Impact on Government Morale		
Improve	36	26
Reduce	3	2
Not Clear/No Impact Discernible	102	72
Impact on Bureaucratic Balance		
Strengthen Line Units of Government	62	44
Strengthen Staff Units of Government	66	47
Not Clear/No Impact Discernible	13	9

Notes

Introduction

1 The phrase comes from Vice President Al Gore, *Creating a Government That Works Better and Costs Less: From Red Tape to Results* (Washington, D.C.: U.S. Government Printing Office, 1993), p. 3.

2 See Matthew Crenson, *The Federal Machine: Beginnings of Bureaucracy in Jacksonian America* (Baltimore: Johns Hopkins University Press, 1975).

3 See Harold Seidman and Robert Gilmour, *Politics, Position, and Power: From the Positive to the Regulatory State* (New York: Oxford University Press, 1986), p. 5.

4 David Mayhew, *Divided We Govern: Party Control, Lawmaking, and Investigations, 1946–1990* (New Haven: Yale University Press, 1991).

5 See Carolyn Ban and Norma Riccucci, eds., *Public Personnel Management: Current Concerns, Future Challenges* (New York: Longman, 1991); Richard Stillman, II, ed., *The American Constitution and the Administrative State: Constitutionalism in the Late 20th Century* (New York: University Press of America, 1987); Barry Bozeman, ed., *Public Management: The State of the Art* (San Francisco: Jossey-Bass, 1993); Patricia Ingraham and Carolyn Ban, eds., *Legislating Bureaucratic Change: The Civil Service Reform Act* (Albany: State University of New York Press, 1984); Patricia Ingraham and David Rosenbloom, eds., *The Promise and Paradox of Civil Service Reform* (Pittsburgh: University of Pittsburgh Press, 1992); James Perry, ed.,

Handbook of Public Administration (San Francisco: Jossey-Bass, 1989); John DiIulio, ed., *Deregulating the Public Service: Can Government Be Improved?* (Washington, D.C.: Brookings Institution, 1994); Donald Kettl and John DiIulio, eds., *Inside the Reinvention Machine: Appraising Governmental Reform* (Washington, D.C.: Brookings Institution, 1995); Patricia Ingraham and Donald Kettl, eds., *Agenda for Excellence: Public Service in America* (Chatham, N.J.: Chatham House, 1990); Naomi Lynn and Aaron Wildavsky, eds., *Public Administration: The State of the Discipline* (Chatham, N.J.: Chatham House, 1990); Terry Cooper, ed., *Handbook of Administrative Ethics* (New York: Marcel Dekker, 1993); George Frederickson, ed., *Ethics and Public Administration* (New York: Peacock, 1993); and Jay Shafritz and Albert Hyde, *Classics of Public Administration* (Oak Park, Ill.: Moore, 1978).

6 John Rohr, *To Run a Constitution: The Legitimacy of the Administrative State* (Lawrence: University of Kansas Press, 1986), chapter 10; Chester Newland, "A Mid-Term Appraisal: The Reagan Presidency," *Public Administration Review* 43, no. 1 (January–February 1983), 1–21; Marver Bernstein, "The Presidency and Management Improvement," *Law and Contemporary Problems* 35, no. 2 (Summer 1970), 505–518.

7 Administrative Conference of the United States, *Federal Administrative Procedure Sourcebook: Statutes and Related Materials* (Washington, D.C.: U.S. Government Printing Office, 1992).

8 General Accounting Office, *Selected Government-Wide Management Improvement Efforts, 1970 to 1980* (Washington, D.C.: U.S. General Accounting Office, 1983).

9 See, for example, United States Senate, Committee on Governmental Affairs, *Management Theories in the Private and Public Sectors* (Washington, D.C.: U.S. Government Printing Office, 1985).

10 Fifteen face-to-face interviews were conducted for this book, including off-the-record conversations with five past or present deputy directors and associate directors of the Office of Management and Budget who had primary responsibility for management reform.

  Products of earlier research include Paul C. Light, *Monitoring Government: Federal Inspectors General and the Search for Accountability* (Washington, D.C.: Brookings Institution/Governance Institute, 1993), and *Thickening Government: Federal Hierarchy and the Diffusion of Accountability* (Washington, D.C.: Brookings Institution/Governance Institute, 1995).

  I was responsible for handling general oversight of the Office of Management and Budget and was the lead staff on the Presidential Transitions Effectiveness Act of 1988, the Department of Veterans Affairs Act of 1988, a biennial budget reform measure that did not pass, and hearings on regulatory reform.

11 Bernstein, "The Presidency and Management Improvement," pp. 515–516.

1. The Tides of Reform

1 See Lynton Caldwell, *The Administrative Theories of Hamilton and Jefferson* (Chicago: University of Chicago Press, 1944), for an illuminating account of the differences in philosophy between these two founders.

2 Matthew Crenson, *The Federal Machine: Beginnings of Bureaucracy in Jacksonian America* (Baltimore: Johns Hopkins University Press, 1975), quotations from, respectively, pp. 3, 68.

3 Crenson, *The Federal Machine,* p. 66.

4 Quoted in Crenson, *The Federal Machine,* pp. 77–78.

5 See William Gormley, "Counter-Bureaucracies in Theory and Practice," unpublished paper, for a definition of the term.

6 See Paul C. Light, *Monitoring Government: Federal Inspectors General and the Search for Accountability* (Washington, D.C.: Brookings Institution/Governance Institute, 1993), for a history of the inspector general concept.

7 See Barry Karl, "The American Bureaucrat: A History of a Sheep in Wolf's Clothing," in Richard Stillman, ed., *The American Constitution and the Administrative State: Constitutionalism in the Late 20th Century* (New York: University Press of America, 1989), pp. 59–82.

8 Crenson, *The Federal Machine,* p. 5.

9 See Lynn Marshall, "The Strange Stillbirth of the Whig Party," *American Historical Review* 72, no. 1 (January 1967), 455–457; Marshall writes that spoils allowed Jackson "to increase efficiency by ignoring pre-existing social criteria like 'character' and 'respectability' and defining office impersonally, entirely by rules and regulation." As such, "individuals could be placed or replaced without upsetting the integrity of the whole. Men were fitted to this system, not it to men. It was the administrative counterpart of the interchangeability of machine parts."

10 Woodrow Wilson, "The Study of Administration," *Political Science Quarterly* 2, no. 1 (June 1887), reprinted in Shafritz and Hyde, *Classics of Public Administration,* pp. 5, 12.

11 Robert Vaughn, "Ethics in Government and the Vision of Public Service," *George Washington Law Review* 58, no. 3 (February 1990), 421.

12 Stephen Skowronek, *Building a New American State: The Expansion of National Administrative Capacities, 1877–1920* (New York: Cambridge University Press, 1982), p. 50.

13 Quoted in Skowronek, *Building a New American State,* p. 51.

14 Donald Kettl argues that linking the Gore reforms to budget savings was a critical first mistake; Donald Kettl and John DiIulio, eds., *Inside the Reinvention Machine,* pp. 16 ff.

15 Quoted in Skowronek, *Building a New American State,* p. 180.

16 Skowronek, *Building a New American State,* p. 182.

17 See Ronald Moe, *The Hoover Commissions Revisited* (Boulder, Colo.: Westview, 1982), for a discussion of the two Hoover Commissions and a more general history of the reform efforts leading to their establishment.

18 Al Gore, *Creating a Government That Works Better and Costs Less: From Red Tape to Results* (Washington, D.C.: U.S. Government Printing Office, 1993), p. i.

19 Luther Gulick and L. Urwick, eds., *Papers on the Science of Administration* (New York: Institute of Public Administration, 1937).

20 Gulick, "Notes on the Theory of Organization," in Gulick and Urwick, *Papers on the Science of Administration,* p. 3.

21 Gulick, "Notes," p. 7.

22 Herbert Simon, "The Proverbs of Administration," *Public Administration Review* 6 (Winter 1946), 53–67.

23 P.L. 80-162.

24 *Congressional Record,* March 7, 1939, p. 2386.

25 Quoted in James Morone, *The Democratic Wish: Popular Participation and the Limits of American Government* (New York: Basic, 1990), pp. 138–139.

26 See Committee on Government Affairs, United States Senate, *Executive Branch Reorganization: An Overview* (Washington, D.C.: U.S. Government Printing Office, 1978); the document was written by Ronald Moe.

27 *Congressional Record,* October 26, 1990, p. S 17259.

28 See P.L. 101-576.

29 "Financial Centralization," *Congressional Quarterly Almanac* (Washington, D.C.: Congressional Quarterly Press, 1990), p. 416; Mark Goldstein, "Chasing Wayward Billions," *Government Executive,* May 1991, p. 20.

30 Quoted in *The Minneapolis Star Tribune,* May 8, 1994.

31 National Academy of Public Administration, *Social Security Administrator Board vs. Single Administrator,* report to the Senate Committee on Aging, transmitted September 13, 1989.

32 Personal communication to the author; see also David Osborne, "Can This President Be Saved?" *The Washington Post Magazine,* January 8, 1995, p. 15, for the same point.

33 Frederick Mosher, *A Tale of Two Agencies: A Comparative Analysis of the General Accounting Office and the Office of Management and Budget* (Baton Rouge: Louisiana State University Press, 1984), p. 21.

34 See Light, *Monitoring Government,* chapter 8.

35 These figures are drawn from Light, *Monitoring Government,* p. 54.

36 Quoted in Mosher, *A Tale of Two Agencies,* p. 81.

37 Allen Schick, "The Road to PPB: The Stages of Budget Reform," *Public Administration Review* 26 (December 1966), reprinted in Shafritz and Hyde, *Classics of Public Administration,* p. 258.

38 Light, *Monitoring Government,* pp. 16–17.

39 Committee on Governmental Affairs, United States Senate, *Legislation to Establish Offices of Inspector General: H.R. 8588* (Washington, D.C.: U.S. Government Printing Office, 1978), p. 4.

40 See Government Operations Committee, Intergovernmental Relations and Human Resources Subcommittee, *Establishment of Offices of Inspector General* (Washington, D.C.: U.S. Government Printing Office, 1977).

41 J. Peter Grace, *War on Waste: President's Private Sector Survey on Cost Control* (New York: Macmillan, 1984).

42 See "HUD Reform Bill Cleared by Congress," *Congressional Quarterly Almanac* (Washington, D.C.: Congressional Quarterly Press, 1989), p. 631.

43 See David Rosenbloom, *Federal Service and the Constitution: The Development of a Public Employment Relationship* (Ithaca, N.Y.: Cornell University Press, 1971).

44 See United States Senate, Committee on Governmental Affairs, *Hatch Act Reform Amendments of 1993* (Washington, D.C.: U.S. Government Printing Office, 1993), for a history of the issue.

45 Gore, *Creating a Government That Works Better and Costs Less*, p. 2.

46 President's Council on Integrity and Efficiency and the Executive Council on Integrity and Efficiency, *Inspectors General Vision and Strategies to Apply Our Reinvention Principles,* January 1994.

47 H.R. 4679, p. 1.

48 See Administrative Conference of the United States, *Federal Administrative Procedure Sourcebook*, p. 2.

49 See John Rohr, *To Run a Constitution: The Legitimacy of the Administrative State* (Lawrence: University of Kansas, 1986), for an excellent history of these events.

50 Walter Gellhorn, "The Administrative Procedure Act: The Beginnings," *Virginia Law Review* 72 (1986), 232.

51 Roscoe Pound, "For the 'Minority Report,'" *American Bar Association Journal* 27 (November 1941), 665–667.

52 Gellhorn, "The Administrative Procedure Act," p. 221.

53 United States Senate, Administrative Procedure in Government Agencies: Report of the Committee on Administrative Procedure (Washington, D.C.: U.S. Government Printing Office, 1941), pp. 191–192.

54 United States Senate, Committee of the Judiciary Subcommittee on Separation of Powers, *Refusals by the Executive Branch to Provide Information to the Congress, 1964–1973* (Washington, D.C.: U.S. Government Printing Office, 1974), p. v.

55 United States Senate, Committee on the Judiciary, *Amending the Freedom of Information Act* (Washington, D.C.: U.S. Government Printing Office, 1974); United States Senate, Committee on Government Operations, *Privacy Act of 1974* (Washington, D.C.: U.S. Government Printing Office, 1974).

56 For an excellent history, see Priscilla Regan, *Privacy, Technology, and Public Policy* (Chapel Hill: University of North Carolina Press, 1997).

57 See Ronald Hopkins, "The Privacy Act as a Partial Repeal of the Freedom of Information Act," *Thurgood Marshall Law Review* 9, nos. 1, 2 (Fall 1983–Spring 1984), 429–466.

58 P.L. 101-552.

59 P.L. 100-648.

60 David Osborne and Ted Gaebler, *Reinventing Government: How the Entrepreneurial Spirit Is Transforming the Public Sector* (New York: Plume, 1993); Tom Peters and Richard Waterman, *In Search of Excellence* (New York: HarperCollins, 1982).

61 Caldwell, *The Administrative Theories of Hamilton and Jefferson*, p. 136.

62 For such a critique of the Gore effort, see Peter Drucker, "Really Reinventing Government," *The Atlantic Monthly,* February 1995, pp. 49 ff.

63 Paragraphs 1 and 3 are from the Gore report, paragraphs 2 and 4 are from the Nixon

message to Congress. Nixon's complete statement can be found in Executive Office of the President of the United States, *Papers Relating to the President's Departmental Reorganization Program: A Reference Compilation* (Washington, D.C.: Executive Office of the President, 1972).

64 See Richard P. Nathan, *The Plot That Failed: Nixon and the Administrative Presidency* (New York: Wiley, 1975).

65 P.L. 103-62.

66 For a discussion of the difference between the two, see Light, *Monitoring Government*, pp. 12–16.

67 Testimony from Office of Management and Budget Director Leon Panetta, referenced in United States Senate, Governmental Affairs Committee, *Government Performance and Results Act of 1993* (Washington, D.C.: U.S. Government Printing Office, 1993), p. 3.

68 Senate Governmental Affairs Committee, *Government Performance and Results Act*, p. 43.

69 *Weekly Compilation of Presidential Documents*, October 17, 1994.

70 Gore, *Creating a Government That Works Better and Costs Less*, p. 89.

71 Gore, *Creating a Government That Works Better and Costs Less*, p. 6; see also Donald Kettl, "The Global Revolution: Reforming Government Sector Management," paper delivered at a seminar titled "State Reform in Latin American and the Caribbes," Brasilia, Brazil, May 16–17, 1996.

72 Working Group on Principles of Organization and Management, "Principles of Organization and Management," draft, November 15, 1995.

73 See Terry Moe, "The Politicized Presidency," in John Chubb and Paul Peterson, eds., *The New Direction in American Politics* (Washington, D.C.: Brookings Institution, 1985), pp. 238–269.

2. Charting the Tides

1 These figures come from a national survey conducted by Peter Hart and Robert Teeter, March 1995, for the Center for Excellence in Government. The survey can be accessed through the Roper Center at the University of Connecticut online system, question ID: USHART.95CEG, RF01-R32.

2 Lake Research, *The Show-Me Nation: Restoring Trust in Government* (Washington, D.C.: Lake Research, 1995), report to the Pew Charitable Trusts, p. 11.

3 Charles Goodsell, *The Case for Bureaucracy: A Public Administration Polemic* (Chatham, N.J.: Chatham House, 1994), pp. 77–78.

4 See Stephen C. Craig, *The Malevolent Leaders: Popular Discontent in America* (Boulder, Colo.: Westview, 1993), for a more detailed assessment of trust in government.

5 This was clearly the theme in focus group sessions conducted for the Pew Charitable Trusts by Lake Research in the fall of 1996; see Lake Research, *The Show-Me Nation*.

6 Lake Research, *The Show-Me Nation*, pp. 31–32.

7 Survey conducted for the Pew Charitable Trusts by Lake Research, unpublished, author's files.

8 Hart and Teeter survey for the Center for Excellence in Government, March 1995. Note that past efforts to tie government pay to performance have been so limited that the liberating effects have been minimal.

9 The answers flow from a careful inspection of the legislative history, whether recorded in the *Congressional Quarterly Almanac,* committee hearings, legislative floor debates, or the popular press.

10 Harold Seidman and Robert Gilmour, *Politics, Position, and Power: From the Positive to the Regulatory State* (New York: Oxford University Press, 1986, 4th ed.), p. 5.

11 United States House of Representatives, *For the Establishment of the Commission on Organization of the Executive Branch of the Government* (Washington, D.C.: U.S. Government Printing Office, 1947), pp. 5–6.

12 See Harold Stanley and Richard Niemi, *Vital Statistics on American Politics* (Washington, D.C.: Congressional Quarterly Press, 1994), pp. 220–221.

13 See Paul C. Light, *Monitoring Government: Federal Inspectors General and the Search for Accountability* (Washington, D.C.: Brookings Institution/Governance Institute, 1993), pp. 12–16, for a discussion of the three types of accountability.

14 Light, *Monitoring Government,* p. 14.

15 The two liberation management initiatives that appear in table 2.2 as compliance accountability involved the replacement of one set of rules with a second, lighter set, both of which passed under Clinton: the Hatch Act Reform Amendments and the Federal Acquisitions Streamlining Act. Much as the 1993 Hatch Act reforms finally freed federal employees to engage in a range of political activities once prohibited, for example, it nevertheless kept the lines clear on what was still outlawed—for example, serving as an officer of a political party, soliciting contributions for a partisan political purpose, and becoming a candidate for public office in a partisan election.

16 See Paul C. Light, *Thickening Government: Federal Hierarchy and the Diffusion of Accountability* (Washington, D.C.: Brookings Institution/Governance Institute, 1995), pp. 38–43.

17 The recommendation for an administrative vice president is not to be found in either the first or second Hoover reports but in Hoover's own testimony before the Senate Committee on Government Operations on January 16, 1956; see U.S. Senate Committee on Government Operations, *Proposal to Create an Administrative Vice President* (Washington, D.C.: U.S. Government Printing Office, 1956).

18 Commission on Organization of the Executive Branch of the Government, *Concluding Report: A Report to the Congress by the Commission on Organization of the Executive Branch of the Government* (Washington, D.C.: The Commission on Organization of the Executive Branch of the Government, May 1949).

19 Commission on Organization of the Executive Branch of the Government, *Concluding Report,* p. 14.

20 P.L. 99-272.

21 See Paul C. Light, *The President's Agenda: Domestic Policy Choice from Kennedy to Reagan* (Baltimore: Johns Hopkins University Press, 1991, rev. ed.), pp. 118–126, for a discussion of these two coding categories.

22 P.L. 104-13; see United States Senate Committee on Governmental Affairs, *Paperwork Reduction Act of 1995* (Washington, D.C.: U.S. Government Printing Office, 1995), pp. 15–19, for a discussion of the rationale.

23 Al Gore, *Creating a Government That Works Better and Costs Less: From Red Tape to Results* (Washington, D.C.: U.S. Government Printing Office, 1993), p. 3.

24 Mathew McCubbins and Thomas Schwartz, "Congressional Oversight Overlooked: Police Patrols Versus Fire Alarms," *American Journal of Political Science* 2 (February 1984), 165–177.

25 *Qui tam* is short for *qui tam pro domino rege quam pro se ipso in hac parte sequitur,* which means, in short, "who brings the action for the king as well as for himself."

26 See House of Representatives, Committee on the Judiciary Subcommittee on Administrative Law and Government Relations, *False Claims Implementation* (Washington, D.C.: U.S. Government Printing Office, 1990); see also Erwin Chermerinsky, "Controlling Fraud Against the Government: The Need for Decentralized Enforcement," *Notre Dame Law Review* 58 (June 1983), 995–1018.

27 Answers to the thickening/thinning question draw heavily on Light, *Thickening Government.*

28 Readers who disagree with this decision are encouraged to recalculate the cell by moving all six cases involved from the "toward Congress" category to the "not clear/no impact discernible" category. In doing so, the percent of liberation management reforms that shift power to Congress would fall to 0 percent, while the percentage that would be declared "not clear/no impact discernible" would rise from 29 to 57.

29 This idea is well supported in an undergraduate honors thesis by Steven Struthers completed under Terry Moe's supervision at Stanford University in June 1990.

30 See Light, *Monitoring Government,* chapter 8.

31 See Steven Kelman, "The Grace Commission: How Much Waste in Government," *Public Interest* 78 (Winter 1985), 65–82.

32 Light, *Monitoring Government,* pp. 222–223.

33 U.S. Senate, Committee on Governmental Affairs, *Civil Service Reform Act of 1978* (Washington, D.C.: U.S. Government Printing Office, 1978), pp. 2–3.

34 Quoted in U.S. Senate, *Civil Service Reform Act of 1978,* p. 3.

35 See Charles O. Jones, *The Trusteeship Presidency: Jimmy Carter and the United States Congress* (Baton Rouge: Louisiana State University Press, 1988), pp. 160–163.

36 Quoted in the *Congressional Quarterly Weekly,* July 22, 1978, p. 1839.

37 U.S. Senate, *Civil Service Reform Act of 1978,* p. 131.

38 U.S. Senate, *Civil Service Reform Act of 1978,* p. 8.

39 *The Federalist Papers,* ed. Roy Fairfield (Baltimore: Johns Hopkins University Press, 1981, 2d ed.), p. 198.

40 *The Federalist Papers,* p. 199.

41 *The Federalist Papers,* p. 160.

42 *The Federalist Papers,* p. 384.

43 Thomas Hobbes, *Leviathan: or the Matter, Form, and Power of a Commonwealth Ecclesiastical and Civil,* ed. Michael Oakeshot (Oxford: Blackwell, 1946), p. 63.

44 Hobbes, *Leviathan,* p. 84.

45 *The Federalist Papers,* p. 432.

46 *The Federalist Papers,* p. 18.

47 *The Federalist Papers,* p. 22.

48 Brutus, "To the Citizens of the State of New-York, 18 October 1787," in *The Anti-Federalist: Writings by the Opponents of the Constitution,* ed. Herbert Storing (Chicago: University of Chicago Press, 1985), p. 116. Unlike "Publius," the pseudonymous author of *The Federalist Papers,* Brutus has never been clearly identified.

49 See, for example, Gordon Tullock, *The Politics of Bureaucracy* (Washington, D.C.: Public Affairs Press, 1965).

50 John Rohr, *To Run a Constitution: The Legitimacy of the Administrative State* (Lawrence: University of Kansas, 1986), chapter 10.

51 Rohr, *To Run a Constitution,* pp. 169–170.

52 Donald Kettl, *Sharing Power: Public Governance and Private Markets* (Washington, D.C.: Brookings Institution, 1993), p. 43.

53 This is the NPR estimate.

3. The Climate of Reform

1 The essential source here is John Bear, *The #1 New York Times Bestseller* (Berkeley, Calif.: Ten Speed, 1992).

2 See Bear, *The #1 New York Times Bestseller,* p. 125.

3 Gallup Poll, *Public Opinion Index, 1935–1971* (New York: Random House, 1972), vol. 1, 1935–1946, pp. 512, 557, 591.

4 Congressional Quarterly, *Congressional Quarterly Almanac* (Washington, D.C.: Congressional Quarterly Press, 1946), p. 116.

5 Frederick Blachly and Miriam Oatman, "Sabotage of the Administrative Process," *Public Administration Review* 6 (Winter 1946), 226.

6 Congressional Quarterly, *The People Speak: American Elections in Focus* (Washington, D.C.: Congressional Quarterly Press, 1990), p. 183.

7 Frederick Mosher, *A Tale of Two Agencies: A Comparative Analysis of the General Accounting Office and the Office of Management and Budget* (Baton Rouge: Louisiana State University Press, 1984), p. 70.

8 Mosher, *A Tale of Two Agencies,* p. 107.

9 See Roger Davidson and Walter Oleszek, *Congress Against Itself* (Bloomington: Indiana University Press, 1977), p. 51.

10 See Kenneth Kofmehl, *Professional Staffs of Congress* (West Lafayette, Ind.: Purdue University Press, 1977).

11 George Galloway, *The Legislative Process in Congress* (New York: Thomas Y. Crowell, 1955), p. 591.

12 Quoted in Roger Davidson and Walter Oleszek, *Congress and Its Members* (Washington, D.C.: Congressional Quarterly Press, 1994, 4th ed.), p. 312.

13 Quoted in Congressional Quarterly, *Congressional Quarterly Almanac* (Washington, D.C.: Congressional Quarterly Press, 1950), p. 363.

14 Congressional Quarterly, *Congressional Quarterly Almanac* (Washington, D.C.: Congressional Quarterly Press, 1949), p. 556.

15 Commission on Organization of the Executive Branch of the Government, *Concluding Report: A Report to the Congress by the Commission on Organization of the Executive Branch of the Government* (Washington, D.C.: The Commission on Organization of the Executive Branch of the Government, May 1949), p. 20.

16 P.L. 81-429. See U.S. Senate, Committee on Government Operations, *Classification Act of 1949* (Washington, D.C.: U.S. Government Printing Office, 1949), for a discussion of the assorted elements.

17 Al Gore, *Creating a Government That Works Better and Costs Less: From Red Tape to Results* (Washington, D.C.: U.S. Government Printing Office, 1993), p. 21.

18 Ronald Moe, *The Hoover Commissions Revisited* (Boulder, Colo.: Westview, 1982), pp. 2–3.

19 I was involved in just such an effort in 1988 as staff to the U.S. Senate Committee on Governmental Affairs, which added a third Hoover Commission to the Department of Veterans Affairs Act.

20 U.S. House of Representatives, Committee on Government Operations, *Department of House and Urban Development Act* (Washington, D.C.: U.S. Government Printing Office, 1965), p. 4.

21 Quoted in U.S. House, Committee on Government Operations, *Administration of the Freedom of Information Act* (Washington, D.C.: U.S. Government Printing Office, 1972), p. 1.

22 Quoted in U.S. House, *Administration of the Freedom of Information Act,* p. 5.

23 Quoted in Congressional Quarterly, *Congressional Quarterly Almanac* (Washington, D.C.: Congressional Quarterly Press, 1966), p. 558.

24 Quoted in U.S. Senate, Committee on the Judiciary Subcommittee on Administration Practice and Procedure, *Freedom of Information Act Source Book: Legislative Materials, Cases, Articles* (Washington, D.C.: U.S. Government Printing Office, 1974), p. 74.

25 P.L. 85-619.

26 Gordon Tullock, *The Politics of Bureaucracy* (Washington, D.C.: Public Affairs, 1965), pp. 21–22.

27 Quoted in Congressional Quarterly, *Congressional Quarterly Almanac* (Washington, D.C.: Congressional Quarterly Press, 1970), p. 463.

28 See Frederick Mosher, *A Tale of Two Agencies,* p. 113.

29 U.S. House of Representatives, Committee on Post Office and Civil Service, *Postal Reorganization Act* (Washington, D.C.: U.S. Government Printing Office, 1970), p. 2.

30 U.S. House of Representatives, Committee on Interstate and Foreign Commerce, *Rail Passenger Service Act of 1970* (Washington, D.C.: U.S. Government Printing Office, 1970), p. 1.

31 This language was particularly evident in the so-called Malek Manual, which contained a broad strategy for controlling both career and political executives.

32 Richard Nathan, *The Plot That Failed: Nixon and the Administrative Presidency* (New York: Wiley, 1975), p. 62.

33 For a history of presidential management reform, see Peri Arnold, *Making the Managerial Presidency: Comprehensive Reorganization Planning, 1905–1980* (Princeton, N.J.: Princeton University Press, 1986).

34 See Paul C. Light, *Thickening Government: Federal Hierarchy and the Diffusion of Accountability* (Washington, D.C.: Brookings Institution/Governance Institute, 1995).

35 Interview, October 1995.

36 U.S. Senate, Committee on Governmental Affairs, *Public Officials Integrity Act of 1977* (Washington, D.C.: U.S. Government Printing Office, 1977), p. 4.

37 Paul Douglas, *Ethics in Government* (Cambridge: Harvard University Press, 1952), p. 98.

38 U.S. Senate, *Public Officials Integrity Act,* p. 22.

39 U.S. Senate, *Public Officials Integrity Act,* p. 31.

40 Robert Vaughn, "Ethics in Government and the Vision of Public Service," *George Washington Law Review* 58, no. 3 (February 1990), 432.

41 Reprinted in U.S. House of Representatives, Committee on Government Operations Subcommittee on Intergovernmental Relations and Human Resources, *Establishment of Offices of Inspector General* (Washington, D.C.: U.S. Government Printing Office, 1977), pp. 831–849.

42 U.S. House of Representatives, Committee on Government Operations, *Inspector General Act Amendments of 1988* (Washington, D.C.: U.S. Government Printing Office, 1988), p. 7.

43 The following discussion draws heavily on Priscilla Regan, *Privacy, Technology, and Public Policy* (Chapel Hill: University of North Carolina Press, 1997), pp. 87–88.

44 U.S. Senate, Committee on Governmental Affairs Subcommittee on Oversight of Government Management, *Computer Matching and Privacy Protection Act of 1988* (Washington, D.C.: U.S. Government Printing Office, 1988), p. 2.

45 Westfall v. Erwin, 484 U.S. 292 (1987).

46 U.S. Senate, Committee on Governmental Affairs, *Presidential Transition Effectiveness Act* (Washington, D.C.: U.S. Government Printing Office, 1988).

47 See Paul C. Light, *Forging Legislation* (New York, W. W. Norton, 1990), for a history of the issue.

48 See Alasdair Roberts, "Command Performance," *Government Executive,* August 1966, pp. 21–26, for a discussion of the NPR's proposal.

49 See Light, *Thickening Government.*

50 Pew Research Center for the People and the Press, "TV News Viewership Declines," news release, May 13, 1996, p. 62.

51 For a discussion of how public distrust shaped the debate over national health insurance in 1993–1994, see Theda Skocpol, *Boomerang: Clinton's Health Security Effort and the Turn Against Government in U.S. Politics* (New York: W. W. Norton, 1996).

52 Donald Kettl, "The Global Revolution: Reforming Government Sector Management," paper delivered at a seminar titled "State Reform in Latin American and the Caribbes," Brasilia, Brazil, May 16–17, 1996, p. 4.

4. The Gravitational Pulls of Reform

1 Al Gore, *Creating a Government That Works Better and Costs Less: From Red Tape to Results* (Washington, D.C.: U.S. Government Printing Office, 1993); Al Gore, *Common Sense Government: Works Better and Costs Less* (Washington, D.C.: U.S. Government Printing Office, 1995).

2 See Bill Waldman, *The Bill: How the Adventures of Clinton's National Service Bill Reveal What Is Corrupt, Comic, Cynical—and Noble—About Washington* (New York: Viking, 1995), pp. 108–114.

3 See Fred I. Greenstein, *The Hidden Hand Presidency: Eisenhower as Leader* (New York: Basic, 1982).

4 *Weekly Compilation of Presidential Documents* 17 (January 26, 1981), pp. 27–28.

5 Paul C. Light, *Monitoring Government: Federal Inspectors General and the Search for Accountability* (Washington, D.C.: Brookings Institution/Governance Institute, 1993), p. 225.

6 Suzanne Garment, *Scandal: The Culture of Mistrust in American Politics* (New York: Random House, 1991), p. 5.

7 Representative Stephen Horn (R-Calif.) called for creation of a White House IG in late 1995.

8 Paul C. Light, *The President's Agenda: Domestic Policy Choice from Kennedy to Reagan* (Baltimore: Johns Hopkins University Press, 1991, rev. ed.), p. 123.

9 John Kingdon, *Agendas, Alternatives, Public Policy* (Boston: Little, Brown, 1st ed., 1984), p. 153. Kingdon's classic has been revised in a second edition published by Harper/Collins in 1995.

10 See, for example, "Execs Eye Reinvention Warily," *Government Executive,* July 1994, p. 6.

11 See Paul C. Light, *Thickening Government: Federal Hierarchy and the Diffusion of Accountability* (Washington, D.C.: Brookings Institution/Governance Institute, 1995), p. 118–119.

12 Ronald Moe, "Traditional Organizational Principles and the Managerial Presidency: From Phoenix to Ashes," *Public Administration Review* 50, no. 2 (March–April 1990), 134.

13 Text of the contract can be found in Clyde Wilcox, *The Latest American Revolution: The 1994 Elections and Their Implications for Governance* (New York: St. Martin's, 1995), pp. 69–71.

14 Quoted in Tom Shoop, "Reinventing Reinvention," *Government Executive,* January 1995, p. 17.

15 See Jeff Shear and Timothy B. Clark, "Suspending Spending," *Government Executive,* January 1995, pp. 11–15.

16 See Light, *Monitoring Government,* p. 109.

17 David Mayhew, *Divided We Govern: Party Control, Lawmaking, and Investigations, 1946–1990* (New Haven: Yale University Press, 1991).

18 Terry Moe, "The Politics of Structural Choice: Toward a Theory of Public Bureaucracy," in O. E. Williamson, ed., *Organization Theory: From Chester Barnard to the Present and Beyond* (New York: Oxford University Press, 1990), p. 138.

19 Moe, "Politics of Structural Choice," p. 137.

20 Mayhew, *Divided We Govern,* p. 199.

21 Light, *Thickening Government,* pp. 181–182.

22 The recommendation was in the August 13 draft of the final NPR report.

23 Gore, *Creating a Government That Works Better and Costs Less,* p. 34.

24 The title of this subsection is adapted from Roger Davidson and Walter Oleszek, *Congress Divided Against Itself* (Bloomington: Indiana University Press, 1977).

25 Charles O. Jones, *The Presidency in a Separated System* (Washington, D.C.: Brookings Institution, 1994), p. 2.

5. The Consequences of Reform

1 Paul C. Light, *Monitoring Government: Federal Inspectors General and the Search for Accountability* (Washington, D.C.: Brookings Institution/Governance Institute, 1993), p. 224.

2 See Stephen C. Craig, *The Malevolent Leaders: Popular Discontent in America* (Boulder, Colo.: Westview, 1993).

3 See Harold Stanley and Richard Niemi, *Vital Statistics on American Politics* (Washington, D.C.: Congressional Quarterly Press, 1994), p. 218.

4 U.S. Senate, Committee on Governmental Affairs, *Civil Service Reform Act of 1978* (Washington, D.C.: U.S. Government Printing Office, 1978), p. 11.

5 James Perry, "Linking Pay to Performance: The Controversy Continues," in C. Ban and N. Riccucci, *Public Personnel Management: Current Concerns, Future Challenges,* pp. 77, 83; see also Donald F. Kettl, Patricia W. Ingraham, Ronald P. Sanders, and Constance Horner, *Civil Service Reform: Building a Government That Works* (Washington, D.C.: Brookings Institution, 1996), for a deeper discussion of these issues as they relate to civil service reform generally.

6 Mark Moore, *Creating Public Value: Strategic Management in Government* (Cambridge: Harvard University Press, 1995).

7 U.S. Senate, Governmental Affairs Committee, *Government Performance and Results Act of 1993* (Washington, D.C.: U.S. Government Printing Office, 1993), p. 3.

8 See Paul C. Light, *Forging Legislation* (New York: W. W. Norton, 1990), for a history of the linkage effort.

9 See Paul C. Light, *Still Artful Work: The Continuing Politics of Social Security Reform* (New York: McGraw-Hill, 1995, 2d ed.).

10 Chester Newland, "The Politics of Civil Service Reform," in P. Ingraham and D.

Rosenbloom, eds., *The Promise and Paradox of Civil Service Reform* (Pittsburgh: University of Pittsburgh Press, 1992), p. 84.

11 Paul C. Light, *Thickening Government: Federal Hierarchy and the Diffusion of Accountability* (Washington, D.C.: Brookings Institution/Governance Institute, 1995), p. 60.

12 Michael Barzelay with Babak Armajani, *Breaking Through Bureaucracy: A New Vision for Managing in Government* (Berkeley: University of California Press, 1992), p. 3.

13 Barzelay and Armajani, *Breaking Through Bureaucracy,* pp. 8–9.

14 Joel Aberbach, "The Federal Executive Under Clinton," in C. Campbell and B. Rockman, eds, *The Clinton Presidency: First Appraisals* (Chatham, N.J.: Chatham House, 1996), p. 180; it is a point also made by James Q. Wilson, "Reinventing Public Administration," *PS: Political Science and Politics* 27, no. 4 (December 1994), 667–673.

15 James March and Johan Olsen, "Organizing Political Life: What Administrative Reorganization Tells Us About Government," *American Political Science Review* 77, no. 2 (June 1983), 77.

16 Quoted in Paul C. Light, *The President's Agenda: Domestic Policy Choice from Kennedy to Reagan* (Baltimore: Johns Hopkins University Press, 1991, rev. ed.), p. 121.

17 Quoted in Light, *The President's Agenda,* p. 120.

18 See Richard Fenno, *The United States Senate: A Bicameral Perspective* (Washington, D.C.: American Enterprise Institute, 1982).

19 See Joel Aberbach, *Keeping a Watchful Eye: The Politics of Congressional Oversight* (Washington, D.C.: Brookings Institution, 1990).

20 Donald Kettl, "Micromanagement: Congressional Control and Bureaucratic Risk," in P. Ingraham and D. Kettl, *Agenda for Excellence: Public Service in America* (Chatham, N.J.: Chatham House, 1992), p. 94.

21 Aaron Wildavsky, "The Two Presidencies," in A. Wildavsky, ed., *Perspectives on the Presidency* (Boston: Little, Brown, 1975).

22 U.S. Senate, Committee on Governmental Affairs, *Inspector and Auditor General Act of 1978* (Washington, D.C.: U.S. Government Printing Office, 1978), p. 14.

23 U.S. Senate, *Inspector and Auditor General Act,* p. 10.

24 Light, *Monitoring Government,* pp. 19–20.

25 Quoted in Light, *Monitoring Government,* p. 62.

26 G. Calvin Mackenzie, "The Presidential Appointment Process: Historical Development, Contemporary Operations, Current Issues," background paper for the Twentieth-Century Fund Panel on Presidential Appointments, March 1, 1994, p. 1.

6. Against the Tides

1 See Paul C. Light, *Thickening Government: Federal Hierarchy and the Diffusion of Accountability* (Washington, D.C.: Brookings Institution/Governance Institute, 1995), p. 29.

2 William J. Clinton, "Memorandum for Heads of Departments and Agencies; Subject: Streamlining the Bureaucracy," September 11, 1993, p. 1.

3 George Downs and Patrick Larkey, *The Search for Government Efficiency* (New York: Random House, 1986), p. 238.

4 Downs and Larkey, *Search for Government Efficiency,* p. 237.

5 For a detailed analysis of the factors involved in grade creep see Samantha Durst, Patricia Patterson, and John Ramsden, "Impacts of Traditional Explanatory Factors on Average Grade Increases in U.S. Cabinet-Level Departments," *Public Administration Review* 49 (July–August 1989), 305–320.

6 General Accounting Office, *Classification of Federal White-Collar Jobs Should Be Better Controlled* (Washington, D.C.: General Accounting Office, 1975), p. 29.

7 See Frederick Mosher, *A Tale of Two Agencies: A Comparative Analysis of the General Accounting Office and the Office of Management and Budget* (Baton Rouge: Louisiana State University Press, 1984), p. 112.

8 Alan Dean, Dwight Ink, and Harold Seidman, "OMB's 'M' Fading Away," *Government Executive,* June 1994, p. 62.

9 For a discussion of OMB's track record in leading reform, see General Accounting Office, *Managing the Government: Revised Approach Could Improve OMB's Effectiveness* (Washington, D.C.: General Accounting Office, May 1989).

10 See Paul C. Light, "Wanted: A New Management Czar," *Government Executive,* February 1994, p. 61.

11 Office of Management and Budget, "Memorandum for All OMB Staff: Making OMB More Effective in Serving the Presidency," March 1, 1994.

12 Al Gore, *Creating a Government That Works Better and Costs Less: From Red Tape to Results* (Washington, D.C.: U.S. Government Printing Office, 1993), p. 89.

13 See Light, *Thickening Government,* p. 190.

14 Charles Goodsell, *The Case for Bureaucracy: A Public Administration Polemic* (Chatham, N.J.: Chatham House, 1994).

15 Harry Hatry, "Determining the Effectiveness of Government Services," in J. Perry, ed., *Handbook of Public Administration* (San Francisco: Jossey-Bass, 1989), p. 481.

16 General Accounting Office, *Managing the Cost of Government: Building an Effective Financial Management Structure* (Washington, D.C.: General Accounting Office, February 1985), p. 3.

17 For a more hopeful view, see the National Academy of Performance Measurement, *Toward Useful Performance Measurement: Lessons Learned from Initial Pilot Performance Plans Prepared Under the Government Performance and Results Act* (Washington, D.C.: National Academy of Public Administration, 1994).

18 For a discussion of the performance measurement movement, see Arie Halachim and Geert Bouckaert, eds., *Organizational Performance and Measurement in the Public Sector* (Westport, Conn.: Quorum, 1996); and Peter Smith, *Measuring Outcome in the Public Sector* (Bristol, Pa.: Taylor and Francis, 1996).

19 United States Senate, Committee on Governmental Affairs, *Government Perfor-*

mance and Results Act (Washington, D.C.: U.S. Government Printing Office, 1992), p. 18.

20 United States Senate, *Government Performance and Results Act*, p. 32.

21 Office of Management and Budget, "Memorandum to the Heads of Executive Departments and Establishments: Preparation and Submission of Strategic Plans," September 14, 1995.

22 See Stephen Barr, "Performance Measurers Expand Their Horizons," *Washington Post,* February 3, 1994.

23 This list draws upon Downs and Larkey, *The Search for Government Efficiency,* chapter 7.

24 Office of the Vice President, "Vice President Gore, Director Panetta Designate Pilot Programs," press release, February 1, 1994.

25 Barr, "Performance Measurers Expand their Horizons."

26 Quoted in Gore, *Creating a Government That Works Better and Costs Less,* p. 124.

27 Eleanor Chelimsky, "The Role of Program Evaluation at the General Accounting Office," remarks before the annual conference of the National Legislative Program Evaluation Society, Minneapolis, May 8, 1992, p. 16.

28 Donald Kettl, *Sharing Power: Public Governance and Private Markets* (Washington, D.C.: Brookings Institution, 1993); James Perry, "Merit Pay Systems in the Public Sector: The Case for a Failure of Theory," *Review of Public Personnel Administration* 7 (Winter 1986), 57–69; Martin Levin and Mary Bryna Sanger, *Making Government Work: How Entrepreneurial Executives Turn Bright Ideas into Real Results* (San Francisco: Jossey-Bass, 1994).

29 Jane Mansbridge, "Self-Interest in the Explanation of Political Life," in J. Mansbrige, ed., *Beyond Self-Interest* (Chicago: University of Chicago Press, 1990), p. 20.

Index